The

POLITICAL DYNAMICS

of

AMERICAN EDUCATION

By

Frederick M. Wirt
University of Illinois, Urbana

and

Michael W. Kirst
Stanford University

McCutchan Publishing Corporation
P.O. Box 774, 2940 San Pablo Ave., Berkeley, CA 94702

ISBN 0-8211-2273-8
Library of Congress Catalog Card Number 97-70792

Printed in the United States of America

Preface

This book is not just a revision but a major overhaul of the most widely used text in the politics of education, *Schools in Conflict*. The many new concepts and the extensive new content are reflected in the new title, which stresses the political dynamics of education.

The Political Dynamics of American Education places more emphasis on the micropolitics of education at the school site, reflecting the political conflict and stress evident in recent reform challenges. The authors expand both on the political interactions within the local setting to address the current increase in bottom-up political activity, and on the external context of local schools to analyze the political momentum behind education standards. At the same time, the limits of both deregulation and centralized strategies are stressed as standards policies confront complex local politics. For example, the local school board has often been overlooked by education reforms, but this book subjects that crucial policymaking body to a new and penetrating analysis.

The most contemporary issues are treated: the debate over the possibility of local control, the expanding role of state government in influencing policy direction, and the development and future of federal involvement in education. One frequent issue arises from the policy debate: Did children's education improve? The book explores a wide range of current political issues, including curriculum, finance, and desegregation. Across this range of conflict there has been the emergence of new pressure groups from conservative elements. The latest school politics research is covered in a new chapter that reviews new "political" research dimensions that point to research gaps and the current state of education politics scholarship.

This text is designed in part for practitioners involved in education--administrators, teachers, state officials, and lay groups. It will also be valuable to scholars of educational administration, political science, and sociology because of its conceptual framework and extensive use of current research. For students, the book provides an overview of the origins, nature, and impact of the political forces surrounding and influencing schools.

The authors have devised an original conceptual framework to organize and chart the increasingly complex political web of American education. These competing forces of challenge and steady state now affect all levels of policymaking and administration. Combined, these conflicting forces constitute the "dynamic" nature of American education.

Contents

Part I

CONCEPTS AND HISTORICAL PERSPECTIVES

1

Conflict, Politics, and Schools

Anyone reading about American schools today must be aware of the conflict in which they are enmeshed. Once there had been a "steady state" of education, in which professionals controlled most aspects of schooling with only minor influence from citizens or school boards. But today there are many signs of challenge to this steady state, indicators of an increased "political" nature to schooling. This book is about the themes of both a professional, producer-oriented organization, as well as a citizen, consumer-oriented conflict over what schools should do.

At the core of this book is an emphasis on politics and on governance of the school system. Many education professionals believe politics should have no role in their work. For many citizens, though, a new challenge reflects their dissatisfaction with their children's schooling. Yet, as we will show throughout this book, all the participants in this conflict engage in politics as they seek to influence public decisions.

THE THEMES OF POLITICS AND GOVERNANCE

It is important that we start with an understanding of the terms *politics* and *governance* before we discuss some of the challenges that now produce conflict in the schools.

Two empirical propositions about human behavior encompass these two terms. The first is that *politics is a form of social conflict rooted in group differences over values about using public resources to meet private needs.* The second is that *governance is the process of publicly resolving that group conflict by means of creating and administering public policy.*

Diversity and Conflict

As we will see in the next chapter, political activity occurs as a result of the inevitable clash between groups with different values about many aspects of life. American society is composed of a diversity of groups that can generate social conflict. Some of this conflict is handled privately; if you don't like the new people in the neighborhood, or the prices of the local store, you can go elsewhere. In an historical example, American youth have left farms and small towns to seek opportunities in big cities that are not found back home. Conflicts can also be resolved within existing social systems without recourse to violence. Thus, the church can help resolve class conflict among its members, the family can deal with generational differences, political parties can resolve ethnic conflict, and so on.

But the political system governs such conflict, in the classic statement of David Easton, by "authoritatively allocating the distribution of values and resources,"[1] as its central characteristic. Note that this definition does not distinguish between democratic or authoritarian systems of government, or between presidential or parliamentary systems of democracy. Rather, the political system is a generic concept that applies to a variety of governing formats.

Conflict and Governing

We can get a sharper focus on both politics and governing if we examine the process by which social conflict is resolved. The conflict potential of value differences arises when a diverse population impinges on the political system. Leaders representing diverse groups seek new values and resources from the political system. In that system, resolution of conflict takes the form of considering program alternatives designed to deal with conflict. In considering policy alternatives, controversy arises over the identification of the problem, the possibilities for implementing programs, and the analysis of their likely outcomes.

Once decisions are made to create public policy, then next they must be operationalized—organization, staffing, and financing in a process of "implementation." In time, implementation can lead to yet another policy stage—evaluating policy outcomes. In turn, the results of these evaluations may precipitate even more demands, more program alternatives, and so on. Governing was once defined sarcastically as doing nothing until someone complains, then adjusting to that complaint, then waiting for the complaint about that adjustment, and then adjusting to the complaint to the earlier adjustment, and so on—eternally.

All kinds of public policy, including education, are surrounded by these twin concepts of politics and governing. In this book we discuss how groups have differed over a long period of time on the issue of "schooling for what." For much of that history answers were provided by school professionals. These professionals were rooted in colleges, government agencies, and school administrations and teaching staff, and they created a consistent pattern of operations we term "steady state." But in recent decades this condition has faced some challenges. These challenges, however, may turn out to be mere "tinkering," which has historically been the norm.[2] Both themes, persistence and challenge, appear throughout this book. As we approach the next millennium, it is still unclear how many of these challenges have affected the existing system.

Exploring Some Current Challenges

Later there will be more details of the persistence and challenges, but some current examples will highlight the politics of school reform. Among the fourteen thousand school districts of the nation, it seems as if everyone is trying something new in the way of curriculum, organization, finances, and so on. But the impression left to the observer is that of disorganized focus on problems and remedies. As Ernest Boyer, a veteran reformer, noted recently, "You could draw a 'Keystone Cops' image here of people charging off in different directions and bumping into each other and, in some instances, having a conflict with one another. There's no overall sense of where the problem is and how we should work together to get there."[3] After completing a series of national opinion polls, the Public Agenda Foundation concluded, righly or wrongly, that the public feels that the schools are no longer theirs, that they have been captured by teachers, by reformers, by unions—someone else. They see leaders and experts as unresponsive to their concerns. As long as these concerns go unaddressed, public resistance will continue to stiffen, ultimately leading them to abandon public education.[4]

A DIVERSE POPULATION

One of the challenges facing education today results from the role of a diverse population and its effects. One measure of the diversity is the ethnic stew of our population.

New Migrants to America

The United States is a nation of immigrants. A chronicler of educational change noted that 20 percent of U.S. senators are grandchildren of immigrants, a claim that can be made by "no other nation . . . about its leading legislative body."[5] As the poet Walt Whitman wrote over a century ago, the United States is truly a "nation of nations."

By the end of this century American society will have been transformed from one in which descendants of white Europeans were an overwhelming majority into one in which many more citizens are members of "minority" groups. This change in demographics is largely rooted in the history of U.S. immigration. In the first wave of immigration in the late-nineteenth and early-twentieth centuries, Europeans accounted for 85 percent of all immigrants. Since World War II, however, European immigration has been eclipsed by a "second wave" of immigration from Latin America and Asia, so that today European immigrants constitute only 10 percent of the total.

One political question is the degree to which new immigrants can be absorbed into American society. Some indicators are optimistic. Rates of home ownership among immigrants are equal to those of the general population, about 59 percent. Many Asians and Hispanics are moving to suburban areas, another indicator of their entry into the middle class.

Because reproduction rates among white Americans are lower than those of other ethnic groups, the Census Bureau estimates that

- by 2010, blacks and Hispanics will be equal in numbers to whites.
- by 2025, half of American youth will be white and half "minority."
- by 2050, no one group will be a majority among adults, producing in the nation a minority majority.

In the dilution of the traditional white majority, the potential for conflict also increases among an increasingly diverse people. However, such conflict will be focused in just a few states; 80 percent of all new migrants in 1990 were in just six states—California, New York, Texas, Illinois, Florida, and New Jersey. California had the largest share, with 44 percent of the total. Moreover, federal agencies estimate that for every legal immigrant to that state there was one illegal immigrant. These immigrants are also seen as a threat by many citizens of the earlier waves who as taxpayers provide schooling and welfare for illegal immigrants. As a measure of this apprehension, in 1994 two-thirds of California's voters supported a referendum limiting public resources for illegal immigrants. Support for the measure was not restricted to whites—almost 60 percent of black and Hispanic Americans also supported the measure.

There is an enormous impact on schools of this second wave of immigration. Languages other than English (mostly Spanish) were the dominant languages spoken in 31.5 percent of homes in California, and in 14 percent of homes in Illinois. Moreover, today's immigrants speak a great variety of languages, and this poses problems for school authorities. The proportion of "minority" teachers to students will decrease in states such as California in which the immigrant school population is expected to increase from 30 percent to 38 percent by the year 2000. Moreover, school graduates from the second-wave of immigrant groups will soon be applying for colleges, thereby placing pressure on higher education. There are already complaints that Asian-American students are "overrepresented" at the most prestigious campuses within the University of California system.

The school problems suggested here will affect all levels of educational governance. Questions will necessarily arise in the school district. Where can teachers be found for non-English-speaking students? Who should represent immigrants on local boards? Where will the local resources for schools be found? There are other questions arising at the state level. Where will funds come from to supplement local resources, especially when white voters dislike paying for education of the children of immigrants? At the national level, how can the limited federal funds for education keep pace with the large number of immigrants? What changes in curriculum and instructional methods are appropriate? All these questions set off conflict and political decisions.

School Libraries and Censorship

Other sources beside ethnic diversity generate school politics. For example, there has always been a surprisingly wide variety of groups that did not like some particular book in the school library. Any hint of profanity or irreligious attitudes was anathema to some, as witnessed by the decades-long criticism of Salinger's *Catcher in the Rye*. Business groups disliked books that were critical of free enterprise. Some in the South objected to being criticized for slavery in earlier times and for segregation in the modern era. Jews objected to anti-Semitic references in literature, as personified by the character of Fagin in Dickens' *Oliver Twist*. Blacks criticized racist terms, like "Nigger Jim" in Twain's *Huckleberry Finn*.[6]

Library protests of this type have grown in recent years. More groups have become critical of books that, in their view, derogated women, Indians, Hispanics, and so on. The American Library Association has documented a growing number of cases of censorship in the nation's schools since 1991. In 1993 there were nearly seven hundred such cases, and in 1994 even more.[7] Those who argue for banning school books claim that their purpose is to protect the young, and they deny any censorship. But the supporters of free speech believe that such measures reflect a lack of confidence in youth and thus charge censorship, pure and simple. Many of these attempts to ban books are instigated by conservative groups, often from the "religious right," who see some books as a challenge to the established order. Tennyson's theme of "The old order changeth" underlies this effort.

Both sides of this debate believe that families should have the right to decide what is best for their children. But librarians want parents to exercise this right at home, while conservatives want the school board to intervene on the ground that no parent can read everything before determining what is acceptable for his or her child. Local events find evangelical Christian clergy and families objecting to one or more books that they perceive as advocating such practices as homosexuality or Satanism (e.g., stories about witches or devils). Occasionally these efforts are made at the state level. In 1994 an Idaho referendum to ban materials that were represented as promoting homosexuality was narrowly defeated. While critics of censorship claim that this effort of certain religious groups to ban books they feel promote values antithetical to their own is only the beginning of a movement to assert control over other kinds of books, some school systems are bending to these new pressures by dropping "objectionable" materials from libraries. Teachers or librarians may come to doubt whether the inclusion of such books in their classes or reading hours is worth the parental pressure that might arise.

Sex Education and "Abstinence Only"

Diversity of thought is also reflected in controversies over curricula. A curriculum is based on an underlying philosophy of certain values and assumptions against which others may contend. Because of this, citizen groups, often religious in orientation, have often challenged the content of specific curricular materials or courses. For decades, challenges have been argued in the U.S. Supreme Court by those opposed to banning school prayers or Bible reading in public schools. Such protests have in the last decade become more overtly political, as local groups won seats on school boards and insisted that their values be incorporated in the curriculum.

Many of these challenges focus on promoting the requirements of sex education courses that sexual abstinence is the only acceptable method of birth control. A recent report found over two hundred cases of this issue.[8] More significantly, over twenty thousand schools subscribe to a three-volume guide advocating only abstinence. These critics argue that existing courses ignore abstinence and instead emphasize the use of condoms, thus implying that premarital sexual intercourse is acceptable. Supporters of the existing curriculum argue that promoting sexual abstinence is not enough. They point to statistics that show that most American youth are sexually active several years before marriage. Supporters of existing sex education also refer to increasing rates of sexually transmitted diseases, including HIV, the virus that leads to AIDS. Against such a real danger among sexually active youth, supporters believe that education in the use of condoms is appropriate.

The tactics of both sides are extremely political in their efforts to match private values to public decisions. Both sides seek to influence the media by meeting with editors, by writing articles, or by seeking coalitions with churches, health organizations, and local businesses. Candidates from both sides run for school boards, hoping to influence local decisions. Losers at the local level can also take their cases to the courts, or they can challenge state laws. A recent Louisiana case overturned the prohibition of curricula that were deemed medically inaccurate or religiously based. In this case, supporters of an "abstinence only" curriculum had won.

Although censorship and sex education are relatively low-visibility issues, they reflect the conflict of values among groups who see schools as a forum for promoting a certain way of thinking. Such conflict has consequences for the governance channels, primarily at the local level. Some school professionals see these parental pressures as a challenge to their own definition of what constitutes good education. From these clashes, the politics of value differences follows.

VALUE DIFFERENCES

As noted, core questions over value differences are relevant to educational policies. Two questions of critical interest underlie such value conflict.

Enduring Schooling Questions

What should children be taught? For much of our early history, the answer to this question came from family and church. They provided the teachers who shared many of the same values. Instruction in both moral and practical lessons guided such teaching. The slow emergence of professional education late in the nineteenth century added new points of view, but teachers still focused primarily on moral and practical subjects. By the twentieth century, new ideas emerged about what should be taught. Later, state law and regulations were promulgated to effect curricular change. These changes originated from the judgments of professionals (e.g., the Carnegie requirements) and later from the judgments of interest groups (e.g., the celebration of the birthday of Martin Luther King, Jr., Lief Ericson Day, or Cinco de Mayo). Today, the centers of decision-making power on such issues are still relatively remote from most parents. But increasingly, challenges to established values in curriculum have generated yet another conflict over schools.

Another continuing question of education lies in *who* should teach. For much of our earlier history, teachers were people— often women—with an interest in teaching and a certain level of education who were hired by family and church. In general, these teachers shared the values of those who hired them. But with the rise of "free public education" after 1840, formal instruction of teachers became the norm. Teachers were trained in "normal" schools, and over time, more education and training were required to teach. In the twentieth century, teachers began to experience the pressures of two sets of values, one from the community and another from the profession, and often they were conflicting. When compatible, these values stimulated teachers; but when opposing—for example in the controversies surrounding sex education—the conflicting values made their work much more difficult.

The Issue of Multiculturalism

These general findings of the history of schooling have contemporary relevance. One question of conflicting values can be found in the current debates over "multiculturalism."[9] Beginning in the late 1980s minority educators and activists were appointed by the New York Department of Education to discuss the formulation of a new curriculum. In their 1989 report this group argued that minority groups "have all been the victims of an intellectual and education oppression that has characterized the culture and institution of the United States and the European-American world for centuries." In light of the growing number of people of non-European descent in the nation, the report called for replacement of the "Eurocentric" curriculum by one that reflected the multicultural experiences of other Americans. This agenda was picked up in the intellectual circles of universities and also generated questions in big-city schools. This new challenge sought to highlight not simply the contributions of minority groups to American life, but also the total control by European-Americans over the curriculum. When elements of multiculturalism emerged in the mid-1990s in a report by a national commission on standards of teaching history, it was criticized by conservatives for its emphasis on minority groups and its allusions to European "oppression."

The response to the challenge of multiculturalism has taken several forms. Schools had traditionally smoothed over ethnic or religious differences in order to produce "Americans" who constitute a nation. "Public schools are the most common shared experience for most Americans, and the public school system has been the key to the Americanization process." It was also argued that the role of minorities in creating and building a new and developing nation was adequately treated in the current curriculum. By the late 1980s a state like Mississippi, with its earlier repressive treatment of blacks, had already required textbooks that reflect the contribution of blacks and other ethnic groups. In another example, a world history text, widely used elsewhere, had separate chapters on Islamic, African, Latin American, and Asian histories. A high school civics text had a chapter explaining equality under law, the earlier inferior conditions of blacks and women, and their movements that changed the law. Similar references to these groups appeared in other chapters.[10]

Criticism of the multiculturalists further insisted that even though not all minorities had contributed equally to the American heritage, "that does not diminish their right to an equal claim to the heritage." According to these critiques, the creative work of artists transcends any considerations of race, class, and gender. The commonality of the heritage taught through the schools is what holds Americans together, not the innumerable divisions of the society. Emphasis on difference will drive groups apart, while a stress on commonality underlies the concept of a nation.

These current examples of the driving force of values in conflict underline how politics and governance shape the nature of school products. We will next explore the agencies of governance in this conflict.

THE AGENCIES OF GOVERNANCE

Agencies at all levels of government are involved in school conflict. Pressures from those attacking or defending the status quo are focused into political channels. Two recent incidents— school prayer and institutional change in Congress—highlight how conflict resolution by such public agencies is a primary function of governance.

School Prayer

The U.S. Supreme Court, in a series of decisions spanning several decades, has decided against the official requirement of school prayers in public schools.[11] Although its line of cases continues to confirm that decision today, more recently its once unified view has weakened. For example, in 1962 the Court overturned (6–1) New York's law encouraging daily prayer recitations. In this and in later cases the First Amendment's prohibition of government promoting or establishing religion was determinative. In 1963 the Court overturned (8–1) Pennsylvania and Baltimore laws requiring prayer and daily Bible recitations. Two decades later in 1985 the Court, composed of a new membership, overturned (6–3) an Alabama law authorizing a daily moment of silence instead of a prayer. The purpose of that Alabama law, the opinion said, was not secular but religious. In 1992 a much narrower split of opinion (5–4) banned a public school in Providence, N.J., from using a rabbi for prayers. School officials who arranged this practice, the majority opinion argued, had created an environment that was coercive to students.

In much of the nation that is rooted in a traditional religious culture, particularly in smalltown and rural areas, these judicial actions had violated a basic proposition of community life. Public opinion polls showed that a majority of respondents believed that the schools should emphasize religious values, especially the right to pray. The Court has recently written that schools cannot forbid the use of school property for meetings of religious groups, if secular groups have similar access. While the Court's stance has softened somewhat, its decisions to prevent prayer and Bible reading have generated political pressure from citizens' groups for passage of a constitutional amendment permitting such practices. However, despite the growing strength of conservatives in Washington since 1981, there have not been enough congressional votes to support the necessary two-thirds majority for passage of such an amendment.

The best hope for religious conservatives was a change in the Court's membership, which could bring about a change in constitutional standards. But some districts in 1997 were still trying new arrangements for prayers that could bypass the Court. However, support for the Court has been rooted in civil liberties groups and major religious organizations—main-line Baptists, Presbyterians, Lutherans, and Jews. When President William Clinton in late 1994 indicated that he might be open to a constitutional amendment, these groups descended on him. The President then hedged his approval as support only for a "moment of silence," which he had endorsed while governor of Arkansas.

The politics over prayer arises from differences in values. Conservative religious groups argued that education and prayer were linked through historical and traditional school practices. Defenders of religion in schools argued that religious values were being ignored in textbooks and in curriculum. Their frustration with the rejection of a traditional set of values led first to the movement to change state laws and later to demands for constitutional change. Were a constitutional amendment to pass, it would be a useful illustration that political questions involving schools are rarely settled definitively. There are always other political arguments and other arenas in which these political fights can be carried out.

The 1994 Election and "Revolution"

Elections represent another means of influencing policy about schools. They are the key to creating legitimacy in the agencies of democracy, and electoral victors assume the authority to implement a political agenda. Elections thus provide one of the most important means of translating public opinion into public policy. When there is considerable conflict over policy, elections can act to maintain or to challenge established practices. Schools have directly experienced the effects of electoral politics in the form of school board elections and referenda. Superintendents and board members, who on an election night see a referendum that they supported has lost, know the reality of the authority of voters.

This linkage between elections and policy change is also apparent at the state and national levels. The state and Congressional elections of 1994 produced what its winners called a "revolution." For the first time in about fifty years the Republican party won both houses of Congress, elected thirty governors, and strengthened their position within state legislatures (one-third Republican, one-third Democratic, one-third split). The Republicans had campaigned on a nationwide theme of a "Contract with America" that called for a vast devolution of authority to the states and a large reduction in federal funds for many social programs. Supporters perceived the election results as consonant with Republican philosophy, namely, a growing disenchantment with federal controls and opposition to large federal spending. So as the new Congress opened in January 1995, there were quick successes in the first one hundred days in bringing to a House vote such measures as a balanced budget and forbidding unfunded federal mandates. But a year later in 1996, many of the "Contract" items had not passed Congress, or if they did, were vetoed by President Clinton. Moreover, criticism of the Contract and Speaker Gingrich dominated Democratic campaigns in the 1996 election that returned Clinton to office and reduced the GOP majority in the house.

The impacts on education of these changes were significant.[12] If programs and funds for education were to be devolved to the states, there would likely be reductions in federal funding. This raised questions about how the states would make up that difference. Moreover, many argued that state programs should be further devolved to local schools and districts. Within such a scenario, the regulatory power of states over local communities would be weakened. Local schools had often failed in the past to use opportunities to challenge state regulations. Rather, they had preferred to allow states to regulate them, even as they complained about the heavy hand of the state. Thus, states became lightning rods to deflect criticism of local officials who blamed state control for their own failure to exercise control. As veteran observers of education politics noted, earlier efforts to decrease federal control under Republican presidents such as Richard Nixon and Ronald Reagan began with great enthusiasm and support from Republican governors. But these eventually failed because less control and more freedom usually translated into a heavier financial burden in state budgets.[13] Although some federal changes in educational finance and administration are likely to occur as a result of recent Republican victories, changes are likely to be incremental.

This recent effort to modify federalism by devolving more authority to the states presents a new opportunity for understanding the politics of education. This opportunity arises from an analysis of the ongoing nature of conflict resolution among multiple authorities, deeply held but opposing values about schools, and a variety of political agencies. Later chapters will explore this intergovernmental dimension of the politics of education.

SCHOOL POLICIES

Policies produced by schools are similar in two respects to those of any governance agency. They involve allocation of values and resources, and they all reflect a common process of policymaking. Almost all of the services provided in schools are regulated by a complex set of policies generated by constitutions, legislation, court decisions, bureaucracies, and elections. This book will later deal with many of these policies in a systematic way, but it would be useful at this point to indicate a few new currents within the realm of public policy that involve schools. This will serve to highlight various elements of politics and governance in the policymaking process that involves stages of initiation, implementation, and evaluation.

Criticisms and Reform "Waves"

One central and national policy initiation within American education has been large-scale programs in the 1980s to improve the quality (or "excellence") of schools. In the 1990s, however, these reforms centered around issues of providing "choice" for parents. Such reform was directed against the steady state of education in all states with its pattern of received knowledge and routine activities by school professionals.

The background of change is relevant here. This steady state had resulted from reform over the last one hundred years, as earlier noted, that was implemented since by generations of professionals. A new feature, particularly after World War II, was the creation of large bureaucracies at the local and state levels to oversee the administration of an increasing number of standards regarding schooling. Again, this steady state existed in every local and state jurisdiction in the nation. Wherever one's children were schooled, there were much the same techniques of teaching, curriculum, special services, and administration—altered, of course, by variations in local context and funding.

This steady state was controlled by a hierarchy of power within each school system. Superintendents, sometimes termed "benevolent autocrats," and their agents in management—the principals— occupied the top of this hierarchy. Until about 1960, teachers,

lacking any collective bargaining power, had very little authority
in the schools. In big-city schools, a central-office bureaucracy
dominated all decisions, including resource allocation. A seemingly democratic channel of popular views—the school board—
was limited by its tendency to accept the definitions of problems
and solutions offered by professionals. Parents had little interest
in these matters, except to support the school's authority and
discipline and to vote for school taxes. When they turned up at
school, usually as members of an acquiescent PTA, parents focused only on side issues, like a cookie sale to provide a projector for the third grade. And as for another constituency—the
students—their closest contact in this organization came only from
teachers, and that interaction was similarly controlled.

But beginning in the 1950s, public dissatisfaction over declining student achievement grew, reflected in opinion polls critical of
schools.[14] Federal laws in the 1950s sought to improve science
quality and teaching, and in the Elementary and Secondary Education Act of 1965 improved education of poor children. In the
early 1980s most states sought "top-down" laws involving a host
of mandates.

But these laws did not satisfy opinion, so even more change
was debated, and state reforms abounded after 1985. There was
much discussion—but little change—about providing "choice" for
parents by moving children within or between districts. Decen-
tralizing authority to the school site was much discussed, but
again, relatively few districts took such measures, despite the
publicity given to the issue. Still, decentralization appeared in
Dade County, Florida, and in Los Angeles. In 1989 in Chicago,
over four hundred decentralized sites were created with local
councils of parents, teachers, and the principal, although there
was little indication by 1996 that these changes had any impact
on student achievement.

Other large reforms were publicized, but little action had been
taken as of 1996. Voucher plans, using public funds to enable
students to attend schools of their choice, had been much discussed for several decades. But little reform of this kind appeared;
indeed, voucher referenda had failed in three states (California,
Colorado, and Oregon) in the early 1990s. But the Republican
success in the 1994 election noted above brought new GOP gov-

ernors who were committed to vouchers, reviving hopes for this reform. Business executives also created a council in the mid-1990s to promote "school-to-work" policies. Another reform, "privatization" of public schools, was designed to decrease costs and found some supporters and a large-scale effort in Baltimore— later withdrawn. But critics of these reforms, primarily teachers' groups, were numerous, although some elements of privatization, for example, contracting for outside technical services, appeared to have benefits. Private foundations also funded the search for school reform successes that might be translated into large-scale public reform. Those foundations that entered the field to improve schools included Rockefeller, Carnegie, Pew, Annenburg, Lilly, MacArthur, and Mott.[15]

These challenges to the steady state of public schools were paralleled by assertions that schools had failed to teach students. The reform policies described above resulted from a perceived need to improve schooling by offering choice, decentralization, vouchers, or privatization. But by the early 1990s some analysis was questioning this charge of school failure as a "myth," that the reforms were directed against a system that had not been broken, as critics claimed. There were national reports of schools with fewer dropouts, higher test scores for both whites and minorities, and greater rates of college attendance by minorities. In 1995 the RAND Corporation reported academic gains, not losses, on standardized test scores over the two decades between 1970 and 1990. Those gains occurred despite such off-setting increases in percentages of teenage mothers, children in poverty, working mothers, or single-parent families.[16]

Reforms, often labeled as "waves" in the last decade, were more likely an artillery attack coming from many guns. But did they hit the target? Many reform ideas were never adopted, or if so, never implemented. Yet school policy, which had once been the province of the professional, had now entered a different political arena. More groups were involved, more effort was made across a wider front of governments, and more new practices were undertaken. But it is still unclear whether any of these efforts have been successful in the first and primary goal—improving student achievement. Moreover, if recent analysis suggests that schools have not been doing as badly as the reformers had insisted, there may not be a need for a complete overhaul of the system.

THE IMPLEMENTATION OF SCHOOL POLICY

Programs approved within the political system are never self-executing and so must be implemented. To meet program objectives, an organization must be created, staff employed, managers appointed, funds provided and disbursed, services dispensed, and results evaluated. There is much controversy surrounding each of these topics. A few of these problems, which are related to politics and governance, are highlighted below.

Examples of the Politics of Implementation

Politics surrounding implementation often shape the administration of school programs. For example, leaders of reform programs in Southeastern states have been unable to stay in place as administrators, so that incumbency turnover has weakened the thrust of change.[17] Since state reforms began in 1983 only two of thirty-six state educational administrators in these states have remained in their positions. On the average, these positions changed hands three times since reform began. Consequently, policy initiatives were interrupted when state economies faltered or state leaders changed.

Another political problem arises in that state mandates have been increasingly used to ensure local compliance. This has generated a local challenge against this control because state governments have failed to provide funds to carry out these mandates. All schools, localities, or municipalities are constitutionally dependent on the state for their own authority, but that dependency has been politically challenged by the mandate revolt. Not only do states want to escape federal mandates, but so also do local districts when they view the state capitol.

The politics of implementation is increasingly evident in the case of school superintendents. Faced with a wider range of state or federal programs to administer, superintendents find growing opposition from particular groups who believe that their interests are not being served. Whereas once the office of super-intendent had great authority over school matters, it now faces criticism from a wide range of minority groups, teachers, taxpay-ers, parents, and students, as well as from other governmental bodies. Today, many groups insist on providing input on major policy questions, and on having their members serve in school offices and oversee details of administration.

The result has been increasing political pressures on the su-perintendency, as a later chapter shows, thereby leading to greater turnover in office. The average term in big cities is down from six years a few years ago to three years in 1995. Length of serv-ice is about double that for other-sized cities, but still less than in the recent past. Working in a world where lay persons are empowered has altered the superintendent's old role of "benevo-lent autocrat" to one of "politician." To undergo a role change in life generates much stress, leading to more change in admin-istrative activity in which sharing, not dominating, prevails. More superintendents spend more of their time involved in public relations activities designed to generate support for school pro-grams, as well as for their own tenure. For many of them—as well as for principals—the result is often being fired or resign-ing, and many leave the profession.

These illustrations suggest that implementation matters are themselves permeated by the aura of conflict over resources and values. The structure and the personnel of organizations are al-tered by various interest groups. For a long time, implementa-tion rested with the professional schoolpeople, but today lay persons participate in these processes with consequences for professional careers.

PROGRAM EVALUATION

Implementation is not the end of the dynamic process of politics and governance. At some point there is evaluation, that is, the effort to deal with the pragmatic question, Did it work? This effort is often linked to "hard" quantitative measures of changing effects. But it is clear that evaluation has a "softer" and highly pol-itical quality. Group conflict arises over such matters in evaluation as the nature of research questions, the data needed to test them, the measurement methods employed, and their interpretation. Evaluators, scholars, and public officials regularly differ over such questions.

The "Effects" of Desegregation

For example, how would we measure the "effects" of desegregation?[18] Many may ask whether the central evaluation question is: Do desegregated schools improve education for blacks? But that evaluation is confounded by the realization that the Supreme Court did not judge that question to be the constitutional measure of desegregation. Rather, the judges unanimously agreed that the mere fact of segregation of resources was itself the central question, and that such segregation violated constitutional values. If segregation is the constitutional question, and not whether blacks learn more under desegregated conditions, other evidence must be used than just test scores.

What if the central research question were this: With resources now integrated, are more black students now obtaining more years of schooling than before? The question does not address the results of learning, but focuses on if there has been an increase in years of study for a specific minority group. By comparing only contemporary data—a method often used in testing desegregation effects—the researcher fails to ignore other improvements that are found in the more schooling, and in the larger allocation of school resources for blacks. Clearly, the data that are sought influence which questions are asked.

Now that ethnic groups understand the political quality of evaluation, many participate in assessing proposed school policies. In a short time these representatives have challenged the validity of tests, including standard IQ tests, and have sought to measure student outcomes other than just test scores. However, this sophistication in evaluation has not been applied to the consequences of desegregation after the *Brown* decision. Does mandatory desegregation actually contribute to a further segregation of races of students, not in schools but in residential areas? Is the white flight from urban centers creating a pattern of "apartheid" that results from changes in demographics within big-city school systems? Such a result would work against a notion of society that is free of racism. As always, schools reflect major aspects of the larger society in which they are embedded.

Knowing Science and Teaching Science

The pages of *Educational Evaluation and Policy Analysis* and other journals closely track the process and effects of school policies. One case will demonstrate how evaluation is affected by noneducational factors, such as administrative contradictions within policy operations, even when professionals wish to do the right thing.

Since the 1950s the effort to improve the teaching of science has been backed by hundreds of millions of federal dollars. Hundreds of university-based scientists have been engaged in research to improve science curricula, and courses based on these curricula have been taught by unnumbered teachers in public schools across the country. By the end of the 1960s universities and scientific institutes had developed solid curricula in earth sciences, physical science, biology, chemistry, and engineering. But by the mid-1970s the adoption rate of these curricula in schools had peaked, and the momentum for change had slowed. Worse, by 1983 national surveys had found a fall-off in student science achievement in all subjects except biology. These results could stimulate a variety of questions, but our attention here is directed to the outcomes and evaluation of science education policy.[19]

In policy evaluation there are always major questions that must be addressed, but at the core of evaluation is the highly pragmatic American question: Did it work? In this case, were high-quality materials for curriculum developed? The answer is a definite yes. Scientists from the best universities and from different fields created solid instructional materials. But if the question is, Did more teachers use these materials? the results are disappointing. The most widely used curriculum (Introductory Physical Science) was adopted by no more than 25 percent of secondary schools (for at least one class), and other types of curricula had only a 15 percent adoption rate. One judgment made by the evaluators was that "other than the content, length, and difficulty of class, little had changed."

Another evaluation question is, Were more students enrolled in science courses? These results are also dismal. Schools often used these new science curricula as alternatives to but not replacement for existing courses, so fewer students took them. These courses also often received the stigma of being for "college-bound" students, hence they were regarded as elitist and avoided by most students. However, one ongoing effect has been the change in commercial textbooks. Many of these texts have incorporated some of the factual content and the emphasis on laboratory work found in these earlier science education projects. Nevertheless, national tests do not reflect any gains in student knowledge of science.

What are the causes of these failures in implementation? First, these curriculum projects were developed by scientists who rarely consulted with teachers. The curriculum developers, then, had little understanding of how teachers might adapt the content of these curricula to suit their own pedagogical styles. Second, few teachers had been trained in the "new" science. Not surprisingly, many found the new material too difficult to understand themselves, let alone to teach to their students. Finally, the scientists who developed these curricula had little understanding of limitations within the school structure or their ability to adapt to the implementation of new curricula. These new science reforms required longer classes and more teacher preparation time. Moreover, many of the changes required by the new curricula were too complex to be handled within traditional teaching formats or in outmoded labs. Because of this, physical changes in the classroom and the school were needed, and these often entailed the construction of new laboratories. So teachers were often stuck with their old textbooks and older facilities, and whatever new courses were offered focused on college-bound students.

The best thing we can find to say of these reforms is that science courses and books were updated, and a new generation of leaders within science education emerged. But the needs of the target group, the larger student body, were not met, and instructional materials had changed very little for most of them. The "political" quality of science curriculum, like many other aspects of curriculum reform, is due to the pressure of inertia within organizations. Added to this pressure was the unwillingness of teachers to accommodate to change, because, after all, teachers feel most comfortable with what they have already done. Efforts to induce change, through such means as salary increases as incentives to undergo course training in universities, often come up against the heavy pressure of inertia.

WHAT CONCEPTS HOLD TOGETHER SUCH DIFFERENT CASES?

In short, the origins, administration, and evaluation of school activities must be seen within the human context of professionals and lay persons who work daily within schools. Human interests shape all aspects of the political system, and it is ideas that move actors in politics and governance.[20] The variety of contemporary cases we have reviewed in this chapter may appear to be unconnected events. We now need to turn to the realm of theory, because it can provide the means to connect and understand the seemingly disparate elements of politics and governance in schools today.

NOTES

1. David Easton, *A Systems Analysis of Political Life* (New York: Wiley, 1965). For a more recent theoretical overview see James March and Johan Olsen, *Democratic Governance* (New York: Free Press, 1995).

2. For major challenges see Diane Ravitch, *The Troubled Crusade* (New York: Basic Books, 1983); for the concept of "tinkering" see David Tyack and Larry Cuban, *Tinkering Toward Utopia* (Cambridge, Mass.: Harvard, 1995).

3. Ernest Boyer, quoted in *Education Week* (December 7, 1994): 13.

4. Deborah Wordsworth, Executive Director, Public Agenda Foundation, as quoted in *California and Their Schools* (Menlo Park, Calif.: Ed Source, 1996), p. 6.

5. Observations below are from Harold Hodgkinson, "A True Nation of the World," *Education Week* (January 18, 1995): 32.

6. For history see Mary Raywid, *The Axe-Grinders* (New York: Macmillan, 1962).

7. *Education Week* (November 10, 1994): 10.

8. Jessica Portner, "Grassroots Warriors Waging Battle Over Sex-Ed. Curriculum," *Education Week* (October 12, 1994): 5.

9. The quotations below are from the critiques of multiculturalism in Willard Hogeboom, "Multiculturalism: Build on What Holds Us Together," *Education*

Week (December 4, 1991); and from Diane Ravitch, "Standards in U.S. History: An Assessment," *Education Week* (December 7, 1994): 48; see also, Arthur Schlesinger, Jr., "The Disuniting of America," *American Educator* 15 (Winter 1991): 14–33.

10. Walter Wallbank et al., *History and Life*, third edition (Glenview, Ill.: Scott, Foresman, 1987); Robert Hardgrave, Jr., *American Government* (Orlando, Flor.: Harcourt Brace Jovanovich, 1987). The changing nature of this curriculum is evaluated in Frederick Wirt, *"We Ain't What We Was:" Law and Civil Rights in the New South* (Durham, N.C.: Duke University Press, 1997), chaps. 5–6.

11. Reviewed in *Education Week* (December 14, 1994).

12. For a review of the new issues and problems immediately after that election see March Pitsch and Lonnie Harp, "Elections Are Likely to Spur Shift in Power," *Education Week* (December 14, 1994): 1.

13. An effort by President Reagan in the early 1980s to arrange a "swap" of medical and poverty programs with the states failed for much the same reason; Thomas Anton, *American Federalism and Public Policy* (New York: Random House, 1989), pp. 217–22.

14. Polls are surveyed for a quarter-century in Stanley Elam, *How America Views Its Schools* (Bloomington, Ind.: Phi Delta Kappa, 1995). See also David Mathews, *Is There a Public for Public Schools?* (Dayton, Ohio: Kettering, 1996).

15. On voucher, foundations, and business leaders see separate stories in *Education Week* (December 14, 1994); for privatization see the symposium edited by Richard Hunter and Frank Brown in *Education and Urban Society* 27 (1995): 107–228.

16. The "myth" claim is found in the columns of Gerald Bracey, in *Phi Delta Kappa* in the mid-1990s; see also *Student Achievement and the Changing American Family* (Santa Monica, Calif.: RAND Corp., 1995).

17. Lynn Olson, "Rapid Turnover in Leadership Impedes Reforms, Study Finds," *Education Week* (January 11, 1995): 6.

18. These questions are pursued in Wirt, *"We Ain't What We Was."*

19. These elements of the reform are developed in Gary Yee and Michael Kirst, "Lessons from the New Science Curriculum of the 1950s and 1960s," *Education and Urban Society* 26 (1994): 158–71; quotations that follow are from this source. For an evaluation of 1958 to 1970 math and science reforms see Peter B. Dow, *Schoolhouse Politics* (Cambridge, Mass.: Harvard University Press, 1991).

20. For a comprehensive review of recent research in education politics see Jay D. Scribner and Donald Layton (eds.), *The Study of Education Politics* (Washington, D.C.: Falmer, 1995).

2 _____

The Apolitical Myth and Recent Turbulence

We have suggested that American schools are "political," partly as a result of their connection to political systems of state and national governments. But schools also act as miniature political systems themselves. Many professionals and parents would prefer to think of schools as "apolitical," having nothing to do with politics. For, as everyone knows, politicians are vile folk, whose status is about that of used-car sales persons.

These differences in interpretation stem from varying conceptions of what constitutes a "political" act. Schools have traditionally been judged as apolitical, meaning that they had nothing to do with political parties. While political party politics was "dirty," schools, on the other hand, were considered sanitized and outside the realm of party politics. For political scientists, though, political parties represent only one facet of political life. The essence of a political act is the struggle of private groups to secure the authoritative support of government for their values. Within this definition of the term *political*, much of what schoolfolk regard as apolitical is highly political.

Let's be clear on our focus. We are not discussing *how* schools should be run nor *what* they should teach and *why*. Our focus is, instead, on *how the process of policymaking in schools has characteristics that can be termed political.* Wc will show how that process is becoming increasingly and more openly politicized as a result of major changes in the ways state and local governments and even citizens relate to the school system. New definitions of school purposes, new claims on school resources, new efforts to make the schools responsive to certain groups and their values—all are giving rise to a larger, more weblike set of political relationships surrounding local schools. Almost any and every element of school governance is subject to political controversy.

THE ORIGINS OF THE MYTH

By a mutual but unspoken long-standing agreement, American citizens and scholars have contended that the world of education is and should be separate from the world of politics. Although *elections* and *referenda* concerning school policies are political, these words did not connote "politics" in the usual sense when applied to educational policy. Two reasons existed for attempting to preserve the myth that "politics and education do not mix." The first was the risk to the school professionals who were covert players of politics when they were expected not to be. The second reason was the relative benefits to them, namely, more legitimacy and money if they preserved the image of the public schools as a uniquely nonpolitical function of government.

At the turn of the century, a nationwide affiliation of "progressive" university presidents, school superintendents, and non-professional allies emerged from urban business and professional elites. One aim of these people was to free the schools from both partisan politics and excessive decentralization. They saw political corruption as the prime cause of educational inefficiency in urban schools. And in fact, at that time many politicians did regard the schools as a support for their spoils systems and awarded school jobs and contracts as political favors.

Municipal corruption was everywhere, and the schools were as bad as any other city office. Muckrakers exposed textbook publishers and contractors allied with corrupt school trustees for common boodle in the common school.

A superintendent in one of the Eastern States writes: "Nearly all the teachers in our schools get their positions by political 'pull.' . . ." One writes from the South: "Most places depend on politics. The lowest motives are frequently used to influence ends." A faint wail comes from the far West: "Positions are secured and held by the lowest principles of corrupt politicians." . . . In Boston, the teachership is still a spoil of office. . . . The worst kind of boss rule has prevailed in San Francisco. . . .[1]

This situation was vigorously reinforced by local control. A decentralized, ward-based committee system for administering the public schools provided opportunities for exercising extensive political influence. In 1905, Philadelphia had forty-three elected district school boards consisting of 559 members. There were only 7 members on the Minneapolis board, while Hartford—with a third as many people—had 39 school visitors and committee persons. Despite such great variations, at the turn of the century sixteen of twenty-eight cities with over one hundred thousand population had boards of 20 members or more.

Reformers maintained that board members elected by wards advanced their own parochial and special interests at the expense of the school district as a whole. What was needed to counter this atomization, they believed, was election at-large. A good school system was good for everyone, not just for one segment of the community. Professional expertise rested on the assumption that schools could be administered "scientifically," namely, independent of any particular group's values. Through scientific administration, schools could be isolated and protected from local political processes.

Reformers also charged that the executive authority of the larger school boards was splintered because they worked through many subcommittees. No topic was too trivial for one more subcommittee, ranging from how to teach reading to the purchase of doorknobs. At one time, Chicago had seventy-nine subcommittees, and Cincinnati had seventy-four. The primary prerequisite for better management was thought to be centralization of power in a chief executive who would have considerable authority delegated from the school board. Only under such a system could large-scale improvements be made and accountability ensured.

By 1910 a conventional educational wisdom of this kind had evolved among the schoolfolk and leading business and professional men who had sought reforms. Sometimes only a very small group of patricians secured new charters from state legislatures and thereby reorganized the urban schools without any popular vote. The watchwords of reform became *centralization, expertise, professionalism, nonpolitical control,* and *efficiency*—all of these terms in practice would inspire the best system. The governance structure needed to be revised so that school boards would be small, elected at large, and freed from all connections with political parties and regular government officials such as mayors and councilmen.

The model for organization and governance of schools and districts was the industrial bureaucracy that emerged in the turn-of-the-century economy. Divorced from the city political leaders, a board elected by the city as a whole would be less susceptible to graft and job favoritism. The centralized power of the superintendent would overcome the bureaucratic tangle and inefficiency of board subcommittees. These reform concepts spread rapidly from the large to small cities and towns, and they found their major forum and vehicle in the National Education Association.

At the turn of the century, urban school reform was part of a broader pattern of elite municipal change. Public rhetoric then pitted the corrupt politician against the community-oriented citizen. The underlying motives of these reformers have since been questioned by several historians. Financial and professional leaders deplored the decentralized ward system largely because it empowered members of the lower and lower-middle classes (many of whom were recent immigrants).

> Underlying much of the reform movement was an elitist assumption that prosperous, native born Protestant Anglo-Saxons were superior to other groups and thus should determine the curriculum and the allocation of jobs. It was the mission of the schools to imbue children of the immigrants and the poor with uniformly WASP ideals.[2]

After reforms were enacted, membership on the governing agencies did change. George Counts's classic study of 1927 showed that by then upper-class professionals and businesspeople made up the centralized boards of education.[3] For instance, in Saint Louis, after reforms in 1897, professionals on the board jumped from 4.8 percent to 58.3 percent and big businessmen from 9 percent to 25 percent; small businessmen dropped from 47.6 percent to 16.7 percent, and wage earners from 28.6 percent to none.[4] These board members then delegated many of their formal powers to professionals who shaped schools to meet the needs of industrial society—but only as defined by one segment of that society.

The no-politics ideal of public education has enjoyed impressive and lasting popularity with the general public. There have been hard-nosed advantages for the professional in nursing this folklore, as summarized by one school superintendent.

1. The higher social status and salary generally accorded schoolpeople by the public is better maintained and somewhat dependent upon a situation in which the schools are seen as unique rather than as a mere extension of the same local government that provides dog catchers and sanitation departments.
2. In maintaining a tighter control over the public school system, the image of "unique function" allows greater leverage by the professional school administrator than an image acknowledging that schools are "ripe for the picking" by dilettante and professional politicians.
3. The "unique function" image also provides the schools with a stronger competitive position for tax funds wherever voters are allowed to express a choice of priorities among government agencies.[5]

The outcome of this nonpolitical ideology is a major irony in our political system:

Thus is the circle closed and the paradox completed. Thus does the public school, heralded by its champions as the cornerstone of democracy, reject the political world in which democratic institutions operate. Thus is historical identification with local government accompanied by insistence on complete independence of any agency . . . of local government, lip service to general citizen activity attended by mortal fear of general politics, the logical and legitimate companion of citizen action.[6]

Continuing Themes and Tensions

As noted, several national trends have today made the public schools more overtly political, strongly challenging the tenets of the traditional steady state. The reforms of the last three decades suggested in Chapter 1 highlight this increasingly political quality. These changes point to the basic ongoing problem in the governance of American schools. That is, *the tension between the community's need for school leadership that can lead and be trusted and the same community's desire to have its own will carried out by the leadership.* Since its inception in the 1840s with Horace Mann's heresy, American public education has sought responsiveness to the public need for what Raymond Fosdick termed the extraordinary possibilities of ordinary people. The changing focus of American civic education over a century shows that the current effort to create "multiculturalism" is only the most recent skirmish.[7] The historical search to ensure public responsiveness ranged from party control of schools, through the progressive model of corporate centralization, to the contemporary call for contradictory modes of leadership such as "site-based management" (bottom-up organization) or "state leadership" (top-down organization).

This brief history shows that there is nothing new under the sun. An intriguing repetition of issues has occurred over the last century: merit pay, school prayer, school closings, dropouts, and the education of the gifted. In large part, we read both the repetition and variety of that history as reflections of the classic political tension existing between the leaders and the led in a democracy. In each case, tensions center on having school policy work in the way that the variety of actors wish it would. Table 2.1 suggests how language changes while basic ideas remain the same.

THE POLITICAL TURBULENCE OF AMERICAN SCHOOLS

The steady state of education in earlier decades and the contemporary challenge to school policy by reformers suggest clearly that "politics" is now a major aspect of the profession of education. Figure 2.1 captures the flow of political forces that impinge

Table 2.1

Education's "In" and "Out" Terms in the Mid-1990s

OUT	IN
Inputs	Outputs
Innate ability	Effort
Rote learning	Mastery
Autocratic	Autonomous
Seat time	Accomplishment
Student as learner	Student as worker
Teacher as lecturer	Teacher as manager of instruction
Longevity	Competence
Administrator as master	Administrator as servant
Centralized bureaucracy	Decentralized management
Technology: bells and whistles	Technology: productivity enhancer
School board: micro-management	School board: stewardship
Time: periods, semesters, years	Time: flexible
Schools: teacher proof	Schools: teacher friendly
Diploma = seat time	Diploma = mastery
Age	Accomplishment
Superintendent = dictator	Superintendent = choreographer
Taxpayer	Shareholder
Standardization	Standards
True and false tests	Authentic assessment
Blue collar	Professionals
Uniform salary schedule	Pay for performance
Education: school's business	Education: everyone's business
School = building	School = learning

Source: Denis Doyle and Susan Pimental, "What's In and What's Out in '93." Reprinted with permission from *Education Week*, Vol. 12, No. 16 (January 13, 1993): 43.

on policy decision making from below and above the governing agency—the school board.

To understand that concept, we must first identify the "actors" in this process, that is, the constituents of both local and external school policymaking. Second, it is also important to understand another aspect of politics—the "squeeze" on the school district that now exists on policymaking from forces both below and above. Both this pressure from newer local constituents and the policy pressures from above strongly influence school administrators. Administrators, obliged to define the nature of their services, are caught up in a new environment of competing forces. Once, schools of education, or continuing inservice training and

Figure 2.1
Paradigm of Turbulent School Politics

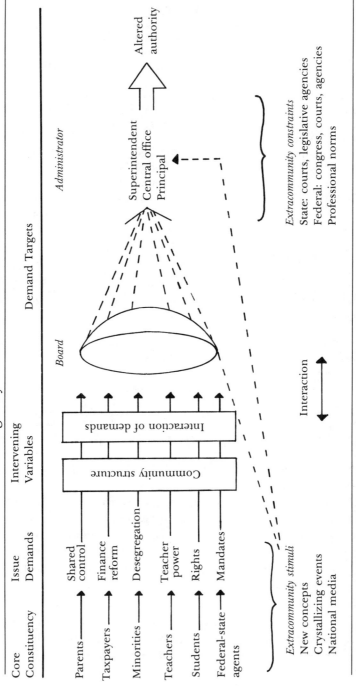

Core Constituency	Issue Demands	Intervening Variables		Demand Targets	Administrator

Parents — Shared control
Taxpayers — Finance reform
Minorities — Desegregation
Teachers — Teacher power
Students — Rights
Federal-state agents — Mandates

Interaction of demands

Community structure

Board

Interaction

Superintendent
Central office
Principal

Altered authority

Extracommunity stimuli
New concepts
Crystallizing events
National media

Extracommunity constraints
State: courts, legislative agencies
Federal: congress, courts, agencies
Professional norms

Source: Reprinted with permission from Frederick M. Wirt, "Political Turbulence and Administrative Authority in the Schools," in Louis H. Masotti and Robert L. Lineberry, eds., *The New Urban Politics,* p. 63. Copyright 1976, Ballinger Publishing Company.

journals, helped provide the administrator with specific definitions of what constituted quality service. Now, though, new definitions have become necessary.

We begin by explaining the set of new constituents who have come to challenge the earlier hierarchy of power and authority that the schooling profession had known. In effect, new school "core constituencies" have emerged. (*Core* indicates that we have separated these groups for analytical purposes although they are not mutually exclusive in experience.) Each group creates special tensions for the school's political authority as exercised by the board and its administrators as each challenges the leadership over special issues that involve reallocation of school resources.[8] These core constituencies and their issues are:

Parents—shared or community control, advisory input, decentralization, or whatever term is current.

Students—rights of governance, expression, dress, behavior, and so on.

Teachers—organization for collective bargaining (hereafter shortened to "teacher power").

Taxpayers—reform of local financing involving a larger assumption of costs by the state.

Minorities—the issues that encompass desegregation, dropouts, and equal employment.

Federal and state authorities—guidelines, mandates, court orders in matters of discrimination, curriculum, finances, and so forth.

Controversy over any issue may vary from locality to locality, but all are subject to certain forces both outside and inside an individual district. The absence of walls around the school districts is a metaphor showing them open to the public and private influences from the external centers of decision making of American national life.[9] New currents outside local schools agitate them. Concepts about how society should be formulated or life enjoyed, the episodic eruption of national events that crystallize local hopes and fears about school matters, and the immediate transmission by media of all these—all are major outside stimuli of school conflict. When such local conflict mobilizes new groups, when national currents are at work locally, and when the rancor and clamor swell, we reach a level of conflict accurately termed *turbulence*.[10]

NEW GROUPS, NEW ISSUES

We provide a fuller treatment of these new power groups throughout this book, but it will help to focus our analysis now to review briefly the roles of these groups.

Parents and Shared Control

The turn-of-the-century triumph of the efficiency doctrine, achieved through centralization and bureaucracy, weakened the ties between school leadership and its constituents. That was acceptable in the pre-World War II decades, when schooling laid minimal claims on district resources, and professionals benefited from their own publicity about education as the key to success. In the two decades after that war, this weakened linkage (as voting studies showed) continued to be acceptable in the rush to obtain schooling for all.[11]

Sometime during the late 1950s, the aura of the professionals began to fade. In 1954 the *Brown* v. *Topeka Board of Education* decision illustrated for the first time the disgraceful failure of Southern educators with their black students. Other complaints emerged that, regardless of race, Johnny could not read, speak languages, or calculate in base ten, and that Russian schools were outperforming our schools. Our rivalry with the Russians generated a vast injection of local and federal funds into schools with the National Defense Education Act in the late 1950s, with university support in the early 1960s, and finally with the Elementary and Secondary Education Act of 1965.

The more voters contributed, though, the more they complained that the educational bureaucracy was not sensitive to parental preferences. Social scientists provided analyses of the unresponsive nature of the school administration. Many of these critiques focused on New York City's central headquarters, now regarded as the prototype of an unresponsive bureaucracy rather than an exception.[12] Suburbanites maintained that administrators were insensitive to their demands either for richer or for plainer curricula, whether in affluent Scarsdale, urban New York, or working-class Maple Heights, Ohio. In the central cities—particularly the newly mobilized black communities—central offices and site principals were increasingly ridiculed for their insensitivity, which was easily labeled "racism." From a surprisingly wide range of social classes, parents-as-voters criticized their lack of connection with school district decision making.

Although reasons for this differed with locale and status, the impulse to participate had clearly increased. Notions of shared control took on different forms during the 1970s. At times participation meant parents having structured input into school decisions, and new structures were created for parental advisory committees at the school site level. In California, for example, community members joined the school principal and teachers to set a budget in tune with their own definition of good education. In Chicago, parent-dominated committees could hire or fire principals.

Parental input also focused on what was being taught in the classroom. The fear of teaching Communism during the 1950s became in the 1980s the anger at teaching about biological evolution or the anger about children reading fiction with harsh language or critical views of American society. By the 1990s AIDS education had become a subject of controversy. Some parents rose to defend the integration of these subjects into the curriculum, and battles were waged in street demonstrations, court suits, state legislative lobbies—accompanied by a steady vilification of professionals and board members.

Parents also challenged the quality of the schools, focusing especially on academic achievement. From the earlier concern with whether or not Johnny could read, growing claims—and some supporting data—suggested that schools were not teaching effectively. National news magazines featured articles on school "failures." Demands arose to hold teachers individually responsible for their pupils' progress, but professionals pointed to numerous factors more potent than teachers in influencing results. By the mid-1980s a first wave of reform involved states' requiring examination of tenured teachers for their basic literacy.

In short, the role played by parents became much more than just participation in parent-teacher organizations, which had loyally supported professionals prior to the mid-1960s. It used to be that teachers and administrators were the highest educated people in a community—in 1960 one in twelve parents had a bachelor's degree, but it was one in five in 1993. In recent years parents felt more knowledgeable and confident in questioning educators and in pushing changes. It no longer worked to keep parents busy with a cake sale to raise money for a projector.[13]

Taxpayers and Financial Reform

Demands for more control of schools have not been restricted just to parents worried about what schools were doing to their children; over the last twenty years, taxpayers have also challenged school financing.[14] A spate of litigation developed from the fusion of the Ford Foundation and university scholars in law and educational finance. It began in California with the famous *Serrano* 1971 decision, which found that the principle of student expenditures based on district wealth was unconstitutional. The United States Supreme Court's 1973 *Rodriquez* case narrowly prevented this finding from being elevated into a constitutional principle. Reform efforts continued though, focusing on state legislatures after the abortive attempts at change through the Supreme Court and statewide referenda.

Pressures to redistribute school financial resources were accompanied by pressures to have the states take on a higher share of local school costs. Since 1900 that state share has grown, stabilizing at around 40 percent after World War II (a figure concealing numerous small shifts up and down). By 1970 it was still at that level, but by 1981 it had jumped to over 50 percent due to recent reform movements and public disapproval of property taxes. Local financial support had also fallen off. The mid-1960s saw the peak for support of local bond and tax issues; thereafter the electorate became increasingly resistant.

A network of school finance reformers appeared amidst this current of protest. Public policy issues emerged on state political agendas for many reasons, but one of the most important and least understood is the role of interstate lobbying networks that sponsor and promote issues in a wide variety of forums. Elements of the network may be entrepreneurs, private nonprofit advocacy organizations, lawyers, interstate technical assistance groups, and often private foundations. Such networks spread ideas and create opportunities for state politicians to champion particular causes or programs. Many of the most interesting educational innovations, such as competency testing, have been promoted by such a lobby network.

By 1981 two of the largest networks—those for school finance reform and spending or tax limits—started clashing with each other. School finance reformers advocated large increases in state and local spending to meet "equity" criteria and special needs, such as those for bilingual, handicapped, or urban students. In contrast, members of the other reform group crusaded for tax limitation, seeking to stop or reverse the growth in state and local spending. Both networks were spawned by different entrepreneurs who generated activity and structured rewards; both acted to unify members from diverse organizations.

The 1983–95 reform era has focused more on academic standards than on finance equity. But expenditures increased nevertheless during 1980–1990 by about 30 percent after inflation as politicians voted to fund higher salaries and academic standards. More science and mathematics teachers were hired, and teachers received more dollars as they moved up their new "career ladders." By 1996 there was a new spate of lawsuits challenging the equity of state school finance formulas, as school expenditures had not grown faster than inflation in the past five years.

Racial Minorities and Desegregation

The core constituency of racial minorities, so intimately involved in school desegregation, has two purposes. First, members seek a status goal, recognition that the Constitution's commitment to equal protection of the law applies to them as well, despite centuries of prejudice and discrimination. As such, desegregation is only one aspect of the "politics of deference," the central struggle of American ethnic politics to gain respect for one's importance and value as individuals and as a group.[15] The second goal of minorities in school desegregation is material, namely, the reallocation of resources to improve schooling opportunities for their children. Desegregation is thus one aspect of the concern for redistributive justice that was sparked in recent decades by challenges to the standards of urban service provided to America's poor of whatever race.

In this effort, almost nothing has been achieved without external pressure on the local district. Everywhere the forces of court orders—and in the South the threat of fund cutoffs to segregated schools—have accounted for any progress. Against local racial barriers, then, a coalition of national and local interest groups, scholars, legal studies centers, and national media interacted with the federal courts to dramatically alter the face of Southern education. Between 1962 and 1972 the South dismantled its de jure segregated schools under the combined attack of private groups and federal action. Year after year the number of all-white schools shrank abruptly to amaze many who thought these changes would take decades. By 1981 Southern desegregation had gone well beyond the publicized stage of parental protest over busing or white supremacists' fears of racial mixing. School problems were now more educational than political; that is, they involved improving the educational services and enhancing the life chances of the poor regardless of race. But in the mid-1980s the rate of desegregation held steady; while higher in the South than elsewhere, stabilization became the norm.

The situation in the North during the 1970s looked a lot like that of the South during the 1950s, with actual segregation increasing. The federal thrust had diminished over the years because of presidents with little political support for the issue, Congresses under great pressure from those who saw busing as the special evil of desegregation, and the lack of support from Northern whites for a range of special programs that originated in President Johnson's Great Society program. Enormous movements of whites out of central cities, recalcitrant local school boards, aroused local political organizations, and hesitant local press all combined at the district level to slow or block a movement that was simultaneously changing dramatically in the South.

But litigation continued in the North, and a rash of federal district judges ordered desegregation planning and busing. Every fall during the 1970s, the opening of Northern schools witnessed some big city in turmoil over beginning this task. Yet much desegregation did take place without publicity, especially in middle-sized places. But for many Americans, the street fighting in Boston was what they associated with such change, although Denver had desegregated quietly that same fall. Wherever such turbulence occurs, there is a formal, almost inescapable, drama that must unfold, with each stage set regardless of locale. By 1981, however, an impressive number of districts existed where desegregation at least extended to the stage at which the outcry dies down, the buses roll regularly, and education begins.

Since then very few court orders have been issued, and Northern cities are now even more segregated. A more conservative Supreme Court in the 1990s ordered the end to desegregation in big-city schools if there had been full efforts made to succeed. Minorities have turned to educational quality and a share of school jobs as this issue seemed to die away.

Students and Their Rights

Core constituencies sketched to this point are based outside the school walls, but two groups that operate on the inside are students and teachers. Both have known the same remarkably brief and recent period during which novel concepts have suddenly flowered to offer them new powers formerly controlled by administrators. Considering their position of relative weakness, students have made strides that contrast dramatically with the background of the law's long indifference to them.[16]

For most of our history, the authority of the school administrator over the student's life at school has been almost complete. Legislatures gave state departments of education broad authority that they in turn passed on to the school board and its professionals. The federal Constitution and statutes had no sway here, for the idea of student rights rooted in these sources did not yet exist. During this era, an administrator's response to any student even politely questioning why he or she had to dress, walk, eat, speak, and otherwise act in the prescribed manner was much like that of writer Ring Lardner when his children questioned him: "'Shut up,' I explained."

The seminal United States Court decision in this field, which typified subsequent thinking by other courts, was another of those abrupt changes in the power context of schools—the 1969 decision of *Tinker* v. *the Des Moines School District.* Here, Des Moines students wearing black armbands to protest the Vietnam War had been suspended even though they had created no disruption. The Court's opinion noted that when a basic constitutional right, such as free speech under the First Amendment, was being exercised, and no evidence showed that the student action interfered with school purposes or disrupted schooling, no punishment could be levied. As later cases demonstrated, such an exercise *could* create disruptions and so be prohibited. Thus, Southern schools could not restrict the wearing of civil rights buttons if the results were nondisruptive, but they could do so if they caused disturbances.

In only a few years, this principle and those of due process and equal protection of the laws have permeated many traditional school practices affecting students. Only a brief listing of judicial restraints on once-conventional disciplinary rules and management decisions is possible here, but recall that these have all emerged since 1969. They include rulings in use of athletic symbols, Confederate flags, and school names; regulating hair length; lack of procedures for suspension and expulsion; corporal punishment; use of bulletin boards; use of achievement or aptitude tests; rules for athletic eligibility; preference for male rather than female sports programs, and so on.

As a result, school authorities everywhere drew up lengthy statements of student rights and school authority. Professional associations helped with model statements related to different fields. None of this meant that students could not be expelled or suspended, their publications controlled, or their expressions banned. They could, but now only according to set procedures and over a longer period of time. All of this constituted an additional challenge to the once unchallengeable school authority, adding another eddy to school turbulence. But students' rights have not advanced significantly after the mid-1980s, as the courts have retreated from the due process concerns of the 1970s. Principals now can check lockers without search warrants and censor student newspapers.

Teachers and Organizational Power

The other core constituency challenging traditional authority from inside the school is teachers—once widely viewed as submissive. A city superintendent or principal today who would regard teachers like that would be hard to find. A change has transpired among teachers in the past thirty years. In part this stems from changes in American education itself and in part from teachers' perceptions of themselves. As with other groups involved with education, things will never be the same again. Teachers achieved a potential for power as education became big business.[17] When more parents wanted their children to have more schooling after World War II, and there were more children to educate, Americans spent more on education. This in turn meant that the schools needed more teachers. As a proportion of the gross national product, school expenditures rose during the period 1949 to 1970 from about 3.5 to 8 percent. Where we spent only $2 billion in 1940, we spent $50 billion in 1970 and over $300 billion in 1996. Riding this massive injection of funds into the schools, teachers grew in numbers from just over 1 million in 1940 to almost 3 million in 1971 and to about 3.1 million in 1996. The number of pupils per teacher declined from 22.3 in 1972 to 17.4 in 1996. Between 1952 and 1968 teachers' incomes increased by over 125 percent, while personal income and employee average earnings rose nationally by about 94 percent. Their salaries passed the average earnings of industrial workers, and the gap increased even more during the 1960s. By the middle 1970s, however, teachers' wage increases lagged behind inflation and private industry only to regain their momentum after the 1983 reform era. As a result, the average teacher salary was $36,500 in 1972 and $37,846 in 1996 after an inflation adjustment.

Concern about wages helped teachers' increasingly conscious efforts to organize for collective bargaining on salary and other matters. The cause-and-effect relationship is ambiguous, however. Did bargaining legislation and subsequent organization precede or follow teachers' dissatisfactions? Were boards and legislatures frightened into voluntary improvements in reaction against successful teacher strikes elsewhere? Did the advent of collective bargaining increase teacher salaries?

There is no question about the growth of teacher affiliations that have become more insistent on improving working conditions. This insistence was seen in the toughening up of the larger National Education Association (NEA), once passive on these issues, and in the rise of the smaller but more militant American Federation of Teachers. These groups both became more active in party politics as well. For the first time, the NEA endorsed a presidential candidate, Jimmy Carter, in 1976, and endorsed Clinton in 1996.

The growth of powerful teacher organizations has been paralleled by the rise of the strike. Despite widely prevalent state laws against public employees using this tactic, some form of strike—"withholding of labor"—has developed as the main instrument used to secure teachers' benefits in recent years. Between 1955 and 1965 there were only 35 strikes in all, but during the one year of 1967–1968 there were 114, and 131 the next year. Coincidental or not, during this first period of strike action, 1966–1968, the number of signed contracts increased by almost one-half. By 1985 the strike threat of teachers was as much a part of autumn as the new football season. But thereafter, the frequency of teacher strikes declined as both teachers and school boards learned to adjust to a new labor environment (e.g., in "win-win" negotiations).

Success has not been without its problems for teachers. As teachers participate more and more in the reallocation of resources at the local, state, and national political levels, they lose the aura of being apolitical. And with their new role as political participants comes all the opprobrium the term signifies in American culture. It was their once mythical quality that helped them claim a large share of resources for so long without having to contend with other claimants. Now, in the state legislatures and city councils, where school budgets are sometimes reviewed, teachers are only one more pressure group whose claim to special treatment must be balanced against others' claims. It follows that other pressure groups will increasingly combine against the teachers' claims and so draw teachers even more into open political conflict. Whatever their form, however, these trends change the traditional interaction between teacher and administrator, adding yet another constraint to the broad authority that school officials once had.

Federal and State Authorities

From the perspective of school boards and professionals who share this turbulence breaking against their walls, probably the most noticed—certainly the most complained of—has been the force of external governments. The movement of core constituencies—demanding new definitions of how schools should be structured, financed, and their services delivered—has often been frustrated by local authorities. The protests have then escalated to higher levels of government within the federal system. This later stage of the conflict resulted in some groups securing state and federal statutes, administrative rulings, or court orders in their favor to change local school practices. This then impinged on the local power structure, meaning more limitations on professional control of the school program.[18]

Each of the constituencies referred to has generated many such external requirements in the form of mandates, guidelines, orders, suggestions, and reporting forms. Sometimes the source is a funded program to enhance educational services, but it can also come in the form of a court injunction not to do something or a court mandate to do something else. These can all become enormously detailed in their requirements. In some cases, regulations or suggestions come without the finances necessary to administer them. And always multiple forms must be filed to show a state or federal authority that what was required has in fact been achieved. That work adds enormously to the volume of services and standards that the schools must maintain.

Some standards work their way into the regular procedures of the district, where they constitute a force generated by a new constituency working against the previous professional dominance. The general rule is that what the district most favors in this flow of external demands becomes what is most implemented. But where the district neither asks for nor accepts the demands, then adaptation of the law becomes the norm. It would be a rare district among the fourteen thousand in the nation where this response did not take place. But bit by bit, across two decades, this extramural force has challenged and gradually altered traditional local control to become another current in the contemporary turbulence of American schools.

Political Forces Outside the Locality

No constituency acts independently; the turbulence of school politics is also affected by extracommunity stimuli. The outside forces noted in Figure 2.1 may be the most important factor in all local politics, whether dealing with schools, high-rise buildings, welfare, ethnic conflict, roads, or other public policies.[19]

Three broad stimuli affect school constituencies today. First, the *state of the economy* greatly influences the amount of resources available and their allocation. Many administrators, particularly older superintendents, have witnessed extremes of bust and boom. The Great Depression of the 1930s shrank all school budgets, preventing new programs and cutting old ones. Under intense constraints the school boards could listen to few if any claims from any core constituencies except the taxpayers. More recently, prosperity and subsequent recession affected every school district in the nation. In the resurgence of public support for school reform beginning in 1983, booming expenditures characterized local politics. With ever-expanding resources seemingly available, claimants for new programs and benefits could be satisfied by boards and administrators. By 1983 the growth in imports and the loss of jobs in autos, steel, and other basic industries made international economic competitiveness a key issue. This concern spawned a massive movement to increase educational standards. But in the early 1990s, another recession hit hard at school reform.

Another extracommunity stimulus is *the power of new concepts*, particularly those centered on social change. Every change mentioned for a core constituency illustrates this process. In addition, education seems particularly subject to faddishness in curricular matters, such as new math, critical thinking, merit pay, and so on. Certainly the concept of "evaluation," given a powerful push by Title I of the 1965 Elementary and Secondary Education Act, has penetrated school activity wherever federal monies are deposited. Most recently, school choice has become such an issue.

Spawned by some scholarly "scribbler," funded by foundations, transmitted by educators' meetings and journals, researched and certified by schools of education, reform ideas sweep through the American school system in recurring tides. Some are transitory, for example, Nixon's Right to Read Program, but others leave a permanent mark on schools, such as desegregation in the South. Behind them all, however small or large, is someone's notion of the preferable, the efficient, the humane, the inexpensive, and the just in matters of schooling.

Another class of extramural stimuli includes highly publicized *crystallizing events* that capture core constituencies and dramatically generate new demands on local school authorities, adding even more turbulence to school politics. The oil-boycott crisis; the death of a prominent athlete due to cocaine; the spread of AIDS; precedent-shattering judicial decisions in the *Tinker, Brown,* and *Serrano* cases; a clash over community control in New York City—these all illustrate the singular event that no one can ignore.

We cannot separate these extramural events from extramural concepts, for each of them emerged from a new full-blown conception about the schools' allocation of resources and values. Yet a concept that is circulated among only scholars lacks both life and influence until an event embodying it grabs national attention. But a concept can also have an effect without the crystallizing event—for example, the spread of the doctorate as a requirement for the school superintendency. The combination of concept and event, though, creates an intensely powerful stimulus for change among the core constituencies that make local school politics so turbulent today.

TURBULENCE AND SCHOOL GOVERNANCE: NOBODY IS IN CHARGE

One consequence of this turbulence has been the emergence of a new question about power. Who is in *charge?* Amid the complexity of new groups and governments, the answer may be—no one.

The Growth of State and Federal Influence

One impact of school turbulence is that the local superintendent has lost his once-preeminent position in setting the district agenda and controlling school outcomes. The superintendent and school board have become reactive forces, trying to juggle diverse and changing coalitions across different issues. Many school reforms such as new math have disappeared, but some left behind structural changes that could be easily monitored but that created a constituency. Consequently, a partial legacy from the 1960–1980 era was tremendous growth in the specialized functions of the school, including administrative specialists in career education, bilingual education, nutrition, health, remedial reading, and so on. Many of these new structural layers diluted the superintendent's influence because the specialists were paid separately by federal or state categorical programs. Hence they were insulated from the superintendent's influence by separate financing and the requirements of higher levels of government.

One element that today is very different for local authorities is the intensity and scope of recent state policy actions. The most striking feature of state-local relations in the last twenty years has been this growth in state control over education. Today organizations of professional educators and local school boards are making suggestions for only marginal changes in proposed new state policies. These trends cede much more control of education to the states. However, there will be enormous variation in how states take control—from the highly aggressive states, such as California and Texas, to the more passive, such as New Hampshire and Wyoming. Dangers attend any aggressive, broad-based state education policy. States can change policy through statutes and regulations, which have a standardizing effect. The focus of state policymaking after 1980 was no longer on categorical groups, such as handicapped or minority students. Instead, current reforms, whether top-down or bottom-up, are aimed at the central core of instructional policy, including what should be taught, how it should be taught, and who should teach it. State-level political actors leading the current wave of reform are legislators, governors, and business interests. The traditional education interest groups—teachers, administrators, and school boards— have been used primarily in pro forma consultative roles.

Also noteworthy of increasing state control is that it has not been limited to such traditionally high-control states as California and Florida. The high tide of state intervention in local instructional policy is washing over Virginia and Connecticut—longtime bastions of local control. National movements and widespread media coverage have played a crucial role in the current reform wave, just as they did with the 1970s issues of school finance reform and minimum competency testing. Some state initiatives, such as high school graduation standards, moved through the states without any federal mandate or organized interest-group lobbying.

The Squeeze from the Bottom

As a result of these changing internal and external forces, the discretionary zone of local superintendents and boards has been progressively squeezed into a smaller and smaller area. The superintendent's discretion is squeezed from the top by increasing regulations from the legislative, administrative, and judicial arms of the federal and state governments, as noted. In addition, there has been the expanding influence of external private interest groups and professional reformers, such as the Ford Foundation and the Council for Basic Education. Moreover, interstate groups, such as the Education Commission of the States, increased their influence, as did nationally oriented organizations, such as the Council for Exceptional Children. All over the nation, networks of individuals and groups sprang up to spread school finance reform, competency testing, increased academic standards, choice, restructuring, site-based management, and other programs.

Moreover, superintendents and local boards also found their decision-making powers squeezed from the bottom by the growth of local collective bargaining contracts reinforced by national teacher organizations. A national study documents the incursion of these organizations into educational policy.[20] And, as noted, the last three decades have been a growth period for local interest groups often resulting from national social movements. This thesis on turbulence from above and below is shown in Figure 2.2.

The social movements of our period differ from those of the nineteenth century, exemplified by Horace Mann, which were interested in building up institutions like the schools. Today social movements are interested in challenging public institutions and trying to make them more responsive to forces outside the local administrative structure. Some would even assert that these

Figure 2.2
Trends in Educational Governance—1950–1995

+ Federal
+ State
+ Courts
+ Interstate networks and
  organizations (school finance
  reform, teacher standards
  boards, tax limits)
+ Private business, Educational Testing Service,
  Business Roundtable, and so on
+ Foundations

- School board
- Local superintendent
- Local central administration

+ Teacher collective bargaining
+ Administrator bargaining
+ Community-based interest groups
    (nonprofessionals)
+ School site councils
+ Charter schools

+ increasing influence
- decreasing influence

movements help fragment school decision making so that schools cannot function effectively. Fragmentation has reached the point where in some districts it could be characterized as hyperpluralist. The litany of the media portrays violence, vandalism, and declining test scores as the predominant condition of public education. It is not surprising that polls rate all schools as weak but individuals rate their own school as much better. What one hears from the media about others is refuted by what one knows intimately at home.

In California, for example, this situation has become so serious that the schools increasingly suffer from shock and overload, characterized by loss of morale and too few resources to operate all the programs that the society expects schools to offer. The issue then becomes how much change and agitation a public institution can take and still continue to function effectively.

Californians are confronted with numerous successive initiatives such as vouchers, illegal immigration, and an extreme version of all the other forces sketched above. Citizens there and elsewhere go to their local school board and superintendent expecting redress of their problems only to find that the decision-making power is at the state or some other nonlocal level. The impression grows that no one is "in charge" of public education.

All of this does not mean that local school authorities are helpless. Rather it means that they cannot control their agenda or shape decision outcomes as they did in the past. The superintendent must deal with shifting and ephemeral coalitions that might yield him some temporary marginal advantages. But many of the policy items on the local agenda arise from external forces, such as state and federal governments, or from the pressures of established local interest groups, including teachers.

The earlier 1920–1960 era of the superintendent as "administrative chief" has passed with profound consequences; the new school politics is much more complex and less malleable. How can we understand as political the seeming confusion of actors and events, emotion and rationality, conflict and conformity described in this chapter? Will this political turbulence lead to an end of American commitment to public education? This question would not have been asked twenty years ago, but now is of great concern to public school supporters who point to declining public opinion polls and a loss of local-civic organizations and community identity.[21] We now turn to a deeper analysis of the political dynamics of American education as a basis for understanding these crucial issues.

NOTES

1. David Tyack, "Needed: The Reform of a Reform," in *New Dimensions of School Board Leadership* (Evanston, Ill.: National School Board Association), pp. 29–51.

2. Tyack, "Needed: The Reform," p. 35.

3. George Counts, *The Social Composition of Boards of Education* (Chicago: University of Chicago Press, 1927).

4. Elinor Gersman, "Progressive Reform of the St. Louis School Board, 1987," *History of Education Quarterly* 10 (1970); 8–15.

5. Lesley Browder, "A Suburban School Superintendent Plays Politics," in *The Politics of Education at the Local, State, and Federal Levels*, edited by Michael

Kirst (Berkeley, Calif.: McCutchan, 1970), pp. 191–94.

6. Roscoe Martin, *Government and the Suburban School* (Syracuse, N.Y.: Syracuse University Press, 1962), p. 89. For a theoretical critique of the Progressive reforms see Jack H. Knott and Gary J. Miller, *Reforming Bureaucracy* (Englewood Cliffs, N.J.: Prentice-Hall, 1987).

7. Gladys Wiggin, *Education and Nationalism* (New York: McGraw-Hill, 1962).

8. For an overview of how this affects the superintendent, see William Lowe Boyd and Robert L. Crowson, "The Changing Conception and Practice of Educational Administration," in *Review of Research in Education*, edited by David C. Berliner, Vol. 9 (Washington, D.C.: American Educational Research Association, 1981), pp. 311–73; and for a survey, see Thomas Glass, *The Study of the American School Superintendency* (Arlington, Va.: American Association of School Administrators, 1992).

9. See Michael W. Kirst, *Who Controls Our Schools* (New York: W. H. Freeman, 1984).

10. This concept is first advanced in Frederick M. Wirt, "Political Turbulence and Administrative Authority," in *The New Urban Politics*, edited by Louis Masotti and Robert Lineberry (Lexington, Mass.: Ballinger, 1976). The larger picture of external influences in America is set out in Norton Long, *The Unwalled City* (New York: Basic Books, 1972); Frederick M. Wirt, *Power in the City* (Berkeley: University of California Press, 1974).

11. See the survey data in Richard F. Carter and John Sutthoff, *Communities and Their Schools* (Stanford: Institute for Communication Research, 1960).

12. David Rogers, *110 Livingston Street* (New York: Random House, 1968).

13. For a broader perspective on the current professional challenge, see Frederick M. Wirt, "Professionalism and Political Conflict: A Development Model," *Journal of Public Policy* 1 (1981).

14. The fullest analysis of the following material is found in Walter Garms, James Guthrie, and Lawrence Pierce, *School Finance: The Economics and Politics of Federalism* (Englewood Cliffs, N.J.: Prentice-Hall, 1988).

15. The ethnic factor is set out in Wirt, *Power in the City*, Pt. V. The fullest analysis of events in this section is found in Gary Orfield, *Must We Bus? Segregated Schools and National Policy* (Washington, D.C.: Brookings Institution, 1978).

16. The following material draws upon John C. Hogan, *The Schools, the Courts, and the Public Interest* (Lexington, Mass.: Lexington Books, 1974). See also David Kirp and Mark Yudof, *Education Policy and the Law* (Berkeley: McCutchan, 1987).

17. Following data are drawn from James W. Guthrie and Patricia A. Craig, *Teachers and Politics* (Bloomington, Ind.: Phi Delta Kappa Educational Foundation, 1973).

18. The fullest review of this current is Tyll van Geel, *Authority to Control the School Program* (Lexington, Mass.: Lexington Books, 1976).

19. Frederick M. Wirt, "The Dependent City?: External Influences Upon Local Control," *Journal of Politics* 47 (1985): 85–112.

20. Lorraine McDonnell and Anthony Pascal, "National Trends in Teacher Collective Bargaining," *Education and Urban Society* (1979): 129–51.

21. David Mathews, *Is There a Public for Public Schools?* (Dayton, Ohio: Kettering Foundation, 1996).

3

A Framework of Analysis for Political Turbulence

Given the turbulence described earlier, it would seem hard to find patterns in the turmoil in what Henry James called the "buzzing, booming confusion of reality." These currents operate in roughly fourteen thousand school districts, a truly indecipherable mosaic without some guide for classifying and explaining what transpires. What analytical scheme can make sense of the diversity and similarity in American education? What political framework of analysis enables us to understand the political nature of school turbulence?

METHODS OF ANALYZING STEADY AND TURBULENT QUALITIES

Some of the explanation that follows has been provided by scholars with different purposes and methods in mind. Educational journals are filled with *descriptions* of the operations of school systems and subsystems, their agents and participants, and their laws and regulations. Description is invariably accompanied by normative *evaluations*, that is, value judgments about whether the object described is worthwhile or workable. Description and evaluation further merge into *prescription*—recommendations for changing the reality to achieve the normative objectives, to close the gap between real and ideal. What has been least common is *explanation*—suppositions and supporting evidence about the causes, consequences, and interrelationships of objects in reality. Causal theory of this kind is frequently found in the psychology of education and sometimes in the sociology of education but seldom in educational administration before the 1970s.[1]

When we look for causal theory in the study of the politics of education today, we find very much where once there was little. The reasons lie in the myth of apolitical schools and the lack of a theory to direct and channel research. This became less true after 1970 as myth was discarded and theory sought. So long as school policy was regarded as "above" politics, its study via political, analytic frameworks was regarded as misguided. As a consequence, theoretical statements of explanatory power were unlikely to develop. Accepted theories of one sort make it difficult to entertain opposing explanations. If the stork is said to bring babies, there is not much room for sex education.

Iannaccone has explained how the profession had once earlier incorporated this orientation by asserting that education was a "closed system," isolated from politics, and that its leaders were free from external control. Also, by controlling what comes in from the outside environment, educators could reduce change within their system. Such effort was clearly useful for professional educators, freeing them from many external constraints and from unsettling demands for internal change that characterize other "more political" institutions.[2] In the past educators were so skilled that they moved the community to adopt the apolitical myth. As Eliot, a pioneer politics-of-education analyst, wryly noted forty years ago, a successful superintendent was one adept in "community relations," but "why not say frankly that he must be a good politician?"[3] Yet most political scientists accepted unquestioningly the educators' closed-system definition, and almost none studied it. Only recently—seeing similarities in education to other policies—have they recalled that "Rosy O'Grady and the Colonel's lady are sisters under the skin."

The most significant reason, however, for the once meager

scholarly analysis of educational politics is probably the lack of an applicable theoretical orientation and methodology. As political scientists pointed out twenty-five years ago, no single theory, simple or complex, guided such research, nor was there agreement on the appropriate methodology.[4] Political scientists, then and now, are severely divided between traditional studies of institutional or legal analysis and quantitative studies of political behavior. Among the behavioralists are a number of partial theories of political behavior, which is another complication. In short, despite the flood of "politics of education" work done in the 1970s, no overarching general theory generated any hypotheses that could be tested by acceptable methods in the crucible of political experiences. Instead there was a grab bag of partial theories and contrasting methods. That this is typical of the early stages in any scholarship is nonetheless frustrating for those who want to create order amidst confusion. The politics of education is certainly not orderly for those who prefer scholarship that explicates established truths, but it is exciting for those who prefer to innovate in the development of theory and hypothesis.

How can we proceed, then, in the absence of an established theory for organizing knowledge? First, we need some definitions. *Theory in its traditional sense is directed toward explanation and prediction* by means of "a set of . . . related propositions which include among them some lawlike generalizations, and which can be assigned specific truth value via empirical tests."[5] Because scholarship, like life, is always imperfect and because all research involves some compromise with ideal requirements, we turn instead to another form of theory—heuristic. *Heuristic theory is not so much a predictive scheme as a method of analytically separating and categorizing items in experience.* Much of what parades in political science as theory of the first type—predictive—is actually heuristic, at best providing a "framework for political analysis." We agree with Easton that "the appropriate question to ask about a theoretical analysis today is not: does this fully explain the functioning . . . or does it offer a fireproof set of concepts toward the end? . . . The appropriate question is: does this approach help us to take a small step in the right direction?"[6]

Easton's comment is appropriate, for it is his heuristic scheme or "framework for political analysis" that we employ in organizing the concepts and data of this book. This framework is termed *systems analysis.* Easton deemphasizes theory in the classical sense and prefers instead to discuss a "conceptual framework" or "categories for the systems analysis of politics."[7] The utility of systems theory is that, like all other heuristic schemes, it enables us at least to order our information or hunches about reality. We can thereby determine what portions of the scheme are clearly untenable in reality, which have some support there, and which need to be further studied. The use of systems analysis has limits, noted later, but presenting the current state of knowledge in the politics of education is our major purpose. For this, systems analysis provides an organizing principle to deal with the current turbulence in school politics. In this fashion only can we "take a small step in the right direction."

THE SYSTEMS ANALYSIS FRAMEWORK

Easton's framework contains the familiar perspective of a society composed of major institutions or "subsystems"—the economy, the school, the church, and so on. Individuals interact with one another and within these institutions in patterned ways that constitute a distinctive culture. One of these institutions is the *political system.* It differs from the others because it alone is the source of, in Easton's classic statements, "authoritative allocation of values, [i.e.,] those interactions through which values are authoritatively allocated for society." This is the subsystem whose decisions—about how individuals and groups will be allocated the valued but limited objects—are generally accepted as authoritative, that is, *legitimate.* The values this system allocates may be *material*—a textbook, defense contract, free land for constructing railroads, or dropout schools. Values allocated may also be *symbolic,* conferring status and deference on favored groups—for example, making Christmas or Martin Luther King's birthday a school holiday. Such an allocative system exists in every society, although its exact forms, inherent values, and public politics differ with place and time.

The link between the political system and other subsystems is a key element in this analysis because Easton is reaching for a general statement about the conditions under which other subsystems interact with the political system. This interrelationship is one in which *stress* in other subsystems of the social environment generates *inputs* of *demands* on and *supports* of the *political system.* The political system then reduces or *converts* these inputs into public decisions or *outputs*, which in turn *feed back* allocated values and resources into the society where the process began. Figure 3.1 is a sketch of this set of interactions.[8] These concepts seek to describe components of a dynamic, interactive, political system that may *persist* in the society in which it is embedded. Easton's concern is not merely with how the political system operates, but with how it persists through time by adapting itself to the host of demands made on it.

The Model Illustrated for Schools

What does all this have to do with schools? The rest of this book will answer this question, but we can briefly illustrate our theme now. Schools allocate *resources*—revenues, programs, professionals—and they also allocate *values*—teaching Americanism or the importance of learning for intrinsic or occupational purposes. If so, then schools are as much political systems as are Congress or the presidency, the state legislature or executive. School systems perform this in a society in which other institutions—economic, religious, family, and so on—themselves seek certain valued resources from the schools. This interaction can take two forms. The most obvious are *demands whose characteristics increase today's political turbulence.* For example, a group wants a special curriculum, more parental authority, or more teacher power, and these wants are directed as demands toward school authorities. A second form of interaction with the schools is *support*; that is, certain groups provide the school with taxes or with intangibles, such as a favorable attitude toward education.

The political system of the school that receives such demands must deal with them selectively because it lacks resources to meet them all. In short, a gap exists between what all groups want and the resources to meet those demands. In all times and places this gap is a powerful generator of social and political conflict. *So school systems must act politically because they must choose which*

Figure 3.1
A Simplified Model of a Political System

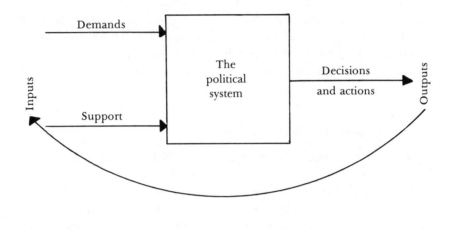

Source: Reprinted from *A Systems Analysis of Political Life* by David Easton by permission of the University of Chicago Press. © 1965 by the University of Chicago Press.

demands to favor and which not. The result of this choice is an *output,* for example, a state or federal law, a school board resolution, or a superintendent's program. An output could even be a principal's memo to the faculty on how the library budget will be allocated between the science and social studies departments. This may not seem to be choosing among resources and values on a major scale—unless you are the science teacher. Whatever form an output takes, all are alike in that they authoritatively allocate values and resources.

After this act, as the arrow at the bottom of Figure 3.1 implies, the output must be implemented in order to cope with the inputs that originally gave rise to it. For example, demand for bilingual education generates a district program, which is implemented by organizing the resources of personnel and material that constitute the program. In another example, the lack of popular support for a school program because it is unproductive or biased—a demand prevalent in American schools—can generate new pressures on the school authorities to alter it. In short, schools can be viewed as miniature political systems because they share certain qualities with large-scale political systems. And, as discussed later, the school professional must operate within this system in a way that shares much with the classical position of the politician. That is, he or she mediates among competing demands from school constituencies that have been organized to seek their share of valued allocations from the school system.

The Concepts Defined

A fuller statement of systems analysis is appropriate here, beginning with the environment of subsystems outside the political system.[9] This environment in Figure 3.1 is of two parts. The first is the environment that exists within a nation (the economy, culture, social structure, and personalities), which represents potential sources of inputs for the political system. The second part is the environment that exists outside the nation; this is a "suprasystem of which any single society is part." It includes the international, political, economic, and cultural systems of the world.

Within either part of the environment—internal or external—challenges arise from changes in existing interactions. Some challenges are in the form of *stress*, which critically impinges on the political system's ability to allocate values for society and to induce most members to accept them. This challenge could be a world war, a major depression, an energy crisis, or a new consciousness of ethnic frustration. Failure of the political system to cope with challenge can be severe. The Greek city-states and the Roman and Aztec empires, as well as various tribal clusters, illustrate political systems that failed to reduce challenge and consequently disappeared. However, so long as the stress is maintained within a limited range, the system persists.

At some point, challenge can move from the external

environment in the form of *exchanges* that penetrate the political system's *boundaries* to inputs that "concentrate and mirror everything in the environment that is relevant to political stress." The inputs, whether *demands* or *supports*, are "key indicators of the way in which environmental influences and conditions modify and shape the operations of the political system."

Demands are pressures on the government for justice or help, for reward or recognition. Behind these demands lies the human condition of longing for something in short supply. However, resources are never plentiful enough to satisfy all claims—a condition of tremendous importance to all aspects of our society, particularly for the political system. *Supports,* on the other hand, are a willingness to accept the decisions of the system or the system itself. A steady flow of supports is necessary if any political system is to sustain its *legitimacy* (i. e., the psychological sense that the system has the right to do what it is doing). So vital is this input that all societies indoctrinate their young to support their particular system, a task that is part of the school's work but is also shared with family and peers.

The whole process of demands and supports can be illustrated in the issue of Southern school desegregation. Demands for desegregation arose from a racially based stress, long endured—but later unendurable— by blacks. Moving from private rancor across the political boundary to create a public challenge, blacks mobilized their resources, first in demands upon courts and later upon Congress but continually upon local school boards. The segregationists' counter demands mobilized other resources to block and delay this challenge. During this process, those seeing too much change or too little began to decrease their support for the Supreme Court's authority to allocate values.

The political system *converts* such inputs: sometimes combining or reducing them, sometimes absorbing them without any reaction, but at other times converting them into public policies or outputs. Clearly not all demands are converted into policy, for the political system is more responsive to certain values, those dominant in the larger society. What inputs get through depends upon which values the conversion process reinforces and which it frustrates. They are also influenced by the values of the political authorities operating within this flow of inputs.

For example, some educators insist that maintaining discipline is a prime value of classwork, while others prefer to achieve intellectual excitement that often looks undisciplined. Which of these values gets reinforced by state authority is the end result of a political struggle. That is, one method will eventually be "authorized," and the school system and its personnel will allocate their resources toward that value. This struggle to have resources allocated authoritatively for one's own educational value is political, much like the process found in other policy fields.

The authorities responsible for running the political system constantly interact in the conversion process with either those outside or those inside the political system. The pattern of their interactions often stems in part from role definitions imposed by the political system itself. Such interactions generate certain pressures inside the political system—or *withinputs*—which in turn shape the conversion process and products. The result is the actors' commitment to a standard way of acting and believing that constitute a systematic way of life. That is a force contributing to its stability. It is also a force that generates challenge by those not benefiting from the outputs, as this book shows.

For example, desegregation reflected a challenge to the systematic way of life of white supremacy in schools in the South. Challenge demands were ignored much longer by Congress and some presidents than by the Supreme Court and other presidents. Border states in the 1950s and 1960s desegregated more quickly than Southern states, and Mississippi school boards resisted most of all. These differing reactions reflected various combinations of power and values in each political subsystem. Each used resources in the political system to advance or impede these challenges, and the resulting conflicts drove the conversion process—which still continues.

The outputs of the political subsystem once achieved require policy implementation that enhances the safety, income, and status of some while it also detracts from those of others. A resulting profile of public policy will mirror the structure of power and privilege and tells us much about what values currently dominate the political system.

Moreover, the authorized purpose of the output will find meaning in reality only through the process of *feedback*. This is the interaction of output with its administration, which becomes in time an established behavior—an *outcome*. For example, the Supreme Court required desegregation at "all deliberate speed," but federal district courts defined that output differently for school districts. In 1965 Congress authorized school aid for schools with *poor* children, but the outcome in the U.S. Office of Education's implementation of that law was aid for *all* schools.

Clearly, the gap between output and outcome becomes a major stimulus to future policymaking. That is, the action of the political system may not result in outcomes. Rather, because outputs can influence society, they generate a subsequent set of inputs to the political system through a *feedback loop*. That is, dealing with challenge causes a response in the system that is communicated to the political authorities, and so a new round of challenge and response begins.

The Concepts Illustrated

The contemporary political turbulence clearly reflects this tension between system and challenge about schooling. These concepts are incorporated in Figure 3.2's educational example of Easton's system analysis. Stresses affect the schools from events as far away as Saudi Arabia or Japan, or as close as meetings of local ministers or teachers. These events emerge in the school's political system as group challenges, for example, to cut school costs or institute school prayers. Whatever their content, these are seeking to reallocate school values or resources. Those in the school political system can reject some of these demands or convert others into formal outputs. The latter can be an act of Congress or a local referendum. The resulting educational policy is then implemented as an administrative decision—for example, busing plans—which in time has outcomes for particular groups, say academic gains for blacks. And the latter group generated the environmental challenge in the first place.

Note that this framework presents the political system as something other than just an allocative process. After all, this structure is an attempt to address the larger question of how any allocative process persists. As Easton notes:

Figure 3.2
The Flow of Influences and Policy Consequences in the School's Political System

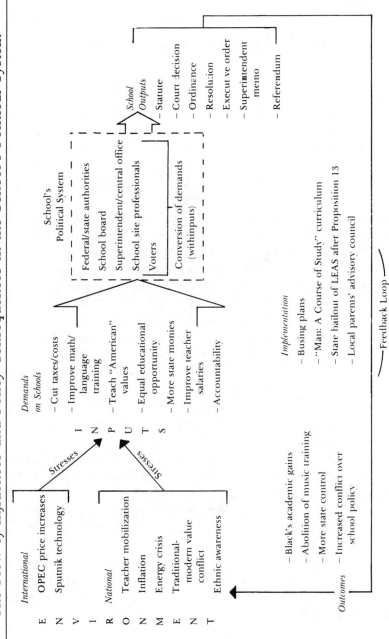

Persistence . . . is intricately connected with the capacity of a political system, as an open, self-regulating, and goal-setting system, to change itself.
The puzzle of how a system manages to persist, through change if necessary, forms a central problem of the analysis of political life.[10]

The belief that schools are embedded in society and responsive to its demands is a truism, perhaps the oldest in the study
of education. We believe systems analysis can help illuminate this
relationship more clearly through such specific concepts as *wants,*
demands, and *supports.* We believe that observing the school systems as converting inputs from subsystems of society in response
to group-defined stresses can lead to considerable explanation.
Further, it seems to us that schools act out conversion processes
like those in other subsystems that are more clearly recognized
as political. That political authorities in schools do seek to maximize support through use of appropriate outputs also seems clear.
Certainly a central question to be explored in this book is the
degree to which the feedback loop operates between schools and
society. In particular, the challenges to systematic qualities of
schools in recent decades is of special interest.

In exploring similarities between schools and larger, more
recognized political systems, with Easton we are seeking to "elaborate a conceptual structure and suggest, where possible, some
theoretical propositions. . . . In the outcome, we shall not have a
theory in the full-blown sense of the term [but] a conceptual
structure which . . . is the most that we can expect in the area of
general theory today."[11]

In this work we seek something more. We want to know how
valid such a general concept is in explaining the systematic structure and processes of American public education as well as the
increased challenge to that system. As the first chapter noted,
old forms and ideas in education are everywhere challenged, and
not only by new interest groups seeking a reallocation of resources. Widespread and increasing resistance to school tax referenda in recent years (about one in three failed during 1969
but three in four in 1979) as well as the waves of reform suggest
disappointment, frustration, or malaise about our schools. Stress,
then, is not an abstract academic concern. Rather, it is a characteristic of contemporary education that affects school boards,

classrooms, administrators' offices, and professionals' conventions, as well as the decision-making forums at state and national levels. And, as polls show, the public's disenchantment with schools creates a nationwide condition of challenge that has motivated recent reforms.

This framework of analysis thus offers a contour map to stimulate thinking and research by scholar, administrator, and layperson alike. We will explore knowledge based on existing research and also provide some of our own. We will also explore major state and national educational policies, not only because systems analysis seems to explain them well, but also because they suggest how adaptation to challenge is important to all those interested in schools.

The precise labels used for these concepts are not the important thing, of course. What matters is whether the concepts provide insight into what is happening and some guide to action. If so, then our contribution, too, must ironically be classified as feedback, which Wiener once defined as "the property of being able to adjust future conduct by past performances."[12]

Uses of Systems Analysis

The links between politics and education are clearly not new, but two disagreements arise over this tie. How *do* schools and politics relate to one another as a matter of fact and how *should* they relate as a matter of value? In many respects, this book focuses only on the empirical question. However, testing an empirical question with reality is no simple matter, for we can make errors in framing the question—as well as in verifying it and estimating the significance of the facts unearthed.[13] Nor do we stand mute on the value questions that lie at the heart of turbulent issues. But to do this, we will use this framework of analysis to organize this wealth of data and values to make sense out of new actors, issues, and resources swirling among the contemporary challenges.

NOTES

1. Fred N. Kerlinger, "The Mythology of Educational Research: The Descriptive Approach," *School and Society* 93 (1965): 222–25.

2. Laurence Iannaccone, *Politics in Education* (New York: Center for Applied Research in Education, 1967).

3. Thomas H. Eliot, "Toward an Understanding of Public School Politics," *American Political Science Review* 52 (1959): 1032–51.

4. Michael W. Kirst and Edith K. Mosher, "The Politics of Public Education: A Research Review," *Review of Educational Research* 39 (1969); Frederick M. Wirt, "American Schools as a Political System: A Bibliographic Essay," in *State, School and Politics: Research Directions,* edited by Michael W. Kirst (Lexington, Mass.: Lexington Books, 1972), pp. 247–81.

5. A. James Gregor, "Political Science and the Uses of Functional Analysis," *American Political Science Review* 62 (1968): 425. For a recent overview of political science theories, see James March and Johann Olsen, *Democratic Governance* (New York: Free Press, 1995).

6. David Easton, *A Systems Analysis of Political Life* (New York: Wiley, 1965), p. 490; hereafter referred to as Easton, *Systems Analysis.*

7. David Easton, *A Framework for Political Analysis* (Englewood Cliffs, N.J.: Prentice-Hall, 1965).

8. Easton, *Systems Analysis,* p. 30.

9. Citations for following unnoted quotations are ibid., pp. 22, 26, 27.

10. Ibid., p. 479.

11. Ibid., pp. vii–viii.

12. Cited in ibid., p. 368.

13. For the problems involved, see David H. Fischer, *Historians' Fallacies: Toward a Logic of Historical Thought* (New York: Harper & Row, 1970).

Part II

POLITICS AT THE LOCAL LEVEL

4

The Origins and Agents of School Demands

The political system is subject to the demands that provide the more contentious stuff of governance. We turn in this section to the exchange, across school boundaries, of wants arising from unsatisfied values. That exchange promotes stress in the school system. This chapter investigates how stress arises through value conflicts and what agents transfer the resulting demands across the system's boundary.

BASIC VALUES IN EDUCATION POLICY

Key Variables Defined

We have noted that groups use political power to satisfy their values, that politics is indeed, in Easton's terms, "the authoritative allocation of values and resources." Now we wish to specify these values as they appear in educational policy. A recent study of such policy in six states by Marshall and colleagues focuses that examination as they posit four values that are pursued in school policy.[1]

1. *Quality:* "a substantial net improvement in the well-being of those affected by policy," best seen in states mandating standards of school performance and then providing resources and regulations to ensure their use. Typical are requirements for staff training, use of instructional resources, or performance by staff and students. This value is instrumental, a means to another value goal, namely, the fulfillment of diverse human purposes, thereby making life worth living and individuals worthwhile.

2. *Efficiency:* takes two forms, economic (minimizing costs while maximizing gains) and accountability (oversight and control of the local exercise of power). The first is regularly seen in such state mandates as pupil-teacher ratios or the minimum needed for kindergarten schools. The second is familiar in the details of procedures that local school authorities must follow (e.g., the budgetary process). This value is also instrumental, serving the end of responsibility for the exercise of public authority—the central operating premise of a democratic nation.

3. *Equity:* "the use of political authority to redistribute critical resources required for the satisfaction of human needs." Two steps in policymaking are required in equity matters— the perception of a gap between human needs and the availability of resources and allocation of resources to close that gap. This value is seen most often in federal compensatory, handicapped, or bilingual programs over the last three decades; but much earlier policy was moved by equity concerns to redress the imbalance in local school finances (e.g., the foundation programs of the 1920s).

4. *Choice:* "the opportunity to make policy decisions or reject them" by local school authorities. Such policies are often mandated but can exist even when no state law does (i.e., what is not prohibited may be done). Law can mandate selecting among alternative allocations of resources (textbook selection), can permit local authorities to use authority or not (program choice by parental advisory boards), and can leave it to special groups to exercise authority (voting for or against bond issues). This value is also instrumental, serving the sovereignty of citizens in a democracy—the most fundamental of all American political views.

Attributes of Values in Operation

Manifest in statutes, these four values generate political conflict because they are not a nicely integrated schema or ideology. Rather, they may oppose, as well as reinforce, one another. These values emerge in a particular sequence during policy conflict.

Choice can inherently oppose all values because nothing in the other values compels one to select them. The exercise of choice can—and has—rejected quality programs and equity programs in education; the South's de jure segregation is a classic example. Efficiency, on the other hand, reinforces all values except choice because efficiency is designed to realize quality and equity goals. Clear illustrations are the "state regs"—heavily oriented to efficiency—that seek compliance with state policy goals. Finally, the quality value opposes all but efficiency; the latter usually reinforces quality, as noted, but quality is unrelated to questions of what should be equitable and what should be chosen. The clash between redistribution policies after 1965 and the quality ("excellence") policies of House Speaker Newt Gingrich is well known.

This brief argument makes a larger point, namely, each value is always pursued in policy in relationship to other values. Also, a tension arises among them because different policy actors back different values. Broadly expressed, professionals have historically left their mark on quality and efficiency values in education, as the modern school system that emerged over the last century demonstrates. They usually defined the quality goals as well as the efficient means to achieve them. The participatory thrust of democracy can get in the way of this activity at times—but not always. This depends on how the force of choice and the search for equity emerges either directly from citizens or from professionals who share these values.

Another attribute of these policy values is the way they are sequenced into law. The history of American education shows that the first efforts to build this service were based on a belief in quality. The movement stems from Horace Mann and other reformers' moral objection to an illiterate population. Decades later it was stimulated further by public reaction against party machine control that had resulted in poor education. Efficiency values in policy would come second in this historical sequence because quality goals are not self-executing. Like all other good aims, they must be worked at to be realized. That necessity prompted considerations of what it would take to administer quality goals and how to ensure compliance. Later, because of the maldistribution of educational services, equity values would be stimulated. The classic example is how the local property tax—a rational means of raising funds—had made the quality of a child's education a function of district wealth; equity-driven funding reforms in the 1920s and 1970s testify to that maldistribution. It is in the effort to redress these imbalances in the distribution of rewards that equity policy arises. Finally, choice values in policy do not follow this sequence; instead they pervade it at every step. Citizens chose the idea of free public education, voters supported elected school boards or tax levies to hold power accountable, and today, professionals must work within a "zone of tolerance," constraints implicitly imposed by local citizens' preferences.[2]

The Infusion of Values in State Education Law

We see the reality of these values when we search state laws. Marshall and colleagues subjected state codes to content analysis within the framework of values. Table 4.1 summarizes their findings for their four values in seven areas of state policy mechanisms, or policy domains, and in two states of differing political cultures, Illinois and Wisconsin. Across the first row, we can see the proportion of each value in the finance laws of each state. The table reports that finance and governance policies are dominated by the efficiency value, although Wisconsin offers more equity-based law. Personnel policy is dominated by different values in the two states, and other policies show more diffuse values. The results challenge any simple notion that a given policy domain is dominated by a single value.

Social Context and Educational Policy

Let us put the preceding discussion of values within the analytical framework of the preceding chapter. How do values and a political system interact to produce educational policy?

Table 4.1

Distribution of Values by State Policy Mechanisms in Illinois and Wisconsin

SPM	Quality		Equity		Efficiency		Choice	
	Ill.	Wis.	Ill.	Wis.	Ill.	Wis.	Ill.	Wis.
Finance	6	10	9	36	68	36	16	19 = 100%
Personnel	47	29	22	29	25	39	7	3
Testing and assessment	45	–	45	50	–	50	10	–
Program definition	34	27	28	30	17	23	21	20
Organization and governance	10	9	17	18	64	53	9	20
Curriculum materials	23	33	39	–	23	–	16	67
Buildings and facilities	26	27	21	27	29	31	24	15

Source: Frederick Wirt, Douglas Mitchell, and Catherine Marshall, "Analyzing Values in State Policy Systems," Educational Evaluation and Policy Analysis 10, no. 3 (1988). Copyright 1988 by the American Educational Research Association. Reprinted by permission of the publisher.

Filtered through the pluralist prism of our society, general values take on specific definitions. At times the private pursuit of these definitions produces cooperation and accommodation among groups. Yet other groups come into conflict because insufficient resources for satisfying their values exist in private subsystems. As a result, some groups are rewarded and others are not. The resulting stress can mobilize the group that went unrewarded to drive for additional resources. This drive can transfer the resource struggle from the private to the political system. That system, in turn, seeks to maintain support for its political objectives by finding different ways of adjusting to such demands for value satisfaction.

Each school district reflects locally prevailing values to some degree. The guardians of community values, for whom schools are important instruments for keeping the faith, operate here. When insulated from outside forces, local guardians of orthodoxy can exist without challenge. But in this century, as mentioned, obstacles to local autonomy abound. Local control over school policy has been weakened by those groups increasingly unwilling to accept the dominance of localism. A centralization to the state level of demands for quality and equity has resulted from this.

This centralization, though, is far from the bland uniformity of the French school system. Certain American schools still hold the theory of evolution suspect, while others teach evolution, calculus, or Asian history. The decentralization impulse of pluralism wars with centralizing national forces, such as professionalism and state and federal laws. In this process, education is not unique but merely reflects the tensions that emerge as well in many other policy areas of a federal system. But whatever the balance among these conflicting values before, it has been tipped by new nationalizing forces in recent decades.

Within this general framework of values and demands pursuing policy, we need to know more specifics about this exchange and conversion process. Who are the agents that transfer demand inputs into the political system from their position on its boundaries? We need some flesh-and-blood referents for these abstract "transfer agents." For our purposes, we focus on the transfer roles that interest groups, electoral mechanisms, and local power structures play in this process. Latently, each mechanism is involved in boundary transfer activities that affect the ability of the political system—in this case the school—to persist as it seeks to cope with turbulent demands. Manifestly, each process speaks for or transmits the variety of American individualism within the swirl and clamor of local school politics. Both functions tell us much about how Americans generate educational values into a political form when they seek to transfer private preference into public policy. Understanding these processes is vital to understanding how current challenges to the system of schools generate new political turbulence.

INTEREST GROUPS AS TRANSFER AGENTS

Interest groups, working between citizens and educational authorities, are involved in the full spectrum of private demands on the school acting as a political system: claims for justice, help, reward, or recognition—all sought in the pursuit of quality, efficiency, equity, and choice. Competing claims for scarce educational budget resources often mobilize them. They do more, however, than just transmit political desires from citizens to officials. As transfer agents for the political system, interest groups often reformulate demands so that they differ somewhat from citizens' desires. Also, interest groups do not confine their activities to just the input and conversion phases of the political system; they provide feedback on the implementation of school policy as well. Despite such political activities, the tradition that overt politics and schools should be separate has shaped these interest groups.

Individuals join interest groups and engage in collective action mostly because they get something for it. Others do not join because they can, without cost, benefit from gains the group may make—the "free rider" syndrome. Leaders mobilize groups for the diverse benefits that group activity provides. Not surprisingly, past decades have witnessed an impressive growth in the numbers and types of educational interest groups. This complex array is part of the greater political turbulence with which educational policymakers must contend. The emergence of a wide spectrum of narrow-based interest groups reflects a weakening national consensus about schooling goals over the last three decades and the diminishing influence of broad-based groups, such as PTAs. Moreover, reforms such as compensatory, bilingual, and special education have created their own separate constituencies to preserve these new school functions. In addition, such programs spawn cohorts whose prime allegiance is to the program rather than to the broad concept of a common school. Categorical programs from Washington and the state have generated a jumble of interest groups that includes local project directors, parent groups, and federal and state categorical administrators.

Educational interest groups also grow as spin-offs of broader social movements, including women's liberation in the 1960s and the Christian Coalition in the 1990s. These movements form political action groups with sections devoted to educational policies. For example, the National Organization of Women (NOW) may urge a state board of education to include a broader variety of female occupations in textbooks, or the Christian Coalition will appear before local boards advocating that the story of creation be taught alongside evolution.

Another type of interest group includes networks of interstate experts and advocates who advocate particular policies, such as school finance reform or competency education. These "policy issue networks," not so broadly based as social movements, emphasize technical expertise and assistance in their lobbying strategy. All of these newer interest groups are added to the collective action groups that have been around for years, including the Council for Basic Education and the school administration association. We will turn to these shortly.

This complex and shifting kaleidoscope confronts educational administration with a much broader range of demands than faced even a few years ago. There is a political wisdom that any contest changes in nature when the number of participants changes. Two tenth-graders engaged in a schoolyard fight, one black and one white, are most likely working out their budding masculinity in a fashion characteristic of that age. But if a hundred students of each color are involved, it is not merely a melee; there are likely to be racial overtones to the fighting. Increasing the number of participants facing the administrator means that he or she is in a different kind of contest than before in which one's role definition will change. Historically, role definitions have altered through this century as a result of new social environments affecting big-city superintendents.[3] A later chapter will explore these role changes in depth. In one sense, the current period is the most exciting since reformers started pulling schools out from under political bosses and machines a century ago, but in another, this period is unpleasant for those involved.

One of the major changes is that the administrator must work with these new interest groups. Sometimes NOW will join forces with a local PTA, but at other times it will oppose local preferences and align with a state organization made up of compensatory education parents. Because education has lost its diffuse support, appeals for loyalty to general public education will be insufficient to mobilize interest group support for many specific changes, including increases in local taxes. Splintered interest groups want a specific "payoff," such as access ramps for handicapped children. The role of the local school superintendent as an administrative chief has long since changed from "benevolent autocrat" to that of a chief political negotiator and coalition builder. The next section categorizes the interest groups that confront policymakers at all levels, explaining their formation and growth, and underlining the necessity for coalition formulation of public school policy.

The Role of Interest Group Entrepreneurs

If the social and structural forces at work in our society create interest groups, why do so many individuals join and contribute to them? The initial simple answer was that people join a group because they agree with the group's goals. Olson, in his *The Logic of Collective Action*, changed this straightforward emphasis on motivations.[4] As an economist, he stressed that individuals will *not* contribute to interest groups if they receive the same benefits through nonparticipation—as a "free rider." Why join the local teachers' organization if everyone receives wage increases through the efforts of those who give time and money? Olson answered this puzzle by focusing on the other benefits an organization can extend to or withhold from individuals. Anything of tangible value—group insurance programs, newsletters, tire discounts—can be contingent upon individual contributions. Interest groups thus attract members and resources by supplying benefits only partly related to politics or specific public policies. Yet interest group political activities are possible because the people who join want private benefits, not because they share common values or goals.

Olson's thesis has gone through several adaptations, which help explain the broad array of motives for individual contributions to groups. Others have demonstrated that ideology, moral principles, and social pressures can also generate collective action.[5] In an analogy to the marketplace, lobbyists form groups because, like entrepreneurs, the benefits they can obtain exceed the costs they must invest in mobilizing others. Members of a group also join because the cost-benefit ratio is favorable. Benefits are not merely material, such as good teacher contracts. They can also be "solidarity," the intangible psychological reward that comes from belonging—the pleasure of sharing the company of like-minded others—as in a group of mothers protecting the neighborhood school against dangerous drugs. Benefits can also be "expressive," so that one's personal goals are incorporated into and expressed by group action. An example would be a belief in the value of education manifested by work in the PTA. Common Cause is one group that is a classic example of all these motivations. Other analysts have emphasized the motive of "imperfect information," as when individuals underestimate their ability to become a free rider or overestimate the importance of proposed education legislation for their job performance. Individuals' motives for collective action in interest groups may arise because they like to go to meetings or have feelings of responsibility.[6]

What inducements will make people join a group? Politics need not be a by-product of membership gained through discounts for auto rentals or tax shelter annuities. Interest group entrepreneurs can attract members through ideological appeal, emphasis on fairness, social pressure, and the structuring of meetings. But we lack empirical studies on the perceptual and value characteristics that motivate membership in education lobby groups. We do know, however, that numerous motivations exist and that the interest group leader is well advised to develop diverse appeals. At the core of this exchange, though, one trades off group dues for individual benefits.

A recent key change in education politics has been the decline of loyalty as a motivation for supporting education interest groups. The PTA and American Association of University Women have lost ground in membership to such groups as state Chapter I ESEA coordinators, the Christian Coalition, and parents of limited-English-speaking children. Selective benefits are increasingly organized around categorical programs or professional specialties. Also, loyalty to the harmony of the education profession no longer inspires the membership it did when National Education Association (NEA) headquarters included administrators, professors, and schoolteachers under one roof.

Reflecting all this activity is the fact that expenditures for group action have grown dramatically since 1980. A state-local "arms race" results in creating Washington or state capital lobby offices for cities, categorical groups, low-wealth school districts, and women's organizations. Two examples illustrate this point. Table 4.2 is a listing of groups on one side of a school issue; they are opposed to vouchers or federal tax credits for private school tuition. This staggering variety illustrates two qualities of current school politics. Education policy touches on a mosaic of American values—religious, ethnic, professional, social, economic—that often clash in politics. Table 4.2 also illustrates the shifting quality of coalitional policymaking; this amalgam will rearrange itself for other school issues. Some groups will drop out, for example, if the issue does not involve federal aid to private schools.

Another perspective on the recent proliferation of interest groups is shown in Table 4.3, a California statewide collective that supports increased unrestricted state aid for local schools. Note how many separate school employee and support groups are represented in Sacramento. Although rarely studied, much the same situation probably exists in most if not all the states.[7]

A CLASSIFICATION OF SCHOOL INTEREST GROUPS

Differences existing among these educational groups parallel those found in interest groups of other areas, for example, in

Table 4.2
Groups in Washington, D.C., Officially Opposing Private School Tuition Tax Credits

American Association of Colleges for Teacher Education

American Association for Health, Physical Education, and Recreation

American Association of School Administrators

American Civil Liberties Union

American Ethical Union

American Federation of State, County, and Municipal Employees

American Federation of Teachers, AFL-CIO

American Humanist Association

American Jewish Congress

Americans for Democratic Action

Americans United for Separation of Church and State

A. Philip Randolph Institute

Association for International Childhood Education

Baptist Joint Committee Public Affairs

Coalition of Labor Union Women

Council for Education Development and Research

Council for Exceptional Children

Council of Chief State School Officers

Federal Education Project of the Lawyers Committee for Civil Rights under the Law

Horace Mann League

Labor Council for Latin American Advancement

League of Women Voters

National Association for the Advancement of Colored People

National Association of Elementary School Principals

National Association for Hearing and Speech Action

National Association of Secondary School Principals

National Association of State Boards of Education

National Coalition for Public Education and Religious Liberty

National Committee for Citizens in Education

National Congress of Parents and Teachers

National Council of Churches

National Council of Jewish Women

National Council of Senior Citizens

National Education Association

National School Boards Association

National Student Association

National Student Lobby

National Urban Coalition

National Urban League

Student National Education Association

Union of American Hebrew Congregation

Unitarian Universalist Association

United Auto Workers

United Methodist Church

United States Student Association

Table 4.3
A California Collective Education Interest Group

American Association of University of Women—California Division
Association of California School Administrators
Association of California School Districts
Association of Low Wealth Schools
Association of Mexican-American Educators, Inc.
California Association of School Business Officials
California Congress of Parents and Teachers, Inc.
California Federation of Teachers, AFL-CIO
California Personnel and Guidance Association
California School Boards Association
California School Employees Association
California School Nurses Organization
California Teachers Association—NEA
The Delta Kappa Gamma Society—Chi State—California
Education Congress of California
League of Women Voters of California
Los Angeles Unified School District
Schools for Sound Finance
United Teachers of Los Angeles

temporary versus permanent organization, special versus broad interests, and larger versus limited resources. The NEA illustrates the qualities of permanent organization, broad interests, and large resources; however, taxpayer-revolt groups exemplify the temporary, narrow, and limited-resource type of group.

A major distinction of all such groups centers on how broad their interest is in the many facets of education. Thus, there are those for whom education is an end and those for whom it is a means to other ends. The first consists of professional educators or those professionally oriented, and the second of those wishing to use the school to serve other values, such as reducing taxes, protecting moral or patriotic values, and so on. Policy issue networks are in some ways an interest group but do not fit any of the conventional definitions. Policy issue networks can encompass several interest groups, but will focus on a single issue such as creation science or a national standards board for teacher certification. In contrast, interest groups are concerned with numerous issues.

Professional Interest Groups

For many years the most numerous interest group—teachers—
exerted only minimal political influence. School teachers had
traditionally hesitated in using collective action for transmitting
demands to political authorities either within or outside school
systems. The doctrine of the school administrator also played
down the usefulness of teachers' collective organizations, stressing instead negotiations by individual professionals. This doctrine also emphasized the authority of the superintendent and
played down democracy and participation, as those terms are
used in the current popular sense. Later, an altered conception
of administration favored teacher participation, but only for its
effects on morale building and consequent improved performance. Not surprisingly, until recently the views of teacher representatives differed only slightly from the administrators' tenets.

A review of the history of the NEA will help to illuminate the
norms of the professional educator.[8] This group wanted a unified profession that would not split into opposing interest groups
competing for scarce educational resources and would not engage in public conflict over competing educational values. As
the leading national organization, the NEA concentrated its efforts at the national and state levels. It gave scant attention either to local teachers' interest groups or to collective pressure
to change local school policy. Educators were inculcated with
the "professional" need for a harmony of interests and thus agreement on educational goals for children. Group activity, when
reinforced by formal arrangements such as interest groups, would
lead only to unnecessary and harmful conflict. With that perspective until 1960, the NEA focused its concern on standards
and ethics and lobbied for general federal aid for buildings and
salaries, conduct and dissemination of research, and technical
assistance for state affiliates.[9]

This national group's resources are not minor. In 1996 it had
over 2.2 million members, representing about 60 percent of our
public schoolteachers. It has an extensive bureaucracy and hierarchy, although the executive staff usually makes policy with the
concurrence of a board of ninety-two directors and an executive
committee of eleven.[10] Every state has its own teacher's associa-

tion, which is frequently a powerful interest group at the state level. Over eighty-five hundred dues-paying local school affiliates filter their money through the state affiliates.[11] Revenue in 1994 was about $785 million.

At the national level, the NEA functions as an umbrella for major segments of the profession. Within the national organization are over seventy-five departments, divisions, commissions, and committees. Separate professional organizations within NEA exist even for audio-visual specialists, as well as for home economics and speech teachers. The Political Action Council of NEA spent $4.2 million in 1994 supporting Democratic political candidates at the national level. In one Washington building the NEA houses groups with specialized orientation and values that increasingly compete with each other in the political system. Principals and counselors feel that they are not well represented by either teachers or administrators and so they get lost in an intermediary position. These divisions over priorities for money and values have spawned professional competitors who argue their cases before school boards and legislatures.

The most noticeable NEA competition comes from within the teaching profession itself. The American Federation of Teachers (AFT) restricts membership to teachers and administrators who have no direct authority over teachers. The AFT has affiliates in one-half of the states and an 875,000 membership concentrated in large cities or nearby. However, it has not been able to take significant numbers of members away from the NEA in the last decade. While the two teacher groups take common positions on some policy issues, for example, increased state aid for teacher salaries, they still have differences on others.

The AFT grew rapidly between 1960 and 1975 by contending that professional unity is a myth because value conflicts are inevitable between teachers and their managers who administer the school.[12] AFT rhetoric was replete with *we* and *they*, terms that reflect an adversarial relationship between an aggressive labor union and its employer. The AFT willingness to resort to a strike proved attractive to urban teachers but shattered the professional ethic of low-profile interest group activity. However, the organizing success of the AFT in the 1960s led to the NEA taking a more militant stance in stressing collective bargaining.

The differences between the two unions are clear in their organization of political efforts. If the AFT has succeeded more in big cities, the NEA has been more effective at the state level, where its affiliates—one of the largest organized interest groups in the states—spend much time dealing with state politicians.[13] The AFT, on the other hand, has few effective state federations, concentrating its efforts at the local level. Both have Washington offices, but under Republican administrations neither has been very successful in getting political demands approved by the president and Congress.[14] NEA support of Jimmy Carter led to his support for a cabinet-level Department of Education, and the Clinton administration has worked closely with both unions. But Republican governors and legislators in some Midwest states reduced the bargaining rights of teachers in 1994 and 1995.

Major administrative groups of superintendents and principals (shown later) frequently make their own distinctive demands on the political system and maintain their own offices at the state and federal levels. The National School Boards Association (NSBA) has traditionally joined forces with the administrator-teacher groups at the state and federal levels. The NSBA has overcome its early reluctance to lobby in Washington and is now the most aggressive of the lay groups in Washington, D.C.

Divisions among professional educators should not be overestimated, because powerful forces work toward their unity. The tradition of a unified profession and the common training and experience of professional educators have led them to agree on many fundamental values, a factor that tends to restrict the range of interest group activity. For example, most administrators move up through the teaching ranks, and accrediting associations are usually staffed by professional educators. Indeed, the faith that the public has in accreditation makes regional accrediting agencies a professional interest group of considerable importance, often bringing irresistable pressure to achieve their standards of faculty, budget, facilities, and curriculum.

Professionally Oriented Interest Groups

Other nonprofessional groups are also interested in educational policy as an end in itself. Like educators, they provide schools with diffuse support, but they also differ as educators do on some aspects of school governance and so present their own demand inputs.

The National Congress of Parents and Teachers is not only the largest group in this category, it is also the largest volunteer organization in the nation, with 7 million members. The PTA is a loose confederation of about twenty-five thousand local units concerned primarily with specific problems facing *specific* schools. It is most influential and active at the local or district level, because its heterogeneous state membership precludes agreement on controversial issues.[15] Although the membership is now one-third men, the organization is still dominated by women.[16]

Analysts of PTA history stress the generally dependent and close relationship it has to school administrators. Koerner expressed it this way:

> The American PTA is rarely anything more than a coffee and cookies organization based on vague goodwill and gullibility. It is chiefly useful to the administration for raising money for special projects and persuading parents who are interested enough to attend meetings that the local schools are in the front ranks of American education.[17]

But as we shall see in the next chapter, such participation can have important positive social and psychological benefits for individuals. Moreover, in the last two decades, the PTA has become more aggressive, asserting that it is a consumer advocate organization. Major PTA issues include reading improvement and opposition to tuition tax credits and TV violence. The PTA is broadening its membership to include more minorities and becoming more active at the state level.

The PTA's local role is amplified at the national and state levels. However, it does not provide an independent source of demand inputs into school policy; rather it proceeds as an instrument of educators who use it to reinforce or implement *their* policy inputs. Indeed, the national PTA is a resolute member of the "Big Six"—a coalition of three professional groups and three lay groups in education: American Association of School Administrators, NEA, Council of Chief State School Officers, National School Boards Association, National Association of State School Boards, and National Congress of Parents and Teachers. Most studies show that legislators view the PTA as a useful friend but not a very bothersome enemy. In effect, the values of the PTA leadership and the school professionals are similar; as a consequence, the PTA does not sponsor many conflict-oriented demands for school policymakers. However, it can produce many letters to legislators on major education issues.

The PTA is not, however, the only professionally oriented lay interest group. The Council for Basic Education (CBE) is an organization that has emphasized different values from those of the PTA and has become known as a "critic of public education." The CBE believes that the schools have neglected the fundamental intellectual disciplines in their purported overemphasis on social adjustment. Its intentions are to increase the amount of academic versus vocational content in the curriculum. The CBE tries to influence school authorities primarily through publications, conferences, and other uses of the media. It does not have local chapters but has provided material to local groups who express an interest. It opposes cutbacks of traditional academic subjects for electives like driver training or photography.

Professionally oriented interest groups also exist among numerous organizations that embrace education as a secondary concern, for example, the League of Women Voters and the American Association of University Women. These groups promote general social improvements, some of which touch on school programs and processes. They usually try to influence the political conversion process for education only when the members are deeply and widely concerned about a particular aspect of school policy. This condition occurs rarely, however, such as when the state constitution for education is revised. Like the PTA, these are non-issue-specific groups that provide support for the ongoing system and so inject little conflict into it. They also constitute a resource for decision makers in times of crisis. They are losing active members as more women are working full or part time, leaving less time for community activity.

Transcendental Groups

Several kinds of interest groups see the schools as a means to ends that transcend the schools, such as reducing the tax burden, eradicating Communism, and so on. Around the turn of the century, taxpayer organizations began to mold support for the elimination of "wasteful" public spending. Of particular interest is the finding that taxpayer organizations have been *supporters*, as well as opponents, of increased tax support—depending on the tax source. They are strongly opposed to local property taxes, but on occasion will support increases in sales or income taxes.

The recent involvement of the prestigious Business Roundtable, representing the chief executive officers of the nation's 201 largest corporations, is potentially of great importance. Under the leadership of IBM's chairman, the Roundtable has committed itself to a ten-year, state-by-state program to restructure schools. A group of major corporations will each adopt a state and work to reform its schools. The corporations in each of these states plan to work closely with the governors and other political leaders in achieving common goals concerning school improvement and reform.

Other important national business groups also are actively engaged in school issues. The Committee for Economic Development, with its three influential reports, *Investing in Our Children* (1985), *Children in Need* (1987), and *Unfinished Agenda* (1992), has made a compelling case for business involvement and support of additional resources for schools, particularly in the preschool years. Other influential national business groups like the National Alliance of Business and the Business Roundtable recently have created centers that focus on education and related issues. Eight major business groups created the Business Coalition for Education Reform with the purpose of working "to elevate the dialogue on the need for changes in education policies at the national, state and local levels. . . ." The Coalition includes the National Alliance of Business, Committee for Economic Development, Business Roundtable, U.S. Chamber of Commerce, National Association of Manufacturers, Conference Board, American Business Conference, and U.S. Hispanic Chamber of Commerce.

Relationships between these new players and the traditional leaders of education are not yet well formed. There is understandable tension, ambiguity, and uncertainty among all parties. It is much too early to assess such long-range business interventions, but the mere initiation of national efforts reflects a seriousness of purpose that should not be underestimated.

Distinct from those whose main interest is material are those whose concern is the moral instruction in schools, which may include banning "immoral" course content.[18] The educational function of moral indoctrination dates from our schools' colonial origins. Concern for religious instruction has not disappeared either, as seen in the continuing outcry against, and disobedience of, Supreme Court decisions banning Bible reading and school prayers. The main focus of these groups is to guard orthodox values. Their support of the schools is secondary to their concern for maintaining certain community norms. The school is only one of many institutions whose moral sanctity must be protected against subversion or direct challenge. The growing influence of conservative Christian organizations deserves more details on these groups. Explored below at some length, they demonstrate how national value concerns are aggregated locally into an impressive national force.

Conservative Christian Groups: Structure and Organization

For the most part, conservative Christian groups are very well organized and well funded, and all of the national organizations have state and local chapters.[19] Focus on the Family is the largest group, with a mailing list of approximately 4 million and an annual budget of $90 million.[20] The Christian Coalition has between 400,000 and 450,000 members in 872 chapters across all fifty states and an annual budget of approximately $12 million.[21] Citizens for Excellence in Education (CEE) has a somewhat smaller membership of 210,000, although it has 1,685 local chapters and church-based Public School Awareness Committees throughout the country.[22] Concerned Women for America claims an annual budget of $10 million, with 600,000 members in 800 chapters.[23]

The organizational structure of these groups is national, with extensive state and local chapters. Observed Reverend Pat Robertson, founder of the Christian Coalition, "We're grassroots all the way, with tremendous autonomy in the states. . . . We're training people to be leaders on their own."[24] This grassroots activity has been focused largely in rural areas or in small towns and cities, but the national leadership plays a very active role in local activities, providing literature, training manuals, legal advice, and speakers.[25] A more critical observer of the conservative Christian groups draws a tighter connection between the national and local chapters, noting "the soldiers in these battles are the local residents, but the generals are from national organizations."[26]

While all of the major Christian groups have chapters throughout the country, there seems to be some informal geographic division between them. The Christian Coalition has a strong national presence, while the Eagle Forum is concentrated in the Midwest, and CEE and Focus on the Family are more heavily represented in the West.

In addition to geographic division, there has also been some suggestion that an "unspoken division of labor or . . . specialization" exists among the major Christian organizations.[27] While these groups often speak on the same issues, particularly educational issues, each does appear to specialize to some degree. Focus on the Family, for example, concentrates particularly on family solidarity and child rearing. Concerned Women for America emphasizes the traditional role of women. The Eagle Forum frequently focuses on sex education, while CEE is concerned with all aspects of public education.

Over the last several years, there have been changes in the targets and strategies used by conservative Christian groups to promote their agendas. Challenges to the public schools used to come from parents, who targeted specific books to which they objected. In the 1990s the movement has shifted toward nationally orchestrated challenges of instructional programs and methods, textbook series, and restructuring efforts.[28] Christian organizations now employ strategies that combine "up-to-the-minute technology with pinpoint targeting of school districts, church congregations, and specific local issues."[29] These strategies can be grouped generally into three different categories: targeting school boards; direct contact through radio programs, pamphlets, and mailings; and legislation and litigation.

The most aggressive strategy employed by the conservative Christian groups in recent years has been influencing and gaining control of school boards throughout the country. This has been a particularly effective strategy for the Christian Coalition and for CEE. School board elections traditionally have low voter participation and limited media coverage, making it easier for groups to organize an effective campaign.[30] As one observer noted, the leaders of the national Christian organizations "know that a few hundred votes can decide almost any school board contest, and they mean to empty their churches to get them."[31] In addition to low voter turnout, election to a seat on the school board is often seen as a good way to enter the political system. Finally, Christian groups have turned to school boards because of limited success with other strategies, especially litigation. In most instances, the courts have upheld school board decisions and policies, whether in defending or restricting instructional programs. Because of this "judicial deference" to school boards, the conservative Christian groups have focused their efforts on influencing school board elections and policies.[32]

One very effective method employed by the conservative Christian groups for gaining control of seats on local school boards is that of "stealth campaigning." This strategy was developed by the Christian Coalition, and has been used by CEE, the Traditional Values Coalition, and Concerned Women for America. The stealth strategy directs conservative Christian candidates for public office to "shun the media and public debate" and to campaign exclusively among those who share their values and beliefs.[33] Candidates are instructed not to reveal their agendas or appear at candidate forums. But most important, candidates are instructed not to reveal their membership in a conservative Christian organization. While candidates do not deny their faith, Robert Simonds, founder of CEE argues, "you don't have to say up front you're a Christian."[34] Although he has since distanced himself from such extreme statements, Christian Coalition executive director Ralph Reed once said, "I do guerrilla warfare . . . You don't know it's over until you're in a body bag. You don't know until election night."[35] The stealth strategy has been extremely effective, as illustrated by the observation of one local official who noted "nobody laid eyes on an elected official until the day she was sworn in."[36] However, recent extensive media coverage of stealth strategies may limit their future effectiveness.

In addition to advising candidates to follow the stealth strategy, the national organizations also provide candidates with ex-

tensive "how-to" materials. CEE has published a guidebook entitled "How to Elect Christians to Public Office," which has been
described as the "war manual" for the CEE movement.[37] Other
groups have also distributed information about how to hide one's
agenda, and how to talk to reporters. And in the 1993 New York
City school board elections, the Christian Coalition joined with
the Catholic Church to distribute more than five hundred thousand voter guides outlining the platforms of those candidates
sympathetic to Christian Coalition values.[38] The Christian Coalition holds workshops focusing on local school issues, such as
one entitled "Influencing School Board Policy." In 1993 the
Christian Coalition held over eighty such seminars for at least
five thousand people nationwide. The Christian Coalition's Ralph
Reed concludes that "we are training thousands of people every
year to seek office if they feel so led by God."[39]

Tactics for gaining control of school boards and school board
policy have been employed with great success throughout the
country, most visibly in California and Florida. In fact, Robert
Simonds of CEE claims that conservative Christians control 2,200
school boards across the country and hold one in seven school
board seats in the United States.[40]

After gaining control of local school boards, Christian conservatives aggressively push their agendas, challenging programs
and curricula that they find objectionable. For example, in Vista,
California, the fundamentalist Christian-controlled school board
pushed to have creation science included in district science curricula. Because of extreme teacher opposition, though, the board
settled for including this topic in the humanities program. The
same board dismantled the district's sex education programs.[41]
In Round Rock, Texas, the conservative Christian-controlled school
board lifted a ban on prayer during graduation ceremonies.[42]
And in Lake County, Florida, the conservative Christian-controlled school board canceled plans to open a Head Start program
because it felt that "the government should not be offering services
that families should . . . provid[e] to their young . . .[and] that
young children should stay home with their mothers."[43]

In addition to attempting to influence policies and gain control of school boards, the national conservative Christian groups
have employed the more traditional strategies of direct contact

through media to further their agenda. These groups use radio extensively to communicate with members and others sympathetic to their causes. Focus on the Family, for example, produces ten radio shows broadcast on thousands of radio stations around the world.[44] Each of the other major organizations have at least one radio program.

The Free Congress Foundation, another conservative Christian organization that focuses on national political issues, has begun its own television network, the "NET-Political Newstalk Network." This twenty-four-hour-a-day, seven-days-a-week broadcast includes both prerecorded and live call-in shows, often featuring interviews with prominent political figures. The network is carried by over sixty stations in twenty-one states, and is also easily accessible by satellite dish. Free Congress Foundation estimates total household coverage of almost eleven million.[45]

All of the major organizations publish newsletters and pamphlets, which include "warning signs" of objectionable curricula as well as courses of action that can be taken to oppose specific programs or texts.[46] Focus on the Family publishes eleven magazines, targeted at specific groups such as doctors, teachers, and single parents.[47] Other organizations publish brochures and curriculum guides designed to convince parents of the "dangers" of particular instructional materials. These kits are distributed to churches to encourage them to establish Public School Awareness Committees, more than eight hundred of which "monitor public school programs and activities around the country."[48] Additionally, conservative Christian groups distribute books and fax weekly church bulletin fillers and suggested sermon topics to thousands of pastors.[49] These groups carefully manage their requests for information in order to build up their mailing lists, which are their main avenues for dissemination of much of this material. Focus on the Family, for example, receives over two hundred fifty thousand letters and phone calls each month, which it records to produce its mailing lists of over four million.[50]

Another strategy employed by conservative Christian organizations to advance their agendas is legislation and litigation.[51] These groups have supported legislative efforts including choice and voucher plans, which would provide state funding for students to attend the school of their choice, public or private, and pupil protection acts, which would require parental approval of all textbooks, materials, and instructional methods. Conservative Christian groups have also supported home-schooling bills, which would require public schools to provide services and materials to educate children at home.[52] Most recently, the Christian Coalition's Contract with the American Family calls for transfer of Department of Education funds to the local level, the repeal of Goals 2000, school choice, and a parental rights act.[53]

Crisis Interest Groups

Despite the broad variety of interest groups in public education, not all interests or values show up in organized groups. Existing groups may choose not to carry certain demands to school officials. Feeling the urge to impress their values on school policies, they create ad hoc and temporary organizations.

A typical illustration of this occurred in a northeastern suburb where two interest groups developed in one year and then dissolved after the school board elections.[54] One was a "taxpayers association," formed to defeat three board members and cut back school expenditures. The superintendent countered with a group called Save Our Schools in order to reelect the incumbent board members and pass the budget. Both groups conveyed their special values and demands in a political system where organized groups had not been important. But quickly formed, they just as quickly fade. More broadly, integration crises across the country frequently spawn "Parents to Preserve Neighborhood Schools" or "Save Our Schools" as a counterweight to civil rights groups advocating integration. Such groups disband after the integration crisis passes.

Testing Agencies and Foundations

Several groups that do not fit the usual idea of an interest group nevertheless do influence local schooling based on national and professional norms. Although this country does not have a system of national exams, we do have several private national testing agencies. The most important is the Educational

Testing Service in Princeton, New Jersey. Most American schools do not have a choice in whether to provide their best students with courses in most of the subjects covered by College Board Achievement Exams. Because high school administrators want their students to score well on these exams, they do not have absolute flexibility to teach what they want. Such external constraints reflect value judgments on school quality urged in the interest of professionalism. This force of professionalism we earlier argued may be a more powerful external constraint on local school policy than are local demands or federal laws.

Further, while private philanthropic foundations are not thought of as interest groups, they do however, exercise a major influence on curriculum reform, teacher training, testing, finance, facility design, educational television, and so on. Foundations have also used their grants to generate stress over value concerns. For example, in the 1960s foundations financed the development of instruments to assess national achievement in education; this effort helped create a political issue that pitted those who opposed national testing against those wanting increased accountability by professional educators. As a result, local school boards, state departments of education, and the United States Congress had to make a decision on whether to permit national assessment. Consequently, the questions and approaches in the approved assessment represented many compromises, including a decision *not* to include interstate test comparisons.[55]

A foundation does not act like a conventional interest group by seeking access to public policymakers and then advocating its case for public support. But, by using grants to start experiments and demonstration projects (often reflecting certain value orientations), foundations may make value conflicts more visible. Then this effort can create a new demand that provides interest groups with an issue. Such groups may modify the content of the demand as they transmit it to the school board or state legislator, but the foundations need interest groups in order to reach the political authorities through collective pressure. They have played a major role in recent debates about the quality of education.[56] In the mid-1980s the Carnegie Foundation for Advancement of Teaching funded Ernest Boyer's major book, *High School*. The Carnegie Corporation funded a major report calling for a national standards board to certify outstanding teachers. Carnegie then provided money to the National Governors Association to promote this concept. Indeed, most major reports outside of government sponsorship involve foundation subsidies.

CONCLUSION

This chapter has introduced major components of the conversion process by examining only the input side. We have suggested some of the basic values in the social environment that influence that process and have indicated how interest groups act as transfer agents for these values.[57] The energizing force that impels demands and challenge is environmental stress arising from unsatisfied values.[58] This process reflects felt needs, and groups or individuals pursue satisfaction by turning to the political system. When such a force is set in motion, it crosses the boundary between private and public systems to create school policy.

NOTES

1. See writings by Catherine Marshall, Douglas Mitchell, and Frederick Wirt in *Culture and Education Policy in the American States* (New York: Falmer, 1989); a symposium on "State Politics of Education," in *Peabody Journal of Education* 62–64 (1985): 7–115; and *Alternative State Policy Mechanisms for Pursuing Educational Quality, Equity, Efficiency, and Choice Goals* (Washington, D.C.: Office of Instructional Research and Improvement, U.S. Department of Education, 1986), Chap. V; following quotations are from this source.

2. William Boyd, "The Public, the Professionals, and Education Policy Making: Who Governs?" *Teachers College Record* 77 (1976): 539–77.

3. Larry Cuban, *Urban School Chiefs Under Fire* (Chicago: University of Chicago Press, 1976).

4. Mancur Olson, *The Logic of Collective Action* (New York: Schocken, 1965).

5. Robert Salisbury, "An Exchange Theory of Interest Groups," *Midwest Journal of Political Science* 13 (1969): 1–32.

6. Terry Moe, *The Organization of Interests* (Chicago: University of Chicago Press, 1980). For a market theory analysis, see Michael Hayes, *Lobbyists and Legislators* (New Brunswick, N.J.: Rutgers, 1981).

7. See Roald Campbell and Tim Mazzoni, *State Policy Making for the Public*

Schools (Berkeley: McCutchan, 1976). For an update, see Marshall et al., *Culture and Education Policy.*

8. Alan Rosenthal, *Pedagogues and Power* (Syracuse, N.Y.: Syracuse University Press, 1969), pp. 6–10. For a full current history, see G. Howard Goold and Arvid J. Burke, "The Organized Teaching Profession," in *Education in the States: Nationwide Development Since 1900*, Edgar Fuller and Jim B. Pearson, eds. (Washington, D.C.: National Education Association, 1969), Chap. 14.

9. James Koerner, *Who Controls American Education?* (Boston: Beacon Press, 1968), p. 26.

10. See Roald F. Campbell et al., *Organization and Control of American Schools* (Columbus, Ohio: Charles E. Merrill, 1985), pp. 253–57.

11. Anthony Cresswell and Michael Murphy, *Teachers, Unions, and Collective Bargaining* (Berkeley: McCutchan, 1980).

12. For a general background on the American Federation of Teachers, see Patrick W. Carlton and Harold I. Goodwin, *The Collective Dilemma: Negotiations in Education* (Columbus, Ohio: Jones, 1969). AFT publishes a monthly newspaper, *American Teacher*, which provides current information on AFT policy directions.

13. See Marshall et al., *Culture and Education Policy.*

14. James Sundquist, *Politics and Policy* (Washington, D.C.: Brookings Institution, 1968), pp. 155–200. Earlier the NEA was a crucial part of the Emergency Committee for Full Funding. This committee was able to persuade Congress to increase the president's education budget by over $500 million. Since then, though, federal monies have declined.

15. For an elaboration on this view, see Koerner, *Who Controls American Education?* pp. 32–33.

16. Campbell et al., *The Organization and Control of American Schools*, pp. 293–97; William T. Kvareceus, "PTA: The Irrelevant Giant," *The Nation*, October 5, 1963, pp. 200–1.

17. Koerner, *Who Controls American Education?* pp. 147–48.

18. See Richard LaPiere, *Social Change* (New York: McGraw-Hill, 1965), p. 197; Mary A. Raywid, *The Axe-Grinders* (New York: Macmillan, 1962); Jack Nelson and Gene Roberts, Jr., *The Censors and the Schools* (Boston: Little, Brown & Co., 1963). The distinction offered here borders on that of the "sacred and secular communities" analyzed in Laurence Iannaccone and Frank W. Lutz, *Politics, Powers and Policy: The Governing of Local School Districts* (Columbus Ohio: Charles E. Merrill, 1970).

19. F. Clarkson and S. Porteous, *Challenging the Christian Right: The Activists' Handbook* (Great Barrington, Mass.: Institute for First American Studies, 1993).

20. S. Roberts, D. Friedman, and T. Gest, "The Heavy Hitter," *U.S. News and World Report* 118 (1995): 34, 39; U.S. Newswire, "Religious Right Campaign Assaults Religious Freedom in America; New ADL Book Details Strategy, Tactics, Personalities," June 9, 1994.

21. Martha McCarthy, "Challenges to the Public School Curriculum: New Targets and Strategies," *Phi Delta Kappan* 75 (1993): 55–60; George Kaplan,

"Shotgun Wedding: Notes on Public Education's Encounter with the New Christian Right," *Phi Delta Kappan* 75 (1994): K1–12; L. Pappano and A. Sessler, "New Right Joins Fight Over Schools Across State," *The Boston Globe*, October 10, 1993.

22. J. Impoco, "Separating Church and School," *U.S. News and World Report* 118 (1995): 30; Kaplan, "Shotgun Wedding."

23. Clarkson and Porteous, *Challenging the Christian Right.*

24. ABC Nightline, "God and the Grassroots," November 4, 1993.

25. Pappano and Sessler, "New Right Joins Fight."

26. E. Shogren and D. Frantz, "Schools Boards Become the Religious Right's New Pulpit," *Los Angeles Times*, December 10, 1993, p. A1.

27. Kaplan, "Shotgun Wedding," p. 4.

28. M. McCarthy, "Conservative Groups' Challenges to Public School Programs."

29. Kaplan, "Shotgun Wedding," p. 9.

30. Z. Arocha, "The Religious Right's March into Public Governance," *School Administrator* 50 (1993): 8–15.

31. Kaplan, "Shotgun Wedding," p. 10.

32. McCarthy, "Conservative Groups' Challenges".

33. S. Rae, "The Fierce, Furious March of the Fundamentalist Right," *Cosmopolitan* 218 (1995): 158.

34. Shogren and Frantz, "School Boards Become Religious Right's Pulpit."

35. Kaplan, "Shotgun Wedding," p. 10.

36. Rae, "The Fierce, Furious March."

37. Shogren and Frantz, "School Boards Become Religious Right's Pulpit."

38. Tom Toch and K. Glastris, "Who's Minding the Schools?" *U.S. News and World Report* 116 (1994): 78.

39. Shogren and Frantz, "School Boards Become Religious Right's Pulpit."

40. Shogren and Frantz, "School Boards Become Religious Right's Pulpit."; Cable News Network News, "Disputed Territory, Part 3—Christian Soldiers," December 4, 1994.

41. Rae, "The Fierce, Furious March."

42. Toch and Glastris, "Who's Minding the Schools?"

43. Shogren and Frantz, "School Boards Become Religious Right's Pulpit."

44. Roberts, Friedman, and Gest, "The Heavy Hitter."

45. Free Congress Foundation, *NET-Political NewsTalk Network: On Screen* (Spring 1995).

46. J. Jones, "Targets of the Right," *American School Board Journal* 180 (1993): 22–29.

47. Roberts, Friedman, and Gest, "The Heavy Hitter."

48. McCarthy, "Conservative Groups' Challenges."

49. Roberts, Friedman, and Gest, "The Heavy Hitter."

50. Roberts, Friedman, and Gest, "The Heavy Hitter."

51. G. Zahorchak, *The Politics of Outcome-Based Education in Pennsylvania*, Unpublished dissertation, 1994.

52. Jones, "Targets of the Right."

53. Christian Coalition, *Contract with the American Family* (May 17, 1995).

54. Lesley H. Browder, "A Suburban School Superintendent Plays Politics," in *The Politics of Education at the Local, State, and Federal Level*, Michael W. Kirst, ed. (Berkeley: McCutchan, 1970).

55. Ralph Tyler, "National Assessment: A History and Sociology," in *New Models for American Education*, James Guthrie and Edward Wynne, eds. (Englewood Cliffs. N.J.: Prentice-Hall, 1971), Chap. 2.

56. For a good overview, see Robert J. Havighurst, "Philanthropic Foundations as Interest Groups," in *Education and Urban Society* 13 (1981): 193–218. See also Ellen Lagemann, *The Politics of Knowledge* (Chicago: University of Chicago, 1989).

57. See James Hottois and Neal Milner, *The Sex Education Controversy* (Lexington, Mass.: Lexington Books, 1975).

58. Larry Cuban, "Determinants of Curriculum Change and Stability," in Schaffarzick and Sykes, *Value Conflict*, pp. 179–90.

5

School Policy Access: Boards, Elections, Referenda

MODES OF CITIZEN POLITICAL CONTROL

Today's school turbulence finds many groups getting into policymaking, as the preceding chapter described. But more direct access occurs when citizens participate through elections. Although many demands originate outside the political system, some enter it when they "are voiced as proposals for decision and action on the part of the authorities."[1] Some demands do not enter the political system, however, for at least two reasons. They may not be valued highly by society (e.g., a Mafia interest), or they lack sufficient resources to move the system to act adequately (e.g., the poor).

Public preferences have concerned school professionals long before recent turbulent times. Given that citizens vote on school officials and finances, it is not surprising that school officials have long sought to defend themselves against such political control. At the turn of this century, reformers tried to depoliticize education by substituting nonpartisan for partisan elections and election at large for election by ward. But citizens still possessed the means to control those given authority over school matters.

For decades, professionals tried to deflect popular control by mobilizing citizen support, as research shows.[2]

Popular participation in school policymaking has traditionally taken two forms—election of officials and referenda on issues. These elections operate independently of political parties. Contrary to popular impression, political parties at the *national* level have sought successfully to serve as a link between citizens and school policy. For almost a century of national party platforms, education has been among "the predominant forces in operation during election years."[3]

Parties aside, direct and indirect popular control still exists. Directly, there is the widespread practice of electing school boards at the local level and boards and superintendents at the state level.[4] Indirectly, control exists in the election of state legislators, executives, and judges, whose broad responsibilities include authority over many aspects of public education. In those elections, then, policymakers must operate within popularly derived limits that are vague, but elected officials know they exist.

THE ARROYOS OF SCHOOL BOARD ELECTIONS

Although 85 percent of local school boards in this country are elective, the politics of these elections was a great unknown until the 1970s.[5] We know that these officials, five to seven on a board, almost always seek their three- or four-year terms on a nonpartisan ballot. We also know that the board appoints a superintendent, usually professionally trained, who operates under its general policy guides and who may also be removed by it. In the usual community, the theory of democratic control makes the board member a pivot between community demands and school operations. First we must see whether the election of board members provides popular inputs to the school political system. Some widespread general impressions about this interaction existed, but recent studies have provided a more highly complex picture of school board representation.

The Unknown Qualities of Board Elections

What was once known about boards raised more questions than it settled. One clear point remains, that school board elections have little voter turnout, even less than that for other government offices. The reasons are not clear. Is it because of the nonpartisan myth of school politics or because school board elections are held in off years and at primary dates when turnout is low for all contests? If there is variation in the degree of citizen participation in different states or cities, what accounts for it? Does the mere requirement of nonpartisanship preclude political parties from playing a direct role, as they actually do in Detroit, or do voters' party identifications influence their choices, as they do in some city council races? Does low turnout benefit some groups but not others? That is, might board elections more often represent the weight of Republicans—who go to the polls more often than Democrats—and consequently more often represent the viewpoint of groups attracted to the GOP?

It is clear, though, that campaigning in school contests is limited, candidate visibility low, and the contest rarely based on specific policies. Is this again attributable to the nonpartisan myth, which requires participants to act as if they were not engaging in political acts? Or is it due to the lack of highly visible issues that might stimulate popular interest? Under what conditions do election contests become visible and the public highly participant? Further, although most boards are elected, a minority in significant American cities are appointed. What difference does this make in representative roles? Is there any difference in policy orientation under the two methods; if so, can we trace such differences directly to the methods? A clue that this difference has policy consequences is suggested by the earlier finding that boards immune from elections were somewhat more able to move toward school desegregation than elected boards.[6]

Recruitment: Few Are Called, Fewer Chosen

In any political system, leaders must be recruited to fill the constitutional positions, but this process is not random. Rather, it is in harmony with the dominant values of the larger system, just as the selection of kings and presidents tells us much about the values of their respective societies.[7] Also, the process by which a mass of citizens selects few decision makers involves winnowing away those who do not meet the dominant values. Successful recruitment must be followed by effective role learning in the new position of authority and that, in turn, by successful role performance before a political system produces its leadership.

Recruitment in North American school elections is a process of many being excluded, few being called to office, and even fewer becoming leaders.[8] Being recruited comes from possessing political opportunities, some formal, some practical. There is always an unequal distribution of these opportunities, a fact that provides a first screening of the total population. Formally, the legal code may set down minimum requirements—being a qualified voter, a district representative—but clearly these screen out from the enormous numbers only those who do not qualify to vote. Practically, eligibility is screened by social status, political resources (the more eligible have more of these), age, and gender (men get elected disproportionately in government). The fact that such opportunities are structured in society, some having many and many having few, means that most citizens are filtered out of the recruitment process.

Note the results of this process found in the social composition of school boards. When the Progressive reforms of nonpartisanship in school matters began across the nation after 1900, the large working-class membership by the 1920s had almost disappeared from school boards, and white middle-class members dominated everywhere. Moreover, most of these members were male, married with children in the public schools, and active in the community. From the landmark study by Counts in 1927 to a replication by the National School Boards Association decades later, all the research substantiates this finding.[9] The 1991 survey in Table 5.1 finds these members with the same demographics of those seventy years ago. A test of the link between representation and the possession of resources appears in the case of blacks.[10] Their representation on the 168 big-city boards was smaller than their resources (i.e., numbers, money, organization); at-large systems effectively widened the gap between resources and board seats.

Table 5.1
PROFILE OF SCHOOL BOARD MEMBERS

	1989 (percentage)	1994 (percentage)
SEX		
Male	68.1	55.1
Female	31.9	40.3
Data unavailable	—	4.6
ETHNIC BACKGROUND		
Black	3.4	4.4
White	93.7	90.4
Hispanic	1.3	1.5
American Indian	0.7	0.6
Asian	0.3	0.6
Other	0.3	2.2
Data unavailable	0.3	0.3
AGE		
Under 25	0.2	0.3
26–35	7.3	5.6
36–40	15.4	11.7
41–50	44.5	46.2
51–60	20.0	20.8
Over 60	12.6	14.4
Data unavailable	—	1.0
INCOME		
Less than $40,000	26.9	17.7
$40,000 – $79,999	51.8	46.6
or more $80,000	17.9	32.1
Data unavailable	3.4	3.6
WHERE BOARD MEMBERS LIVE		
Rural	28.7	22.0
Small town	26.1	26.7
Suburb	29.0	25.9
Urban area	10.8	9.4
Did not specify	5.4	16.0
CHILDREN IN PUBLIC SCHOOL		
Yes	—	58.9
No	—	40.7
Did not specify	—	0.5

continued on page 104

Table 5.1
CONTINUED

POLITICAL CLASSIFICATION

Conservative	—	64.1
Liberal	—	27.1
Other	—	8.9

BOARD MEMBERS' WORRIES

1989	1994
1. Lack of financial support	1. Lack of financial support
2. Declining enrollment	2. State mandates
3. Parents' lack of interest	3. Poor curriculum/standards
4. Finding good teachers	4. At-risk students
5. Teachers' lack of interest	5. Parents' lack of interest
6. Use of drugs by students	6. Increasing enrollment
7. Poor curriculum/standards	7. Collective bargaining
8. Lack of discipline	8. Management problems
9. Pupils' lack of interest/truancy	9. Crime and violence
10. Disrespect for students/teachers	10. Personnel problems

Source: Reprinted with permission from *The American School Board Journal,* December 1994. Copyright 1994, The National School Boards Association. All rights reserved.

High social status alone does not give entry to the school board, but community activity—whether civic, business, political, or educational—joined with high social status, provides training for office that few of the well-off actually use. Clearly, though, in the recruitment stages the eligibility processes of our democratic system leave out a vast majority of Americans who cannot or will not seek entry or who simply don't care for the game.

Using elections to select unrepresentative school boards always generates questions about the validity of those elections. Thus the continuing criticism of the unrepresentational nature of board membership just noted has implied that without such "virtual representation" the people cannot be well served. This then implies a theory of democracy in which only those with like characteristics can speak for like-minded constituents. On historical grounds alone this is simplistic, for leaders in expanding civil liberties or social policy for the less favored have largely been drawn from higher social status groups. Franklin D. Roosevelt and John F. Kennedy were far removed in status from the millions of poor and ill-favored who saw them as their leaders.

In the waves of reforms in the 1990s, advocates of new ideas emerged in local board elections. They advocated choice, charters, curricular changes, and family values. What has emerged in the recent turbulence over school board elections has been another force of instability affecting the role of the superintendent. That change may account for the reduced tenure of this office in some cities or for the increased superintendent effort at public relations in the community. Quite common have been superintendents elected by one board finding shortly thereafter that a new board emerges—often with different agendas with which one must deal. Often too, such board changes precede changes in that office. That increased turbulence from the board also contributes to the new superintendent's role, not as the "benevolent autocrat," but as working in a "political" context with others who are empowered.

Time and again, what emerges from board elections is, however, that they are little-used channels to the political system. Like arroyos in the Southwest, only rarely does intense turmoil surge through these channels. Certain occasions can, however, have the effect of flash floods through desert courses—enormous conflict followed by altered features in the immediate environment. Much more often, however, these election campaigns offer only slight variations in ideology or policy orientation, and voting for this office, if dominated by nonpartisanship, depresses turnout. These conditions make the democratic model of informed choice between significant policy options by a sizable electorate more a pleasant fiction than a hard fact. A study of school boards summarized the issue:

> I found it compelling to read how much the public believes in the need for school boards, how much it remains attached to the concept of grassroots educational self-governance. But it was equally disturbing to note, from this report, that the same public evidences essential illiteracy about the actual role and activities of school boards. Moreover, the public turns out in appallingly thin numbers to vote for the school boards it otherwise believes to be so essential. We are left with the disturbing question: If the school boards' popular constituency misperceives their role and doesn't care enough to exercise its franchise in their selection, how fully or forcefully will the boards *ever* be able to function?[11]

Competition and Responsiveness

This pervasive condition is greatly affected by history from the nonpartisan reforms begun a century ago and now commonplace in American local government. Many scholars report that such reforms as nonpartisan ballots and at-large elections actually lower electoral school conflict, particularly in metropolitan areas. Research in these areas demonstrates that changing elections from at large to subdistrict also changes the behavior of board members. They become oriented more to concerns and allocations for their own subdistrict, rather than to districtwide policy.[12] But subdistrict elections do create more minority winners.

Nonpartisanship has a more qualitative effect on the nature of school elections in both city and rural districts. The nonpartisan approach and at-large elections affect the degree of competition, however one measures it. Is competition measured by whether candidates are fighting over a major change in school policy, by the degree of differences among candidates over a range of policy issues, or by whether they differ about the board's role? None of these attributes of competition increases if there are nonpartisan ballots or at-large elections involved. Partisanship, on the other hand, can increase turnout and competition.[13]

In short, political scientists have found that what applies to nonpartisanship in other aspects of the local political scene holds true for school politics. Such reforms increase the cost of citizen participation, make the bridge between representative and citizen more tenuous, and consequently muffle expression of the full range of political interests within a community. Those constrained citizens who are affected tend to be of lower socioeconomic status, so governing structures are clearly not value free. Rather, these reforms actually encourage the access and satisfaction of another group, middle-class and higher-status people. The rhetoric of Progressivism a century ago proclaimed the expansion of democracy—"the cure for the evils of democracy is more democracy" was their standard. The reality has been otherwise, filtering out those who cannot use the cue of political party to decide among complicated public issues, including those involving schooling. Such reforms ensure that—until recently at any rate—the game of school politics was played by a few and mostly by those whom fortune favored. It is not yet clear in 1996 that the recent criticism of public schooling has changed that judgment.

The citizen-board linkage in elections is not simple; it must be differentiated for different issues, times, and communities. A rich research demonstrates this variability for the 1960s and 1970s.[14] But we do need more analysis of the last decade of reform and its effects on local elections, a point noted in the preceding chapter.

One of the matters that make a difference is status. The exact nature of the status alignments in voting may depend on the particular issue. No one has yet tried to classify board elections in such terms, reflecting a modification of the concept that different policies generate different kinds of politics.[15] Some work on desegregation suggests that such an issue rearranges electoral coalitions. At the other extreme, and during the same time period as desegregation, sex education has been an area in which professionals have changed the curriculum without much controversy until recently.[16] However, critics have called to add abstinence as a preferred student response that may have affected board elections. Education about American society, however, seems to generate fierce status conflicts between ideologues, who also come into conflict over science; for example, the current evolution-creationism dispute.[17] But financial reform conflict as an issue seems to unite all status levels, as in California's Proposition 13 mood of the late 1970s. A theoretical analysis of various policy effects has yet to be done, but a rich diversity is available in the recent challenges to school systems.

Policy Dissatisfactions and Community Conflict

A theoretical framework needed to understand the citizen role in local school policymaking must turn away from a static view of community context as an explanation. The "dissatisfaction theory" of Iannacconne and Lutz, on the other hand, provides a dynamic model of both quiescence and turbulence as sequences in community life.[18] At one point in a community's life, rough agreement will exist among citizens, board, and superintendent on the course of school policy. Citizens are satisfied with what they have, and their participation in such access channels as elections is quite limited because they support the whole system.

This satisfaction can suddenly break down with growth in the local population that brings newcomers whose policy demands differ from what prevails, but these are rejected by the oldtimers. The result is dissatisfaction with existing school policy. A new protest then ensues before the school board, which is now less a reflective council than an arena where advocates for old and new policy views clash with great rancor. Another outlet for dissatisfaction is the channel of elections. Its use by newcomers in time will produce new board members; a new majority then fires the superintendent, and finally the new policymakers act in congruence with newcomers' policy preferences. At that time, citizen participation falls off due to satisfaction with the new system.

The advantage of this theoretical approach, like all longitudinal analyses, is that it captures shifts or sequences that researchers can explore further. The theory is dynamic, as the time quality is central to explaining what occurs. The traditional cross-sectional approach, on the other hand, permits analysis at only one point in time. Dissatisfaction theory has generated qualitative research in a few communities. A study of Santa Barbara from 1930 to 1980 found that the theory did explain what happened, but it needed to be specified more clearly. That is, all the old board members had to be replaced, the new superintendent had to understand the new mandate, and he or she must be able to express and implement it. Those conditions flow from a realigning election that ends with the voting public's influence evident on new school programs.[19] Similarly, a three-district study over two years, using the same exhaustive search of records and interviews, found that dissatisfaction varied with the object or focus of the feelings. Dissatisfaction with board, superintendent, or both created different outcomes of challenge, as Table 5.2 summarizes. For example, if board and superintendent are a common focus of dissatisfaction, a high chance exists of arena-like council behavior and subsequent board and superintendent turnover. Table 5.2 predicts that the superintendent will be thrown to the wolves if the focus of dissatisfaction is on that person. That theory underlies the reality of an increase in that office's turnover in recent years, as noted later in Chapter 7.

Table 5.2
Policy Dissatisfaction and Political Challenge

Challenge Consequences	School Board	Focus of Dissatisfaction Board and Superintendent	Superintendent
Increased rate of school board member turnover	High	High	Low
Shift to arena-like council behavior	High	High	Moderate
Involuntary superintendent turnover	Low	High	High

Source: Modified from Roger Rada, "Community Dissatisfaction and School Governance," *Planning and Changing* 15 (1984): 246.

Why Citizen Participation?

During the period after the mid-1960s, many people called for more participation in school decision making. This call ran beyond seeking greater voter turnout in board and referenda elections. Rather, this movement sought a qualitative change in the process of policymaking by expanding the number who sit on the boards. This could be done directly, as in the New York City decentralization movement of the 1970s, which created thirty-three neighborhood school boards in place of one. Or it could be arranged by attaching "citizen advisory councils" to existing boards or local school sites. This change created great scope when an Illinois law in 1988 created over five hundred school site councils of different school constituencies in the city of Chicago. This movement was not restricted to the United States, as it surfaced in France, Australia, Canada, Italy, England, Sweden, West Germany, and China.[20]

Several purposes motivated these changes. Some wanted increased participation for instrumental reasons, for example, to achieve specific policy changes. Thus, if more black or Hispanic parents were put on such councils, they could influence the system to be less racist by securing more sensitive teachers and administrators, a multicultural curriculum, and so on. A second purpose for greater participation was psychological, that is, the process itself would improve the participant's sense of value as a person. There might not be much policy change, but participation would stimulate others to act and so permit the emergence of a "community will." A third reason was to avoid the bureaucracy of the central office that critics claimed had interfered with learning and was wasteful of dollars.

Social context is everywhere important in defining who participates and what participation means.[21] Mothers with children, those deeply rooted in the community, the upper social strata—not all in these categories participate, but those with these characteristics are more predisposed to participate than not. The amount of participation does not seem to be highly influenced by family background and socialization. But having children in school is important, and participation itself leads to more intensive participation. Participation has traceable but highly complex effects on one's personal development, level of information, social interaction, and subsequent civic involvement.[22]

Participants in school politics are more distinguished by *what* they do rather than *how much* they do. Some only go to meetings, some specialize in contacting public officials, others talk to fellow citizens about school matters, and still others work primarily in school elections. These types of participants work through different institutions—family and neighbors, political parties, voluntary organizations, the elections system, and school officials. Those who participate support public education, with trust in the honesty and effectiveness of its administrators; they are also sanguine about their own ability to influence local school policy. As an analyst concluded:

> There is broad support in these findings for the ancient view that the active citizen would also be the confident and effective citizen.... The central finding is that ... the more people participate, the greater will be the impact on them, and the greater the impact, the more likely it will take the form of enhanced personal growth and development.[23]

All this participation unfolds in a school politics that is dynamic—constantly changing actors, participants, issues, and conflicts. The changes that accrue from such participation are not dramatically large or abrupt; rather they are small and incremental. But over time, these subtle shifts add up to massive changes in the amount and quality of a policy service like education.[24] For example, the average number of school years attended in 1900 was 6.0, in 1990 it was 12.2 years. The change arose from no single decade, but from the incrementalism of small changes each year.

Those entering the policy world expecting fast, big changes are doomed to disappointment. No system, by definition, changes in this way short of violent revolution—and not even then, as the Soviet system illustrates. However, those entering the school policy world with a sense of developing their capabilities and generating challenge are much more likely to have small effects. Persistence with small effects can achieve major change if, as the poet Graham Greene noted, there is "patience, patience everywhere like a fog." Over time, as the American experience has shown, these people can transform an institution and thus benefit their children immensely.

NONLOCAL PARTICIPATION

To this point, we have focused only on the local channel of the school board's authority. Yet partisan elections for state and federal office can certainly impact local schools because of the resources those levels transmit to schools. Increasingly, the budget fight in the legislature over funds for local schools becomes an annual drama in every state. Governors and legislators thus have a direct bearing on school quality, equity, efficiency, and choice. As we will see in a later chapter, this state role and its mandates make "local control" more imaginary than real. Further, what the legislature says about the taxing authority of local units is vital to local schools and citizen pocketbooks. In 1983 public opinion showed dramatic increases in concern about education quality, so that state governments were galvanized to enact numerous reforms. The same but limited response occurred later for "choice" plans.

One other nonlocal channel for popular participation exists, namely, the elections of Congressional members and the president.

When the range of issues facing political authorities is extensive at the state level, the reach becomes enormous nationally. This should mean that the importance of school issues goes down when most persons vote for higher governmental offices. That is, concern over school taxes or curriculum is less than for issues of war and peace or the national economy. However, citizens follow national affairs more closely than local affairs, but state affairs the least, when they pay any attention to public affairs at all.[25] As yet we have little research on citizen efforts to affect national authorities on school policy. Citizens may have *opinions* on Washington's policies, as we shall see, but the gap between popular opinion and action on many issues rivals the Grand Canyon. And even then, citizen demands, or even attitudes on federal policy, may be so diffuse as to be nonexistent.

Some input is provided, however, through party channels in the form of issue stands. Rather consistently in the past, those identifying with the Democratic Party have been stronger supporters of federal aid to education than have Republican identifiers. Professional politicians of either party were even more widely separated on these issues than average party members.[26] After 1965, as federal funds became increasingly available to local school budgets already straining under an overloaded property tax, this partisan difference began to disappear. It reemerged in the Carter administration over creation of the Department of Education. In 1980 Ronald Reagan campaigned for its abolition and sought to do it after his election, including cutting federal funds for schooling. Forceful opposition frustrated both efforts, however; by 1995 the department still stood, but school funds had been cut from a high of 8 percent down to only 6 percent. Clearly, the 1995–96 Republican "Contract with America" called for cutting even those funds and channeling them to the states as bloc grants.

Diffuse attitudes on federal school policy can crystallize, however, under certain circumstances. For example, there was intense support for the GI Bill after World War II; to oppose this was to oppose our soldiers' efforts in that war. Similarly, during the later 1960s national attitudes coalesced in profound opposition to school busing during the desegregation controversy. On the other hand, citizen input into national arenas deals rarely with educational policy, and little evidence shows that it flavors the decisions of voters in federal elections. Yet, if a perceived threat to a closely held value exists, opinions can have electoral impact. After all, some of the support for Ronald Reagan, and later George Bush, was from foes of busing, especially in the South.

In summary, then, although elections in the United States serve as potential channels for citizens to have school inputs in a way that is rare among nations, they seem little used. Board elections are barometers, normally reflecting little dissatisfaction in the environment, but subject to sudden change. Additional examination of changes that produce dissatisfaction or "rancorous conflict" would be immensely valuable.[27]

Such analyses would have several uses. Practically, they would describe the conditions under which school administration can trigger public concerns. Theoretically, they would help develop an understanding of the links between private wants and public outputs under stress conditions that yield to equilibrium. These practical and theoretical concerns generate interesting questions. Practically, how much can the superintendent support external demands for quality or equity from the profession and state when community standards reject or resist them? Does the frequency of superintendent turnover—chronic in the profession and especially so in larger cities—inhibit or enhance this executive's efforts at financing, curriculum and staff improvement, or desegregation?[28] We will return to the superintendent's situation in Chapter 7.

Any theoretical questions we posed are in contrast to the available evidence that American schools receive a minimum of significant input through the direct channel of elections. Yet from this, one must *not* conclude that the political authorities of School or State ignore the wants of citizens. The possibility always remains that a school issue that agitates the community or the nation deeply enough could suddenly focus on the channel of elections, suddenly displacing the old with the new. Dissatisfaction theory research substantiates this possibility. In the satisfied stage, school officials are confined by a "zone of tolerance" that is based on community expectations. But in the dissatisfied stage, voters use elections to focus their demands and restructure the local policy system. In either case, school officials must keep tuned for public signals, no matter how muted they are. A 1992 survey

found that while nearly 60 percent of Americans thought parents and other members of the community should have more
say in allocating funds and deciding curriculum, less than 15
percent of administrators and 26 percent of teachers shared this
view.[29] Clearly, the profession is not tuned in.

REFERENDA AND POLICY CONVERSION

Numerous channels carrying demand inputs pour into the
miniature political system that the schools form. We have seen
this in electoral inputs. Yet a second input channel is the referendum by which citizens vote directly on such school policy matters
as budgets, bonds, or levies. The referendum is a device for reg-
istering the extent of public support for specific school policies.
Unhappiness with excessive spending, insensitive teachers, lack
of student discipline, objectionable curriculum, or even the losing football team can all generate lack of support. Simply voting
"no" is a convenient way of expressing this dissatisfaction, so school
boards and administrators have to pay attention to this potential
support. In short, they must become "political" by seeking to
mobilize group support within the community for what they see
as necessary funding. But in recent decades, school authorities
have found that this support is drying up. This development is
yet another part of the current political turbulence that fills
American schools today.

Background and Significance

By the end of the nineteenth century, many Americans were
disgusted with the greed and corruption of local government.
Reformers in the Progressive movement at that time altered many
forms and practices in local policymaking.[30] More significantly,
they altered the dominance of the political party in the "nonpartisan" movement noted earlier.

However, the use of referenda to pass budgets, levies, and bonds
in education did not arise from progressives. School referenda
were the handiwork of *conservatives* seeking to *prevent* passage of
bond issues and to keep property tax rates down by state law.

These laws made school referenda to be voted on only by property owners, and these required extraordinary majorities to pass. Conservatives thought that few such efforts would succeed, given these barriers, but that is not what happened. The unintended consequences of this reform were that local revenue sources dried up and pressures escalated on the state to bail out the locals. After 1900, this process generated pressures for new state taxes and later led to the widespread adoption of the sales tax and new grant and taxing arrangements for the local schools. This reaction occurred again in the educational finance politics of the 1970s. Consequently, "the tax limitation schemes begat fiscal policy centralization and a web of state-local fiscal relationships and interdependence."[31]

In two respects the referendum is more significant for education than for other areas of public policy. It is the necessary device for securing financial support of schools in all states except Alabama, Hawaii, and Indiana; however, certain districts are exempt in fourteen other states. Also, this device may be viewed as a process that bypasses the school board and authoritatively allocates values, *a direct policymaking process*, while it also allocates school resources in levies and bond issues. The act of voting thus links the individual citizen to the school in a direct and intimate way that is unparalleled for other major public policies.

LINKAGES AMONG VOTING AND REFERENDA SUCCESS

These conceptual distinctions are well illustrated by voting patterns for bond issues in recent decades. Figure 5.1 traces these dynamics over the turbulent years of three decades featured throughout this book. What it shows is that popular satisfaction with the steady state school system of the 1950s and 1960s is seen in the high degree of support for referenda; about four in five supported these across the nation. But the dissatisfaction with schools we have noted earlier was associated with a sharp decline in referenda support; in 1986 only about 35 percent showed support. Indeed, the curve on elections is a mirror of the politics of education in these decades.

Figure 5.1
Three Decades of School Bond Approval, 1957–1986

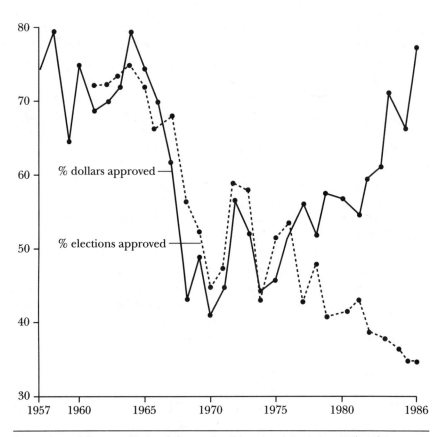

Source: Annual Reports, National Center for Educational Statistics, 1957–1976; combined report 1977–1986 (August, 1987).

A citizen's vote on a secret ballot does not tell us much about his or her motivation. But that knowledge is important for officials who must cater to the diverse feelings of citizens. Analysis of differences employs a rough model of their behavior. Policy events in schools move voters—at least some—to turn out to pass or reject referenda. But how a citizen votes may be affected by his or her own characteristics, by the school district or site, or by school events. Personal influences may lean heavily on the voter as the "rational actor," that is, one who evaluates what is gained or lost by a vote. Or voters may lean heavily on the reinforcing nature of the district, so that, as research shows regularly, a wealthy district reinforces support while less wealthy districts may not. These independent variables explaining voter turnout are displayed by this model seen in Figure 5.2. Some summary results of such research are useful in understanding the complexity of voting on a referendum.

Who Votes and Why?

Research *historically* pictures voters who are supporters, those who do turn out and support these referenda.[32] The largest explainer of voter turnout is *status*—voters are mostly the middle- and higher-status members of the community. Measures of income, education, occupation all show much the same thing, indicators of a descending cascade of turnout and support running down from upper to lower statuses. This research topic was widely explored prior to 1970, but since the growing defeat of referenda (noted in Figure 5.2), there has been little research interest in this matter.

Other factors confound, however, the influence of status, for example, *ethnicity*.[33] In the absence of political parties' providing cues for voters on how to vote (given schools' nonpartisan elections), ethnicity may be a cue to voting. Earlier research showed differences among ethnic voters (Irish and Polish give less support, blacks more). But a large research agenda remains untouched after the turbulence of the last several decades. Does the ethnicity of those who have newly come to power in big cities (blacks, Hispanics, Asians) vary with status—particularly among supporters and opponents? Or does status within these groups differ, so that middle-class ethnics support referenda and poorer members do not? Does support vary with the school issue at hand, such as curriculum, teachers' salaries, and so on?

A largely abandoned reason for voting on referenda was that citizens vote in response to an *ideology* or ethos that is centered around the school in the community.[34] Those who hold a "public-regarding ethos" (primarily Protestant, middle-class, Anglo-Saxon) were thought to support the community's general interest

Figure 5.2
Model of Research into Financial Referenda

Individual-Level Explanations →	Turnout →	Voting Outcome →	Subsequent Policy Events →
Vote Characteristics:			
Variable - status - ethnicity - ideology - school attitudes	Percent of eligibles Social composition	Size of support Social composition of yeas and nays	Future frequency of referenda Results of future referenda Amount of funds in future referenda Board turnover Superintendent turnover Board policy (program changes)
Economic—optimization Ethos—other-regarding Psychological—alienation school age cohort			
System-Level Explanations: Environmental—macroanalysis			
Political access—legitimation			
Community conflict			
District Characteristics: Demand levels: resources school age cohort			
Structural requirements: - voting - majority submission			
Amount of politization			

Figure 5.3

Personal and Community Orientations to Voting in School Referenda

	Voter Motives	
Direction of vote	*With Children in Public Schools*	*Without Children in Public Schools*
For	Mixed	Community
Against	Personal	Personal

Community =	Has first commitment to community, second consideration for economic costs of referendum, and consequently reasons in voting: Community benefits > personal costs
Personal =	Has first commitment to self-family-ethnic group, second consideration to community, and consequently reasons in voting: Personal costs > community/personal benefits
Mixed =	Motives may be either personal or community benefit as primary consideration, but not both, and consequently reasons in voting: Indeterminate

in school support. However, those who held a "private-regarding ethos" (primarily immigrants, lower-class, or working-class) centered on supporting their own special interests in their family or group.

These private versus public orientations are suggested in Figure 5.3. The types of voters implied there suggest that self-interest looms large when community interest fades. What accounts for such fading? Fewer children in public schools is a growing fact of school demography today as birth rates decline and childbearing is postponed, especially in the middle-class segments.[35] Also, constant criticism of the "failure" of schools would weaken the public-interest motivation for referenda support. Or, a decline in disposable income would cause private interest to loom even larger over that of a public interest in school support. Much of that research in the new era of the challenge to schools has not yet been undertaken. But the wide availability of computer-based voting data suggests a relatively easy analysis.

These attitudes about schools involve the citizen's perceptions and sense of worth about schools. What the school system communicates to its public can generate support or opposition. Even direct involvement by parents in schools generates much more support and greater credibility to schoolpeople.[36] Or, citizens' sense that expenditures for schools is "a good thing" or that government taxes are a "bad thing"—vague as these feelings seem— may move citizens at their deepest level to affect turnout and support. As polls of the last decades show, when citizens come to increasingly distrust government in general, they may accept the concept of any governmental expenditures as bad. Indeed, as elections are channels for funneling many kinds of attitudes, one attitude—personal alienation—may be salient for schools. The sense of being ignored by a society that is seen as control-led by a conspiracy of a few (who are quite different from one's self) would weaken any support for school referenda. We should not overestimate the number of citizens so alienated, but nei-ther should we underestimate their role in defeating referenda.

These are new possibilities about voters' attitudes, quite different from the traditional analysis of district qualities affecting the vote. While we are far from knowing the origins of these attitudes and perceptions, future work on these cognitive maps of voters may well provide information to school officials and boards with funding needed for school programs and facilities.

There is an underlying support of goodwill for public schools. By the late 1990s polls showed that Americans liked their schools somewhat more, especially those they knew close to home. As one scholar of polls noted, "Despite all the outcry about school 'failures,' public confidence in those responsible for education ran ahead of all other institutional leaders except doctors."[37]

But that underlying support may mean less in the face of a changing demography of voters. Fewer public school parents today means fewer motivated to vote for referenda out of personal or community interests. The striking factor is the growing number of citizens without children in public schools. Both the young and oldest voters and those with children in private schools are unlikely to support referenda. The result must be the erosion of the once stable and continuing base of public acceptance for the steady-state school system and its referenda.

THE LOCAL CONVERSION PROCESS IN TRANSITION

This chapter has pointed to the dual interest by officials and professionals, who must rely on referenda for continued sustenance, and by scholars of democratic politics. School officials do not like the device, although they express little of that feeling publicly, but no evidence suggests that it will be abolished any time soon.[38] Low-key community relations used to be the norm in affecting school decisions. The professionals' decisions withdrew somewhere into the crevices of their world; supporters inside and outside the system were maintained and reinforced; and a closed world of policymaking existed for a select few. There was only a limited citizen control over schools, exceeded only occasionally by episodic events. In that context, one sees much of systems analysis and democratic theory in operation. As one scholar concluded, "There is reason to believe that the reduction of public conflict is something of an ideal toward which school systems tend."[39] Much of this is done to anticipate community demands. The result is an output reflecting both public and professional needs and wants.

Yet the recent turbulence has affected traditional systems. The decline of the total number of referenda seen earlier in Figure 5.1 shows the desperate efforts of school authorities to anticipate the voters' reduced zone of tolerance in the 1970s. These new forces at the local level require adaptation, and often new training, in administrative roles as well.[40] Training administrators has shifted somewhat from an emphasis on organizational theory as explaining their decisional environment to an emphasis on political context.[41] Certainly the superintendent today needs to understand much more than just the old notion of keeping the referenda campaign low key in order to win. Partial theories of explaining what goes on in voters' minds in these elections abound, as we have shown. Indeed, the professional needs to know much more about the politics of decision making, and for this, one must grasp other political theories—rational, incremental, implementation, and so on.

Finally, whatever new role the professional adopts within this current turbulence, he and she will have participated in the most recent skirmish of our historic clash between participatory and meritocratic values. James Madison, Alexis de Tocqueville, or Lord Bryce, brought back to life and observing the events discussed in these last two chapters, would understand quite well what they meant. These observers and many others have grasped the basic underlying dynamic of American politics and policymaking. That is the tension generated by a nation of diverse groups seeking to realize their values through the subsystems of society, including the political.

NOTES

1. David Easton, *A Framework for Political Analysis* (Engelwood Cliffs, N.J.: Prentice-Hall, 1965), p. 122.

2. H. M. Hamlin, "Organized Citizen Participation in the Public Schools," *Review of Educational Research* 23 (1953): 346–52. Compare this with the study fifteen years later by Otis A. Crosby, "How to Prepare Winning Bond Issues," *Nation's Schools* 81 (1968): 81–84.

3. Richard J. Brown, "Party Platforms and Public Education," *Social Studies* (1961): 206–10.

4. Roald F. Campbell et al., *The Organization and Control of American Schools* (Columbus, Ohio: Charles E. Merrill, 1975); Peter J. Cistone, ed., *Understanding School Boards: Problems and Prospects* (Lexington, Mass.: Lexington Books, 1975); Tyll van Geel, *Authority to Control the School Program* (Lexington, Mass.: Lexington Books, 1976).

5. Charles R. Adrian and Charles Press, *Governing Urban America*, 3d ed. (New York: McGraw-Hill, 1968), p. 434.

6. Robert L. Crain et al., *The Politics of School Desegregation* (Garden City, N.Y.: Doubleday-Anchor, 1969), and David Kirby et al., *Political Strategies in Northern School Desegregation* (Lexington, Mass.: Lexington Books, 1973).

7. Lester G. Seligman, *Political Recruitment* (Boston: Little, Brown & Co., 1972).

8. Peter J. Cistone, "The Recruitment and Socialization of School Board Members," in Cistone, *Understanding School Boards*, Chap. 3, and Cistone, "The Ecological Basis of School Board Member Recruitment," *Education and Urban Society* 4 (1974): 428–50.

9. George S. Counts, *The Social Composition of Boards of Education* (Chicago: University of Chicago, 1927).

10. Ted Robinson, Robert England, and Kenneth Meier, "Black Resources and Black School Board Representation: Does Political Structure Matter?" *Social Science Quarterly* 66(1990): 976–82.

11. Neal Peirce, Preface in *School Boards: A Strengthening Grass Roots Leadership*, by Lila N. Carol et al. (Washington, D.C.: Institute for Educational Lead-

ership, 1986). See also Jacqueline P. Danzberger, Michael W. Kirst, and Michael Usdan, *Governing Public Schools* (Washington, D.C.: Institute for Educational Leadership, 1992).

12. Jacqueline P. Danzberger, Michael W. Kirst, and Michael Usdan, *Improving Grass Roots Leadership* (Washington, D.C.: Institute for Educational Leadership, 1986).

13. Sande Milton, "Participation in Local School Board Elections: A Reappraisal," *Social Science Quarterly* 64: 646-54; Sande Milton and Robert Bickel, "Competition in Local School Board Elections: Findings in a Partisan Political Environment," *Planning and Changing* 13: 148-57. For a recent overview of national voting see Warren E. Miller and J. Merrill Shanks, *The New American Voter* (Cambridge, Mass.: Harvard, 1996).

14. The earliest studies (before 1960) included Richard Carter, *Voters and Their Schools* (Stanford: Institute for Communications Research, 1952). Analysis after 1960 included L. Harmon Zeigler, M. Kent Jennings, and G. Wayne Peak, *Governing American Schools: Political Interaction in Local School Districts* (North Scituate, Mass.: Duxbury, 1974), pp. 60–62; David Minar, "The Community Basis of Conflict in School System Politics," *American Sociological Review* 31 (1966): 822–34; William Boyd, *Community Status and Conflict in Suburban Schools* (Beverly Hills, Calif.: Sage, 1975); and Christine Rossell, "School Desegregation and Electoral Conflict," in *The Polity of the School*, Frederick Wirt, ed. (Lexington, Mass.: Lexington Books, 1975), Chap. 4.

15. Theodore Lowi, "American Business, Public Policy, Case Studies and Political Theory," *World Politics* 16 (1964): 677–715.

16. James Hottois and Neal A. Milner, *The Sex Education Controversy: A Study of Politics, Education, and Morality* (Lexington, Mass.: Lexington Books, 1974).

17. Paul Goldstein, *Changing the American Schoolbook* (Lexington, Mass.: Lexington Books, 1978).

18. Frank Lutz and Laurence Iannaccone, eds., *Public Participation in School Decision Making* (Lexington, Mass.: Lexington Books, 1978).

19. Ruth Danis, "Policy Changes in Local School," *Urban Education* 19: 125–44.

20. Fred S. Coombs and Richard I. Merritt, "The Public's Role in Educational Policy Making: An International View," *Education and Urban Society* 9 (1977): 169–96.

21. The following paragraphs rely upon Robert H. Salisbury, *Citizen Participation in the Public Schools* (Lexington, Mass.: Lexington Books, 1980).

22. For reviews of the literature on the impact of participation on the participant, see David H. Smith and Richard D. Reddy, "The Impact of Voluntary Action upon the Voluntary Participant," in *Voluntary Action Research, 1973*, David H. Smith, ed. (Lexington, Mass.: Lexington Books, 1973), pp. 169–239; and Dale Mann, *The Politics of Administrative Representation* (Lexington, Mass.: Lexington Books, 1976), Chap. 5. For an overview of the field see Steven Rosenstone and J. Hansen, *Mobilization, Participation, and American Democracy* (New York: Macmillan, 1993).

23. Salisbury, *Citizen Participation*, pp. 177, 199.

24. Charles E. Lindblom, *The Policy-Making Process*. (Englewood Cliffs, NJ.: Prentice-Hall, 1968). For particular evidence of the proposition as it applies to changes in education, see Diane Ravitch, *The Revisionists Revised: A Critique of the Radical Attack on Schools* (New York: Basic Books, 1978); and Frederick M. Wirt, "Neoconservatism and National School Policy," *Educational Evaluation and Policy Analysis* 2, no. 6 (1980): 5–18.

25. M. Kent Jennings and Harmon Zeigler, "The Salience of American State Politics," *American Political Science Review* 64 (1970): 524–27.

26. Herbert McClosky et al., "Issue Conflict and Consensus Among Party Leaders and Followers," *American Political Science Review* 54 (1960): 413; Thomas A. Flinn and Frederick M. Wirt, "Local Party Leaders: Groups of Like Minded Men," *Midwest Journal of Political Science* 9 (1965): 82.

27. William Gamson, *Power and Discontent* (Homewood, Ill.: Dorsey Press, 1968), although the focus here is not upon school issues.

28. Joseph M. Cronin, *The Control of Urban Schools* (New York: Free Press, 1972); and Larry Cuban, *Urban School Chiefs Under Fire* (Chicago: University of Chicago Press, 1976).

29. Steve Faskar, *Educational Reform: The Players and Politics* (New York: Public Agenda Foundation, 1992).

30. On Progressivism and the quotation, see Eric F. Goldman, *Rendezvous with Destiny* (New York: Vintage books, 1956), p. 338. For origins and results of direct legislation, see William Munro, ed., *The Initiative, Referendum and Recall* (New York: Macmillan, 1913), and Joseph G. LaPalombara and Charles B. Hagan, "Direct Legislation: An Appraisal and a Suggestion," *American Political Science Review* 45 (1951): 400–21. On zone of tolerance, see William Boyd, "The Public, the Professionals, and Educational Policy Making: Who Governs? *Teachers College Record* 77 (1976): 556–58.

31. Howard D. Hamilton and Sylvan H. Cohen, *Policy Making by Plebiscite: School Referenda* (Lexington, Mass.: Lexington Books, 1974), p. 3.

32. Philip K. Piele and John S. Hall, *Budgets, Bonds, and Ballots* (Lexington, Mass.: Lexington Books, 1973) and Hamilton and Cohen, *Policy Making*. An updating through 1980 is found in Philip Piele, "Public Support for Public Schools: The Past, the Future, and the Federal Role," *Teachers College Record* 84 (1983): 690–707. For a national perspective see Raymond E. Wolfinger and Stephen Rosenstone, *Who Votes* (New Haven: Yale, 1980)

33. Piele and Hall, *Budgets, Bonds, and Ballots* provides the major review; see also, Gerald Pomper, "Ethnic and Group Voting in Nonpartisan Municipal Elections," *Public Opinion Quarterly* 30 (1966); J. Lieper Freeman, "Local Party Systems: Theoretical Considerations and a Case Analysis," *American Journal of Sociology* 64 (1958): 282–89. On ethnic attitudes, see Nathan Glazer and Daniel Moynihan, *Beyond the Melting Pot* (Cambridge, Mass.: MIT Press, 1980); Emmett Buell, Jr., *School Desegregation and Defended Neighborhoods: The Boston Story* (Lexington, Mass.: Lexington Books, 1981); Dianne Pinderhughes, *Race and Ethnicity in Chicago Politics* (Champaign: University of Illinois Press, 1987).

34. James Q. Wilson and Edward C. Banfield, "Public Regardingness as a

Value Premise in Voting Behavior," *American Political Science Review* 58 (1964): 883; Piele and Hall, *Budgets, Bonds, and Ballots*, pp. 105–7.

35. Michael Kirst and Walter Garms, "The Political Environment of School Finance Policy in the 1980s," in *School Finance Policies and Practices*, James Guthrie, ed. (Cambridge, Mass.: Ballinger, 1980). See also Samuel Popkin, *The Reasoning Voter* (Chicago: University of Chicago, 1991).

36. For example, Thomas A. McCain and Victor D. Wall, Jr., "A Communication Perspective of a School-Bond Failure," *Education Administration Quarterly* 12, no. 2 (1974); 1–17; for a review of this aspect, see Piele and Hall, *Budgets, Bonds, and Ballots*, pp. 83–91, 130–34.

37. Piele, "Public Support for Public Schools," pp. 690–95.

38. Hamilton and Cohen, *Policy Making*, pp. 271–73.

39. Minar, "Community Basis of Conflict," p. 285

40. Cuban, *Urban School Chiefs Under Fire*, App. 2.

41. For a review of this shift, see Norman Boyan, "Follow the Leader: Commentary on Research in Educational Administration," *Educational Researcher 12* (1981): 6–13. For an analysis of the recent contributions of social science to administrators' knowledge and training, see the essays in Glenn L. Immegart and William L. Boyd, eds., *Problem Finding in Educational Administration* (Lexington, Mass.: Heath, 1979), and Jack Culbertson et al., *Preparing Educational Leaders for the Seventies* (Columbus, Ohio: University Council for Educational Administration, 1969). For a less encouraging view see Roy A. Teixeira, *The Disappearing American Voter* (Washington, D.C.: Brookings, 1992).

6

Local School Boards, Politics, and the Community

Elected school boards and appointed professionals alike are criticized, removed from office, and, in general, as distrusted as all institutions of American life have been in the last two decades. These views are captured in the poll data of Table 6.1, where the contrasting evaluations of school problems are exhibited by the board and superintendents, on the one hand, and by the general public on the other; compare the first, second, and third rankings in each column.

These anecdotal and poll data indicate an important challenge to how school officials operate that is unlike the usual dry arroyo of school politics set out in the preceding chapter. To understand this challenge, we need to know more about how the school system operated when stress arose in the environment and fastened on school governance. In the next two chapters, we will explain the behavior of boards, superintendents, and teachers and how they have adapted to the crisis challenge to their authority.

We can understand these events within the analytical framework set out in Chapter 3. Our focus here will be on the formal school system—board, superintendent, and principals—where

Table 6.1

School Board Presidents' Attitudes About Public Schools
(in percentages)

	All School Board Presidents	Superintendents	General Public
What grade would you give public schools in the nation *as a whole?*			
A	2%	5%	3%
B	31	66	20
C	51	25	48
D	9	1	13
Fail	2	—	3
Don't know	5	3	13
What grade would you give the public schools *in your community?*			
A	23	32	9
B	56	58	31
C	18	8	34
D	1	1	10
Fail	0	—	4
Don't know	1	—	12

Source: Profile of School Board Presidents in the U.S., National Center for Education Information, 1989.

most policymaking and implementation activity takes place on a day-to-day basis. Their work is to routinize activity in order to rationalize objectives and economize resources. The consequence of such exorts is to maximize system persistence. But such decision making also has varied consequences for different groups. A second major local force—voter influence—provides episodic inputs to the school system, as described in the preceding chapter. The best way to think of that force is that it generates a set of potential limits on school authorities. In this chapter, we move from the outside to inside the political system of American schools.

THE SCHOOL BOARD'S COMPOSITION AND HISTORY

The school board and professional educators authoritatively allocate values in creating and administering public policy for the schools. Service on the board was once an extremely low-profile, low-conflict position, but in the last two decades, board members have been thrust into the middle of politically turbulent issues. In the process their roles changed; some became champions of lay groups, but others supported professional groups. A board member now needs to know and judge issues in finance, discrimination, textbook values, teacher demands, and so on—a lengthy list of crucial and excruciating claims on school resources. Board membership has become exciting in terms of the ancient Chinese *curse*, "May you live in exciting times."

But, whether meeting or blocking a demand, the board is not static nor are its members value free. They modify, regulate, innovate, or refuse political demands in response to a variety of value preferences. On the one hand, they are somewhat controlled in this conversion function; local groups may conflict within the system, higher system levels can constrain, and voters may disrupt. In short, board members and administrators are not "passive transmitters of things taken into the system, digesting them in some sluggish way, and sending them along as output."[1] Rather they reflect a highly personal element in the interplay of school politics. Policy output, then, partly depends on the feelings and values, failures and successes of human beings. Consequently, it is important to know something about what school board members are like.

Their social characteristics have changed little since the famous Counts survey of 1927.[2] Most are still owners, officials, and managers of businesses, or else they are professionals, but increasingly teachers appear with them. Their income is well above average. Only a fraction are women, and even fewer are workers. The reforms that began over a century ago resulted in the replacement of one class—workers—by others—middle class and professionals—who had generated those reforms.[3] Their motives are a mix of orientations to self, group, and community.

We cannot understand the meaning of the social qualities of this governing agency without some sense of its political function. A historical sketch will help set the framework for understanding the school board's current role.[4]

The Local Conversion Process

When public schools began, no administrators intervened between teachers and board; the board itself was an administrative body. Each member undertook responsibility for a special school task, much as the commission form of local government operates today. Growing enrollments and new professionals transformed the board into a legislative body. Its major function altered to set broad policy guidelines and act as watchdogs over their implementation. Yet even that function was transformed in this century with the increased control over local schools from state and national laws and the increased power of professional administrators and teachers unions.

Prior to the mid-1960s a description of the board's function would be something like this: School boards most often mediated major policy conflicts, leaving determination of important policy issues to the professional staff or to higher external levels; if no evidence of community concern showed up, they might do something. In the process, they legitimated the proposals of the professional staff—making only marginal changes—rather than representing citizens. Board members spent the bulk of their time on details but established a policy zone of consent for the administration to act.

Beginning in the 1960s, the board found that this picture of low conflict was disrupted, but many believed that the school board still could not do much.[5] This picture of a weakened board is partially true. Missing is an explanation of how the board usually operates in its relationship to the community and to the professionals. It must represent both; yet it must control both. A pivot between community notions of schooling and professional standards of service, the board must be seen in some larger perspective.

BOARD SUPPORT FROM THE COMMUNITY

Boards are small political systems, reflecting the ever-present tension in a democracy among the demands of quality, equity, efficiency, and choice. We expect education to be decided by and be responsive to people's choice in general but also, and simultaneously, to be technically advanced and determined by standards of quality.[6] Despite fervent wishes to the contrary, the two expectations do not always coincide. So the board is caught up in an ideology of an informed citizenry participating in democratic decision making.

In fact, citizens are poorly informed on such matters and seemingly disinterested in acquiring such information; hence they participate little. But even if this does describe citizen inattention and inactivity, this does not mean that citizens do not affect schools. For, some argue, this lack of citizen information and participation has generated a massive public loss of support for schools that is potentially devastating. Actually, the evidence can support both the pessimist and the optimist on this matter.[7] Pessimists can point to:

- Gallup polls that show declines in the high rating of schools, especially in big cities;
- decreasing votes for tax and bond referenda;
- and evidence from other nations of criticism, disenchantment, and loss of funding for some public schools.

Optimists can point to:

- the failure to evaluate confidence in schools or achievement records over long enough periods of time;
- growing funding for most schools;
- education's relative vote of confidence compared to other American institutions (much better than for big business, news media, Congress, and organized labor, and a bit better than for the Supreme Court);
- high support for maintaining or increasing current service levels by those also voting to limit taxes and expenditures; and
- movement of blacks into college and of more people into adult education.

One must understand the school board's role partly in terms of this system support for education as a whole. Media fastened on evidence of "failure" or "crisis" and accentuated—maybe even stimulated—this perception of breakdown. This signal did not jibe with many boards' perceptions of their problems, though.[8] Consequently, serious problems of support exist for some aspects of schools, particularly in an era when the public is far more critical about everything in public life and uninterested in looking for success in that area.

Strong evidence suggests that our schools may have done a better job with more people, compared to earlier eras and other nations.[9] But in politics what is important is what citizens *think* is reality—not reality. The 1990s has been, as the 1980s were, a period of skeptical challenge to boards and professional educators for the job they are doing. What occurred was that the usually dry arroyos of community-board linkage became flooded by challenges over a disparity between expectations and reality in school services.

What are the consequences of this gap for the school board, the system's authoritative local agency? There is evidence of what Lutz and Iannaccone have termed "the dissatisfaction theory of democracy." Their study is unusual for its effort to modify theory by testing it in successive analyses in different contexts and locales.[10] It asserts that voters' dissatisfaction rises as the gap between their values and demands and those of board members and superintendent increases. In districts characterized by rapid population shifts—either expanding or contracting in size—dissatisfaction is particularly strong. Newcomers' values, expectations, and demands differ sharply from those of older residents. At some point, the dissidents become strong enough to defeat board incumbents, and a new board replaces the superintendent.

Rare in its use of longitudinal research, this study presents convincing evidence from over fifteen years of testing, thereby leading to a strong affirmation that school boards are indeed democratic. As Lutz has argued, it depends on the question put to the system. Who governs? Do administrator actions coincide with citizen preferences? Who has access to modify the governance, under what conditions, and how?[11] If that is the critical question, it seems likely that once the public knows, it can redefine the needs they want the school system to meet. It is much clearer that continued dissatisfaction with board efforts to meet these new needs produced not simply changes in board membership but also new agendas, new constituents, new resources, and in time even new structures of governance.

THE BOARD AND STATUS POLITICS

Another conceptualization of the community and board linkage stems from status differences between the two. If a community were homogeneous in status, board members' tasks would be simple—just consult one's own preferences, which would largely reflect the community's. Studies of small town school politics show such congruence between citizens and their boards. This also shows up in the pervasive role of the high school within the rural black community, where the school embodies most aspects of the latter; among whites, the school is only one aspect of institutional community life.[12]

However, American community life is becoming much more varied than this, as boards face competing demands arising from needs of a diverse community. The historical record of such a process is clear, although there is debate about which groups were favored or not as a result. We already noted the shift from working class to middle class and business domination in board composition. For some scholars this was evidence of industrialists controlling schools in order to provide a trained labor pool; for others, this was evidence of capitalists foisting education on a proletarian in order to control them. But historical analysis of this shift in board role demonstrates something else. The spread of professionalization in the schools was actually encouraged by trade unions; it attracted the middle class to the schools; and at least in the case of three major regional cities, it was welcomed, not resisted, by the middle class.[13] In the past this status context underlay the control of schools in our cities. Reformers focused on changing the structures of power, which are never value-free but rather dispense varying rewards to different groups. Certainly this was what the business groups who supported such reform believed.[14]

In the contemporary period this status orientation to understanding school conflict undergirds some research.[15] The role behaviors of superintendents differ in working-class, as opposed to middle-class, suburbs and are associated with different political turbulence. Before the 1970s higher-status districts had fewer political conflicts (that is, votes for losing candidates), lower electoral participation in board elections, and less challenge to superintendents' administrative decisions than did lower-status districts. Associated with these differences were dissimilar cultural norms about citizen involvement with schools and school professionals.[16]

These findings were qualified by later events. Thus, when an issue becomes significant to the traditionally low-conflict, higher-status community, its members can actively challenge boards and school professionals. This has been the case in Northern cities in the matter of desegregation, where higher-status elements became just as vocal as South Boston working-class citizens.[17] Both status groups were protecting their social neighborhoods, on racial grounds in this case, although it was also done for other matters such as freeways, low-income housing, or heavy-industry location.[18]

Further, some evidence suggests that the status of the district affects the "board culture" of that school.[19] Homogeneous districts develop a board style of "elite" councils—small in size, seeing themselves as guardians of the public but separate from it, making decisions privately, consensually, and in limited range, and exhibiting administrative, judicial, and legislative functions. On the other hand, "arena" councils exhibit the opposite qualities within a heterogeneous community. However, the elite cultural system has usually prevailed, modifying inputs from different ethnic, religious, and status groups so as to subordinate them.

The Special Stimulus of Consolidation

Consolidation is a factor that has increased not only the volume but also the conflict of status demands on boards enormously. What was once an archipelago of districts in America, each island homogeneous with board and community in harmony, has been fused into larger, more varied districts. The 89,000 districts of 1948 became 55,000 five years later, 31,000 by 1961, and 14,000 by 1996. During the 1970s, on any given day, three districts disappeared forever between breakfast and dinner. But even earlier in the 1960s that many had evaporated between breakfast and the morning coffee break, with another seven gone by dinner.[20] As a result, not only are there now more diverse values and broader status bases confronting board members, but there are also fewer board members to handle this increased input. By the early 1970s, as one scholar calculated, "Where a school board member once represented about 200 people, today each . . . must speak for approximately 3,000 constituents."[21]

This problem in accommodating increasingly diverse views underlies the Lutz-Iannaccone dissatisfaction theory of democracy noted earlier. Evidence of this mixing of districts is suggested by the finding that a greater rate of interest groups is coming to board attention in metropolitan areas and a lesser rate in nonmetropolitan districts.[22] We will return to this shortly.

The Mosaic of Status Politics

No consensus about what the board's link to the community should be appears from the research mainly because the literature spans different periods and issues. However, the view that a board's openness to its community is a variable does emerge. That is, the linkage should be different under conditions of low versus high community dissent over school policies. We could expect that when little conflict exists, boards are less receptive to community input. When more intense community conflict exists, however, the board becomes more receptive to challenging established policies.[23] This linkage appeared in four possible styles of board politics, illustrated in Table 6.2.

Like all typologies, this is a still life of reality that nevertheless covers many communities, but it hints at a dynamic process. That is, the four board styles shown represent different stages of the Lutz-Iannaccone model of longitudinal school conflict. Both typology and model have their respective uses, but the more dynamic model is capable of generating more powerful hypotheses. That is, boards do not merely transmit what the community says, for often it says very little; nor do boards dictatorially block off any signals not on their wave lengths. Rather, when issues heat up the local environment, considerable evidence shows that boards become much more receptive to citizen inputs and more willing to oppose the traditional direction of school policy. There is a

Table 6.2
Styles of School Board Politics

Numbers in Conflict

Skills of Opposition	High	Low
High	I. Reform ideal of citizen democracy	II. Challenge by takeover group
Low	III. All-out battle	IV. Continuity under traditional ruling group

Source: Reprinted with permission from Leigh Stelzer, "Institutionalizing Conflict Response: The Case of Schoolboards," Social Science Quarterly 55 (1974), in Frederick Wirt, The Polity of the School, table on p. 81. Copyright 1975 by Jossey-Bass Inc., Publishers. First published by Lexington Books. All rights reserved.

particularly political quality to this response of school boards, best caught in the aphorism of V. O. Key: "Public opinion is that opinion which politicians find it prudent to pay attention to." In this and other respects, board members are true politicians.

THE BOARD AS A DECISION-MAKING AGENCY

A question that is analytically separate from the role of community inputs is how boards make decisions, although the two merge in reality. Several older models of this process were characterized by their naivete. One was that the school board necessarily reflected the social composition of its members. As we have just seen, that does not work as an explanation of who governs and, as we will soon see, it does not answer the further question, How does it govern? Another naive model was found for a long time in education administration literature. This described the board as the maker of school policy and the superintendent as the administrator of that policy, with a clear separation of function. Empirically, that has not been the case, for the two stimulate and affect each other. Thus, a national sample of superintendents showed in the early 1980s that their policy involvement had become greater by two-thirds, and one-half reported that their professional judgments were increasingly accepted by their boards. Similar results were found for city managers and planning directors.[24]

Multiple Currents of Decision Making

Another, more sophisticated way of viewing board decision making is to see it as different processes for different kinds of issues. In Figure 6.1 we see that any naive model of decision making is confounded by a more varied reality. In the *null response model* we are looking at what happens to most environmental demands made upon a political agency—the agency does not respond. The blocked arrow symbolizes this process, and extensive evidence validates this model. Thus only a small fraction of proposed bills ever become laws in legislatures at any level of American government, and only a fraction of appellate court appeals are ever accepted for hearing and decision. As for the school board, its time is primarily spent elsewhere, as noted below.

Under special conditions, the *negotiated model* of Figure 6.1 describes other board decision making. The several arrows here indicate the flow of competing demands into the political system over an emerging issue; in time these demands become narrowed as alternatives are formulated and a decision is authorized in the form of board policy (output). Here, the board member's role is that of negotiator among competing community groups, "working out things" over time, seeking compromises that create a coalition majority. Such action, though, is episodic, an occasional decision rather than a regular agenda.

The third model, *prompt response,* moves us to two quite different occasions when the political system responds that way to community demands. One of these occasions occurs during a *crisis,* a sudden combination of threats either to the school system or its constituents. The crisis might arise from physical causes—buildings burned, flooded, or blown away—or from social causes that generate conflict over values the schools serve and the resources they distribute. A crisis has a curious quality in that most political actors must agree that a crisis exists or else the third model does not describe what happens. The danger must be

Figure 6.1
Models of Decision Making in a Political System

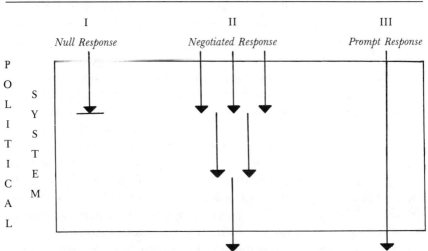

clear to those helped or those helping, and the remedy must be relatively simple, understood, and accepted by all. If not, then some group or board member will question the necessity of taking fast action. Much of the conflict in local school politics arises from some claims that a "crisis" exists while opponents deny it and then redefine the situation to agree with their own interests.

There is a second and quite different aspect to the prompt response model that involves *routines.* These include filling in the details of major policy decisions and are found in reports received and acted on, procedures for implementing a given policy, budgetary support for accepted programs, and so on. The unusual aspect of this context is that there are so many outputs of this kind. Indeed, much political decision making, including board actions, consists of routines as measured by the volume of personnel, funds, paperwork, and so forth issuing from a political agency.[25]

As noted earlier, in every typology a longitudinal model is crying to get out, and so it is with Figure 6.1. If these three models are seen as a sequence, they form a rough chronology of policy evolution. That is, many demands begin as the unthinkable of the first model, supported by only a few "crackpots" and ignored by the political system. An illustration would be blacks seeking equal resources for their segregated schools decades ago in the South. Then, later, the second model starts to work. New combinations of societal events generate more support for the now "reasonable" idea so that its opponents must exert large energies to block it; over time, however, opposing sides move toward resolutions that yield a new output. For example, under Supreme Court threat the Southern school systems first moved to deny discrimination, then to equalize resources for black education without desegregating, and then reluctantly and under pressure to accommodate external pressures by desegregating. A nationwide example is the pattern of invasion of city folk into rural areas where they succeeded in developing new suburban school systems after World War II.[26] Given enough time, resolution of conflict results in opinion closure, in which what was unthinkable is now conventional, so that schools in the South and suburbia show few signs of formerly raging conflicts. At this stage, the third model dominates decision making—routines.

Rational and Other Decision Making

Another conceptual framework exists for analyzing the decision making of school boards; this focuses on the degree to which officials use "rational" versus other methods of arriving at decisions.[27] During the 1970s this became a major inquiry about public policy, but only one scholarly study of school boards has been done from this analytical base.

Peterson's powerful analysis of three major decisions by the Chicago school board over several decades uses alternative perspectives, set out in Table 6.3. Depending on the issue, decision making could take the form of bargaining among members. This could be of two kinds, protecting or promoting relatively narrow organizational or electoral interests ("pluralist bargaining") or involving broader interests rooted in protection of race, class, or a regime ("ideological bargaining"). Alternatively, decision making could take different forms within a policymaking body, that is, a "unitary" model, as found in organizational theory or in assuming rationality in decision making. In this last, Peterson made a highly useful adaptation to an intense debate over the

Table 6.3
Models of School Board Decision Making

Pluralist

Theme: Decisions are the result of a contest among groups lacking much common interests.

1. *Pluralist:* decision the result of a contest among board members representing narrow-purpose groups and designed to defend and enhance as many group interests as possible, for example, budgetary contests among curriculum interests.
2. *Ideological:* decision the result of a contest among board members representing broad-purpose groups designed to defend and enhance interests of a class or a race, for example, affirmative action policy on teacher promotions or principal appointments.

Unitary

Theme: Decisions are the result of interactions among groups that share some qualities which presume an overreaching unity among them.

1. *Organizational:* decision the result of board members motivated by desires to promote objectives of the school organization, for example, maintenance of professional standards against challenges by laypersons.
2. *Rational:* decision the result of board members agreed on a set of educational objectives, which are referred to in decisional debate and which are consistent with the decision itself.

Source: Abstracted from Paul E. Peterson, *School Politics Chicago Style* (Chicago: University of Chicago Press, 1976).

possibility of "rational" policy in a definition that was more realistic. That is, it meant that "board members agreed on certain objectives, that reference to these objectives was made during the course of policymaking, and that policy outcomes were consistent with these objectives."[28] Prior to this, any discussion of rationality was so bounded by unrealistic empirical requirements that no decision could be termed rational; yet thousands of board members thought they were, in fact, acting rationally.

Such models of decision making provide alternative perspectives of a complex process without dictating which is "correct."[29] They also provide the means for testing competing causal theories. Such variety, laid across preceding typologies of board actions, provides a rich pool of analytical constructs to research amid the mosaic of school boards.

JUSTIFICATIONS FOR A STRONG LOCAL POLICY ROLE

The school board is the public's main vehicle for continuing local control of education. Consequently, strengthening the school board is vital to the public interest. Why should the local role in education policy be maintained and even strengthened in certain states where it has declined precipitously? As one scholar notes:

1. Public opinion still supports more local influence and less influence for higher governments.
2. Local school politics tend to be more democratic in several important ways than are decisions made at higher levels.
3. While there will be tension between state and local policymakers, the result is policy that is better adapted to diverse local contexts.
4. Further erosion of the local role risks diminishing public support for the schools.[30]

Figure 6.2 shows the results of a recent survey that indicates that the public believes local government is the most cost efficient level, but is concerned about state government's ability to spend tax money wisely.

Advantages of Local School Policymaking

Numerous and conflicting positions express how well school politics meets the democratic ideal. The issue here is whether school politics is more democratic than control by federal or state authorities. Most citizens have a greater opportunity and chance of policy influence in their local district than they do with policymakers or administrators at the federal or state level. Local school policymakers serve fewer constituents than state officials and are much closer both geographically and psychologically. After all, it is longer and harder to get to the state capital.

Local board elections also provide a much more direct means to influence local policymakers than through a state legislator representing many areas. In the nation's thousands of small school districts, a significant proportion of the community knows at least

Figure 6.2
The Public's Perception of Which Level of Government
Spends Tax Money More Wisely

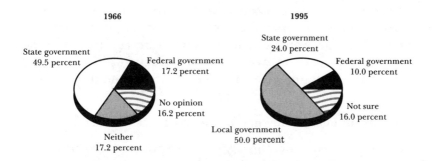

1966

1995

State government
49.5 percent

Federal government
17.2 percent

No opinion
16.2 percent

Neither
17.2 percent

State government
24.0 percent

Federal government
10.0 percent

Not sure
16.0 percent

Local government
50.0 percent

Source: 1966 Survey by the Gallup Organization, December 8-13, 1966;
1995 survey by the Hart and Teeter Research Companies for the Council for Excellence in Government, March 16–18, 1995.

one board member. Local media provide better information on education and can capture the citizen attention more effectively than reports from a distant capital. All of this is not meant to claim that local school politics approaches the democratic ideal. But local school officials can better anticipate the zone of tolerance that local school constituencies permit than can state policymakers.

Most states are too large and diverse for uniform policies to be effective in all areas. In policy area after area, there exists a "nested policy in which the states provide the general contours and the local districts fill in with more specified policies."[31] This condition creates a "functional tension" that tends to provide more appropriate and adaptable policies than statewide specification. There are large areas, however, like civil rights and equal opportunity, where local flexibility must be restricted. Yet most states, for example, prescribe teacher certification requirements but leave hiring and compensation issues to local districts.

The final argument for enhancing local discretion is based on the linkage between political efficacy and public support of schools—citizens will participate in politics more if they believe that they can have an impact on policies. The local level offers the best opportunity for efficacy; therefore, a lessening in local efficacy will lead to less overall citizen participation in education policy. The reasoning here is that people's satisfaction with the results of collective decisions will be greater if they have taken part in making those decisions. Consequently, less local control leads to more citizen dissatisfaction. In California, for example, local parents are told that the school board is too constrained to remedy their grievances. The citizen is referred to a state office or in some cases to a court order. This kind of inaction could lead to alienation from the local public school.

Increasing Local Influence by Institutional Choice

How can one evaluate the arguments favoring redistributing power from higher levels to lower levels? One useful concept called "institutional choice" focuses on the crucial policy decision of which institution should be the decision maker. For example, courts have been reluctant to delegate civil rights protection to the institution of local schools. Another type of institutional choice is whether to place various functions in the hands of markets (e.g., vouchers) or politics (e.g., school board elections). The recent state reform movement has included an institutional choice to enhance the curricular and testing role of state government.

There are two general characteristics of institutions that are important: agreement on substantive goals and the capacity to achieve them. Substantive goals are crucial because of the need to insure support for a policy. Courts may be more supportive of civil rights than school boards, but its support must be buttressed by capacity. Courts cannot run school districts. So which institution should be chosen? A method for choosing can be called "comparative institutional advantage," that is, "the distrust directed at one decision maker must be carefully weighed against the advantages of that decision maker and both the advantages and disadvantages of alternative decision makers. . . . The logic of comparative institutional advantage also implies the futility of seeking perfect or ideal implementation of a policy. . . . The real world offers a 'least worst choice' of imperfect institutions."[32]

The preceding sections point up the complexity of the seemingly simple proposition of local control of schooling. Values and actions on the local scene reflect the influence of diversity that affects all aspects of the political system and its policy outputs. As system and policy grow ever more complex, local control becomes less and less a real description. But in this change, much may have been lost for the citizen's role in democracy.

SCHOOL BOARDS AND EDUCATION REFORM

Why is there so much concern about the effectiveness of boards at this time in our history? One major reason is the lack of attention to school boards in most recent national and state reports on education reform. For example, rather than not discussing school boards, the reform reports could have said that the school board is the crucial agent for school improvement and that state reforms should be directed at strengthening the local school board's capacity to bring about and monitor change. Instead, the unstated implication of many reports is that school boards are part of the problem and have not exercised leadership and authority to improve education.[33] This message further implies that boards need to be circumvented, if not through direct state regulation, then certainly through vastly increased state prescriptions and monitoring. Many state reformers felt that the school board agenda, as they understood it, did not match state policy priorities. That is, mismatched priorities exist in curriculum content, years required in academic subjects in high school, review of student academic standards, teacher evaluation, and rigorous testing of students' advancement through elementary and secondary schooling.

This suspicion about the inability of school boards to provide academic leadership was exacerbated by the predominant emphasis of these reports on effective schools.[34] It was the school site that was the crucial focus for improvement, and the principal was the key catalyst. Where did school board stimulus and assistance fit into this view? The answer was unclear and vague compared to the checklists and criteria for effective schools. This relative lack of emphasis in the reports on school district policies is surprising, given the research on successful school improvement.

Thus, an apparent paradox characterizes the education reform movement. On the one hand, reformers have felt free or obliged to circumvent local boards; on the other hand, reformers focus on improvement at the school site that is governed by a school board. To this point, local school boards have seemed to be either ignored or cast in a passive role as weak reactors or even deterrents, rather than as partners, in shaping educational improvement. Many school boards contend, however, that they initiated and enacted most of the reforms in local districts prior to state action.

RETHINKING THE SCHOOL BOARD ROLE

One major problem plagues all attempts to understand and prescribe policy for school boards: There are too many school boards (about fourteen thousand) and too many board members (some ninety-seven thousand) to be able to generalize about the behavior of all boards. Consequently, the research base is confined to the study of a single case, a few comparative cases, or some nonrepresentative sample chosen for a particular purpose. Moreover, the research techniques employed range from surveys to self-assessments to full-scale case studies. Most research focuses on metropolitan areas or big cities. Horror stories dominate the media, and special attention is paid to conflict and operational failures. We know the least about the most common type of school board—the board of small districts. However, the body of comprehensive self-assessment data collected by the Institute for Educational Leadership (IEL) from 266 rural/small town, suburban, and urban school boards between 1987 and 1990 is an exceptionally large database reviewed below.[35]

If we wait for representative data on all school boards, it will be a very long time until any changes are made to improve board policymaking. However, one way to analyze the need for and direction of school board reform is to analyze overall trends that affect most school boards noted by the IEL. In this section we summarize these trends and stress the way they cause major changes in school board roles, functions, and operations.

Evaluating the Role of School Boards

The last major change in the roles and operations of urban school boards took place between 1900 and 1920. That the basic structure and role were established so long ago suggests strongly the need for a radical overhaul as we near the twenty-first century. By 1910 the conventional wisdom had evolved among the schoolmen and the leading business and professional men who spearheaded the reforms. The governance structure needed to be revised so that school boards would be small, elected at large, and purged of all connections with political parties and officials of general government, such as mayors and councilmen.

While the turn-of-the-century reformers tried to model the revamped school board on the big corporations, they left the board with a mandate to oversee and become involved in all areas of local school operation. The American school board combines the legislative, executive, and judicial functions of government. This role is too expansive and often leads boards to try to do everything by not doing much of anything in depth.

School boards play a legislative role when they adopt budgets, pass regulations, and set policies. Moreover, they provide the constituent-services component of a legislator's district office. Parents will phone board members about fixing showers in locker rooms, relocating school crossing guards, and reclassifying children placed in special education. Many board members believe that an essential part of their role is to "fix" these individual complaints, because failure to respond may mean defeat at the polls.

School boards play an executive role when they implement policy. Many school boards approve not only the budget, but also almost every expenditure and contract for services. For example, a half-day consulting fee for a university professor must be approved by the school board. The board performs the same role as the U.S. Department of Education's contracting office and the General Accounting Office. Many boards approve the appointments of principals, vice principals, categorical program administrators, and even teachers.

Judicial hearings concerning student suspensions, expulsions, interdistrict transfers, and pupil placements can consume an enormous amount of time. After all administrative remedies are exhausted, the board is the final body for appeal, though citizens may still turn to the courts in some cases.

Can School Boards Do It All?

Can any school board composed primarily of part-time laypeople perform all these functions well? Moreover, state sunshine laws require boards to conduct all business, including many personnel matters, in public sessions. Does the essential policymaking role of the board suffer as other roles and functions become more important? Again, we simply do not know about all school boards, but the IEL data and logic suggest that, in many districts, it is difficult to perform all these roles well. The turn-of-the-century reformers attenuated the board's role in providing connections between city and county governments for the delivery of integrated services for children. In trying to insulate school boards from city politics and political parties, the reformers severed the board's connections with other service providers. Today, worsening conditions for children and the interrelated nature of their family problems require some to consider undoing the work of the early reformers. If boards are to play a larger role in such areas as children's services, their existing role must be cut back. Playing a smaller role in some executive, judicial, and constituent-service functions would give boards more time to influence children's policy.

Another policy area requiring more board time has to do with the growing movement for adopting new curriculum standards as part of comprehensive reform. School boards will need to spend more time on systemic policies that help implement curriculum frameworks based on national standards. Boards will need to ensure that their assessment, instructional materials, staff development, categorical programs, and fiscal policies are aligned with the curriculum content standards that embody what students need to learn and be able to do. Secretary of Education Richard Riley emphasized in a recent speech that the school board must play a crucial and unique role as the vital link in making sure that systemic reform actually happens. He emphasized that the school board is the only entity which can ensure that various components of restructuring are linked coherently and do not become merely disjointed projects.

To do this, the school board's consistent message to the entire school system must be that reform is its main mission and

not just an experiment. The board has a major role in orches-
trating numerous policies and looking for gaps in policies and
conflicts between them. The state assessment requirements, for
example, might conflict with local categorical programs, or board
curriculum requirements might conflict, for example, with local
categorical programs.

Can a school district in a large city lead systemic reform and
continue to perform the entire range of legislative, executive,
and judicial roles? The overall task for the board becomes even
more burdensome in large districts where decentralization to the
school site is under way. The IEL study emphasizes that at least
every three years boards need to conduct comprehensive reviews
of school site performance using both district-wide and site-spe-
cific indicators. This effort takes time and involves much more
than a few school visits by board members. The IEL school site
review requires that the board take a comprehensive look at the
objectives of the local school community and examine progress
toward meeting state and central district objectives. Comprehensive reform implies some central district oversight of the curricular framework, of testing, of staff development, and so on.
Decentralization to the school site implies enhanced flexibility,
but it also requires periodic accountability for the overall system's objectives.

Change in Electoral Districts

The turn-of-the-century reformers were adamant in their belief that school board members needed to be elected at-large
and not by subdistricts. They contended that board members
should represent the entire community and that policy should
not be based on the particular needs of subcommunities or ethnic groups. Boards were urged to view the district as a *unitary
entity* and not differentiate the curriculum for particular neighborhoods. All of this was part of the notion that centralization was
desirable and that schools should not be influenced by the
particularistic concerns of politics. Both of these positions are
now being questioned, but the current all-encompassing school
board role evolved from this background.

Dramatic changes have taken place in school board elections

since the last era of reform. In 1996 more than fifty-three thousand board members were elected at large and thirty thousand were elected by district. Many communities use a combination of district and at-large elections to choose board members.[36]

Since 1991 the civil rights movement has increased its pressure to improve minority representation through district/ward elections—at least one hundred school systems have switched to district elections since 1994. This dramatic transformation of the electoral base suggests the need to rethink the roles of the school board. Perhaps the turn-of-the-century reformers were partially correct. A board that appoints personnel at the school level or second echelons of the central administration and approves contracts for supplies will be more prone to base its decisions on politics if that board is elected by ward or district rather than elected at large. For example, board members elected by subdistricts in the IEL studies became concerned with how school policy could improve the economic development of their own districts.

Another major change in board selection since 1920 has been the active participation of teacher unions in board elections. Unions were not major players in school board elections until the 1970s. Today, unions can be the most influential participants in school board campaigns, in terms of both money spent and campaign workers supplied. With the turnout for board elections often falling below 15 percent, it is possible for unions in some localities to elect both sides of the collective bargaining table. This raises again the question of whether we should re-evaluate the appropriate role of the school board in personnel decisions and other administrative areas.

Suggesting that changes may be needed in the structure and roles of school governance cannot be equated with a conspiracy to remove the schools from citizen control. Whether one agrees with specific ideas for structural changes or not—ideas that range from municipal authorities appointing school boards to state licensing of individual schools—the debate does not exclude citizens from exercising some type of political control of the schools. School boards are deeply embedded in U.S. political culture, and proposals for radical change in their roles will encounter well-organized grass-roots resistance.

NOTES

1. David Easton, *A Framework for Political Analysis* (Englewood Cliffs, N.J.: Prentice-Hall, 1965), pp. 132–33.

2. George S. Counts, *School and Society in Chicago* (New York: Harcourt, Brace, 1928).

3. L. Harmon Zeigler and M. Kent Jennings, *Governing American Schools* (North Scituate, Mass.: Duxbury, 1974), pp. 39–42. A similar finding exists for municipal councils.

4. For a review of this agency's functions, past and present, see Peter J. Cistone, ed., *Understanding School Boards* (Lexington, Mass.: Lexington Books, 1975). For a more recent overview, see Patricia First and Herbert J. Walberg, *School Boards: Changing Local Control* (Berkeley, Calif.: McCutchan, 1992).

5. Robert Bendiner, *The Politics of Schools* (New York: Harper & Row, 1969), p. 165.

6. Dale Mann, "Public Understanding and Education Decision-Making." *Educational Administration Quarterly* 10, no. 2 (1974): 1–18.

7. Michael W. Kirst, "Loss of Support for Public Secondary Schools: Some Causes and Solutions," *Daedalus* (September 1981), assembles the contrary evidence noted below.

8. For the poll data from both sources see ibid.

9. See the evidence in David C. Berliner and Bruce J. Biddle, *The Manufactured Crisis* (Reading, Mass.: Addison-Wesley, 1995).

10. Frank W. Lutz and Laurence Iannaccone, eds., *Public Participation in Local School Districts* (Lexington, Mass.: Lexington Books, 1978).

11. Frank W. Lutz, "Methods and Conceptualizations of Political Power in Education," in *The Politics of Education*, 76th Yearbook of the National Society for the Study of Education (Chicago: University of Chicago Press, 1977), p. 32.

12. Frederick A. Rodgers, *The Black High School and Its Community* (Lexington, Mass.: Lexington Books, 1975). See also Catherine Marshall, eds., *The New Politics of Race and Gender* (London: Falmer, 1992).

13. Paul Peterson, *The Politics of School Reform* (Chicago: University of Chicago Press, 1985).

14. Raymond E. Callahan, *Education and the Cult of Efficiency* (Chicago: University of Chicago Press, 1962). See also Jane Hannaway and Robert Crowson, eds., *The Politics of Reforming School Administration* (London: Falmer, 1989).

15. David W. Minar, "The Community Basis of Conflict in School System Politics," *American Sociological Review* 31 (1966): 822–34; William L. Boyd, *Community Status and Conflict in Suburban School Politics* (Beverly Hills, Calif.: Sage, 1975); and Hannaway and Crowson, *The Politics of Reforming*.

16. Zeigler and Jennings, *Governing American Schools*, Chap. 6.

17. Christine Rossell, "School Desegregation and Community Social Change," *Law and Contemporary Problems* 42 (1978): 133–83.

18. Emmett H. Buell, Jr., *School Desegregation and Defended Neighborhoods: The Boston Controversy* (Lexington, Mass.: Lexington Books, 1981).

19. Boyd, *Community Status*, and Marshall, *The New Politics*.

20. Carol Mullins, "School District Consolidation: Odds Are 2–1 It'll Get You," *American School Board Journal* 11 (1973): 160.

21. James W. Guthrie, "Public Control of Public Schools," *Public Affairs Report* (Berkeley: University of California, Institute of Governmental Studies, 1974), p. 2.

22. Rossell, "School Desegregation," and James Cibulka, ed., *The Politics of Urban Education in the U.S.* (London: Falmer, 1992).

23. Leigh Stelzer, "Institutionalizing Conflict Response: The Case of School Boards," *Social Science Quarterly* 55, no. 2 (1974).

24. Frederick M. Wirt and Leslie Christovich, "Administrators' Perceptions of Changing Power Contexts: Superintendents and City Managers," *Education Administration Quarterly* (1989).

25. Lila N. Carol et al., *School Boards* (Washington, D.C.: Institute for Educational Leadership, 1986).

26. Frederick M. Wirt et al., *On the City's Rim: Politics and Policy In Suburbia* (Lexington, Mass.: Heath, 1972), pp. 161–66.

27. For an introduction to these concepts in an educational context, see Dale Mann, *Policy Decision-Making in Education* (New York: Teachers College Press, 1975).

28. Paul E. Peterson, *School Politics Chicago Style* (Chicago: University of Chicago Press, 1976), pp. 134–35. See also Alan Peshkin, *Growing Up American* (Chicago: University of Chicago Press, 1978) for a small-town district.

29. William L. Boyd, "The Public, the Professionals, and Educational Policy-Making: Who Governs? *Teachers College Record* 77 (1976): 556–58. See also First and Walberg, *School Boards*.

30. Fred S. Coombs, "The Effects of Increased State Control on Local School District Governance" (paper presented to the annual meeting of the American Educational Research Association, 1987).

31. Ibid.

32. William H. Clune, *Institutional Choice as a Theoretical Framework for Research on Education Policy* (New Brunswick, N.J.: Center for Policy Research in Education, Rutgers University, 1987), p. 4.

33. See Lila Carol et al., *Improving Grass Roots Leadership* (Washington, D.C.: Institute for Educational Leadership, 1986). The major recent data base is contained in Jacquelin Danzberger, Michael W. Kirst, and Michael Usdan, *Governing Public Schools* (Washington, D.C.: Institute for Educational Leadership, 1992). See also First and Walberg, *School Boards*, pp. 177–95.

34. Michael W. Kirst, "The State Role in School Restructuring," in *Education Reform in the 90s*, edited by Chester E. Finn, Jr., and Theodor Rebarber (New York: Macmillan, 1992), pp. 23–35.

35. Danzberger, Kirst, and Usdan, *Governing Public Schools*. The following observations and quotations are drawn from this source.

36. Del Stover, "More School Boards Switch to Electing Members by District," *School Board News* 16, no. 22 (December 10, 1996): 1.

7

The Chief Administrator as Professional and Politician

THE PROFESSIONAL AS DECISION MAKER

If the community is only occasionally active and the board has strong limitations, school professionals should retain a greater influence on policy issues. After all, professional educators have their resources, too. They define choices, produce research, provide specific recommendations, and shape the formal agenda. Using these resources, professionals generate pressures and information that can affect, if not determine, the board's deliberations and decisions. In Easton's framework, the school superintendent and staff provide withinputs to the school board and the bureaucracy. Many specific policy issues, however, may never reach the school board if the superintendent and staff act under broad discretion from the school board. Consequently, both board and superintendent are authorities seeking to gain support from the community through appropriate outputs like budget, curriculum, teacher selection, and so on.

The professional staff does operate under certain constraints, however. They must anticipate reactions of board members to their actions because the board does have the basic power to

151

fire them.[1] They also know that the ultimate power of a pro-
voked electorate is to remove them by changing the board, as
noted earlier. It is also likely that the superintendent would act
in keeping with the school board's wishes on many issues even
without the threat of job loss. It is natural to assume that board
members would hire a person whose values were similar to their
own. An example of this is the low rate of turnover in smaller
districts, which tend to be more homogeneous in their values.[2]
In effect, the board's impact on specific decisions may be more
indirect than direct, but it is nevertheless real. The superintendent operates with considerable latitude as long as he or she stays
within the board's ideological zone of tolerance.

Do superintendents mold school boards by control of
policymaking through socialization to professional values? Answers from research seem to change over the last decades. Studies of suburbs in the 1960s found that to be the case. But during the 1970s, a larger Canadian sample of board members challenged that belief, finding that socialization to professional values had little effect on their decisions.[3] The biggest study was
done in the 1970s, in which Zeigler and Jennings looked at eighty-
eight districts.[4] Their findings on this linkage were modified by
the social context of the district, noting that

1. Board demands on and opposition to the superintendent
   increase, but board victories decrease as one moves from
   small town to suburb to city school district.
2. Superintendent interaction with the board is positively related to board opposition in city and suburban sites but
   less so in rural locales.
3. The superintendent's socialization of board members reduces board opposition in both urban and small-town places.
   But both interaction and socialization effects have little effects on board victories against the superintendent in smaller
   districts, although high association exists in urban districts.

A more diverse urban social context generates more potential
conflict over school decisions and is more likely to place the
board in opposition to the superintendent. Ironically, then, Zeigler
and Jennings found that effective opposition to professional in-

fluence by the board occurred in small districts with their limited political conflict and consensual elite board. Urban boards, on the other hand, were more contentious but had only limited effect against professional power. As other studies demonstrate,[5] these new currents raise the consciousness of policymakers to the sharpness of the issue and so alter their behavior; this is more the case for board members than for administrators. In all the research reported here, the distinction between urban board behavior and values and those in other locales—while sharper on some issues and in some contexts than others—can be seen to work against board dominance by the professional.

Administrator control over the board is highly contingent on other matters like the kind of policy or the size and homogeneity of the district.[6] Administrative power is increasingly limited by new constituencies and government rulings, as noted previously.

The fragmentation of delivery systems for local transportation, welfare, or pollution control makes citizen access to any of these a feat only slightly easier than the labors of Hercules. At least a citizen knows where to go to register a complaint against the local school, although few choose to do so.[7] So an early 1970s study of big cities and public agencies found that education ranked highest on responsiveness and innovation compared to the others (except for the War on Poverty agencies especially designed to maximize client input).[8] Studies like this fail to tap what political scientists term the "law of anticipated reaction." This is the capacity of the administrator to estimate the limits within which to act without board concern—the "zone of tolerance" in organizational theory. That is, superintendents inhibit their own behavior by knowing the controls these boards may exert. Subtle and hard to measure, this influence is still a reality that superintendents will detail in endless anecdotes. We will question that control in a later section.

NEW ROLES FOR THE SUPERINTENDENT

Much research has put the professional at odds with the community,[9] the antihero of school democracy; but it is instructive to consider an alternative perspective. This views the professional role as being a representative of something other than the profession.

Many of the challenging trends set out in this book have affected other professions besides education. A "revolt of the client" appears not only in education but also in law, medicine, among clergy, and in other areas. This is happening not only here but in other English-speaking nations as well.[10] A consequence of this tension between the professional and a mistrustful client is that training schools have begun to redefine the professional role so that graduates are more sensitive to citizen needs. One aspect of this in schools of education is the growing attention to defining the "political" role that the educator must play. The traditional apolitical myth still holds for many, but future school administrators are often being taught that they operate in a web of external demands to which they must respond and balance in some fashion.[11]

Studies of how social and political forces reshape superintendent roles in our big cities reach some significant conclusions.[12] Role definitions change under external challenges by pressure groups, traceable back to school consolidation around World War I and the urban crisis three decades ago. One consequence of this challenge is increased turnover in these positions; in the early 1970s twenty-two out of twenty-five big-city superintendents were replaced. Another obvious outcome is that old role concepts become outmoded. Under political turbulence, by adopting the role of "negotiator-statesman" one is more effective than any notion of being a neutral technician. The first role sees conflict as inevitable in human affairs and regards interest group demands as legitimate, to be dealt with and reconciled as part of the job. The superintendent is not just a leaf floating helplessly on the flood of turbulent politics. Yet note how far this role brings us from that of the earlier school administrator as an omnipotent, insensitive figure. We can see in the actual careers of many superintendents success while yielding to insuperable organizational and resource obstacles in other matters.[13]

Yet superintendents today face a conflict in theories of leadership. From "top down" to "bottom up" reforms, leadership is confused by the decisional context. Unintended consequences have wrecked many in the last quarter-century. Many and more complex tools of management and leadership are needed to do the job. One analysis of how superintendents spend their time stresses the large amounts of verbal interactions with many people for a short period of time. Little time exists for reflection, while much time is spent on the persuasion and discussion that are the essence of building internal coalitions of subunits—that is, a political role.[14]

SUPERINTENDENTS, POLICY PRESSURES, AND CONFLICT MANAGEMENT

In this section we wish to explore the kinds of pressure on superintendents. In Chapter 2, Figure 2.1, all the issue demands from new core constituencies were shown to impact first on the school board, which then focused them on the superintendent. How does this person act when political shot and shell explode around the school? First we provide superintendents' own perceptions of high-pressure milieu and their judgment of its effect, and then conceptualize the new roles and skills in order to manage this conflict.

Evidence of Pressure

Pressure shows up indirectly in the turnover figures among superintendents. A summary of this measure in the twenty-five biggest cities shows that this rate was 8 percent in the 1950s, 12 percent in the 1960s, 16 percent in the 1970s, and in the first half of the 1980s lower than the peak of 1965–1979.[15] Nevertheless, in the 1980s New York, Chicago, Cleveland, Boston, Seattle, and Denver each had three superintendents in less than five years! By the mid-1990s the average tenure in big cities was three years, and elsewhere, six years.

What specifically was creating this job stress? A comparative study of hundreds of school administrators in Oregon and Tennessee before and after 1980 found the prime pressure was adapting to new state and federal organizational rules and policies.[16] The second largest stress came from trying to get public backing for school programs, and the third from involvement in collective bargaining. Note that all these stress sources are also aspects of the job becoming ever more political; that is, all three sources affect the emerging political tasks of the position.

However, there are costs to administrators for learning a new political role. A 1981 study of over 270 administrators in the West found that half had some psychological or physiological stress-related illness, including ulcers, cardiovascular problems, and so on. This group, too, cited as reasons for such illness, in order, teacher negotiations, community pressures, and school finances in general and specifically.[17] The response to heavy stress like these pressures is "burn out," and the record of shortened tenure makes that point. One superintendent recently committed suicide, leaving a note about the great pressure of "politics" in the job.

A national sample of superintendents in the 1980s identified many specific groups from which they had experienced pressures that were significantly greater than earlier in their careers. Table 7.1 summarizes the answers. Almost 60 percent found four or more groups had increased their demands (more than that re-ported for city managers and planning directors in the same study). Was this greater citizen pressure? Using three different ways of defining citizens, Table 7.1 reports that this pressure is not much different from traditional and official groups; one sus-pects the high percentage for "lay opinion" might have been professional deference to the democratic image. The point is that, aside from elected local officials (e.g., school boards), all groups were increasing their demands, especially teachers. In an open-ended question about what aspect had most changed since starting their career, the answer was overwhelmingly "politics," often written with exclamations.

Does this mean that increased group pressure had weakened acceptance of the superintendent's policy judgments? Quite the contrary. One-half reported an *increased* acceptance of those judg-ments by board and citizens; only 12 and 7 percent, respectively, reported that their acceptance had declined. One might think the answer to such influence would vary with the kind of com-munity. However, regression analysis reported no significant re-lationship among measures of communities, unlike the findings of Jennings and Zeigler's 1960s data discussed earlier. One might infer from the two data sets that as group pressure on this office

Table 7.1
Superintendents' Perceptions of Group Pressures

1. From how many groups have you perceived increasing demands?

8	7	6	5	4	3	2	1	0	N
5.8[1]	3.3	20.0	12.5	20.0	15.8	11.7	7.5	2.5	131

[1]That is, 5.8 percent perceived that all eight groups had increased demands on them; 3.3 percent perceived seven groups, and so on.

2. Which groups in particular have increased demands?

Group	Percent Replying "More" and "Much More" Demands Perceived*
Traditional:	
Business	48
Labor	62
Citizen:	
Clientele	52
Minorities	50
Lay opinion	61
Officials	
Elected local	34
State	50
Federal	54

*More than one choice was possible.

Source: Frederick Wirt and Leslie Christovich, "Administrators' Perceptions of Policy Influence: Conflict Management Styles and Roles." *Educational Administration Quarterly* 25 (1989): 5–35. Reprinted with permission of Sage Publications.

expanded so, too, did the need for conflict management techniques of this professional.

But because not all superintendents can win all the time, one cost of the job is undoubtedly professional stress, reflected in the shortened job tenure and the pervasive illnesses they reported. Yet the findings support two ideas usually seen as contradictory, namely that the superintendent is "beleaguered" but also dominates school decision making. The reality may well be that this professional fits both descriptions but pays considerable costs for both activities.

These results agree with the dissatisfaction theory of democracy discussed earlier. That is, administrators can operate with minimum concern until an issue reflecting popular dissatisfaction with professional decisions arises. Whether it is the big-city milieu—where single-issue or district-oriented board members insist on power sharing[18]—or smaller districts that face school closing, a new policymaking environment for superintendents emerges. Rather than executive leadership, this new context requires the professional to act in a representative, coalition-building way— actions well known to "politicians" in government. Caught as they are between old role definitions and new demands, no wonder that superintendents have suffered more turnover and illness.

ROLE, STYLE, AND CONFLICT MANAGEMENT

As professionals are not simply reflexive responders to the demographic and political structures of their communities, we need to describe the varieties of superintendent behavior today amidst so much educational change.

A Dynamic Model of Superintendent Response to Change

Much of what any executive does involves managing routines to implement decisions about allocated resources. Each profession provides training in such routine management (budgeting, personnel, planning, dissemination), and its practitioners fill their early careers with these tasks. But even routine management is not without its potential for conflict. The fight each year to get more personnel lines out of budget sessions is a typical example. This routine conflict has become a conflict that looks like a standard dramatic play in which "actors" play their roles in pursuit of resources. Such interplay still operates within bounds set by authority (e.g., deadlines), by reality (e.g., revenue limitations), and by the compromise principle (nobody gets everything, nobody gets nothing, everybody gets something.)

How do superintendents manage the conflict that comes from the outside and from groups not usually active in policymaking, that is, "conflict management"? In theoretical terms, our concerns are with two questions: What variation exists in the general roles and styles of conflict management, and how does one explain that variation? For the practitioner, the research question is, Can managing conflict advance district and personal objectives, such as survival and career enhancement? The questions are evident from reports of superintendent dissatisfaction and turnover.[19]

Encompassing these major questions is the basic paradigm of administrator forces and change:

> Change generates *demands* in *policymaking* arenas to which *superintendents respond* with *differing roles and styles* of conflict management.

We will provide some ideas about each of these emphasized terms.

THE INFLUENCE OF CHANGE

As changes in the decision-making environment of the schools' political system generate new demands, there is conflict with which the superintendent must deal. What forces of changes are there?

Population Alteration: Changing the Players

Change in the social composition of the population has been a constant in urban history, everywhere transforming political, economic, and social institutions and programs. Thus, recent transformations stemming from the growth of minority and poor populations in the biggest cities have had a major impact on city resources needed to cover the high-cost problems of welfare, crime, and education. Or the suburban exodus after World War II transformed politics on the city's rim from rural quiescence to conflict over better services brought on by the upwardly mobile.[20] In short, changing the players in the community means changing the games and thus changing the rewards.

The grand transformations in school politics lie partly with population growth or decline. Growth has curious effects on social structures and their performance. For example, an *arithmetical*

growth of population inevitably brings on a *geometrical* increase
in demands for services, both in quantitative and qualitative terms.
A familiar case for the city manager is that as population grows,
the ratio of police to citizens increases. Another example is suburbanites flooding the urban fringe who want better, not simply
more traditional, services. On the other hand, population decline
also has different effects on urban services and their administrators. The major point is that change in the social mix of the
population has consequences for the administrative environment
of superintendents in new demands and pressures, and hence
generates conflict.

Fiscal Context: Living with Boom or Bust

Recent decades have witnessed a "riches to rags" story for
schools and superintendents. Prosperity makes for easy leadership, whether as president or superintendent. Recessions, though,
make all leaders look bad. But in either case, local conflict is
generated.

However, even when prosperity grows and superintendents hit
it rich, conflict can still develop. As property values inflate, paying the property tax (the main source of school revenue) becomes ever more burdensome. The "tax revolt" in the late 1970s
arose from just this problem. Also, while addressing problems of
equity, the appearance of federal riches in the form of categorical and bloc grants over the last thirty years has also created
conflict. Bigger cities fell into greater fiscal dependency on federal grants that often carried requirements that altered the local
policymaking context. Under the stimuli of such programs, public participation was enlarged,[21] minority and poor gained influence in the urban power structure,[22] and consequently public
demands on urban delivery systems altered. More significantly,
these grants brought state and local officials into local systems;
state and federal intervention was the most reported problem
among superintendents and city managers in the 1980s.[23]

In short, prosperity introduces conflict to superintendents in
the form of new conflicts of distributive and regulatory policies.
Conversely, when recession tightens local budgets, superintendents face another conflict over redistributive policies that involves

taxing one group for the benefit of another—always a hotly contested issue. Consequently, changes in the national economy send waves into the local economy and political system that generate conflict for the suprintendents.

The Elected: Living with Political Masters

These changes alter superintendents' own interaction with their political masters. Over time, the policy process of many communities moved beyond protest to newly politicized minority cadres, altered power structures, sensitized superintendents and bureaucrats, and new kinds of administration. Protests and elections over personnel and programs everywhere characterize the school district most often studied—the big city and its "urban school chiefs under fire."[24] These reports also presented scenes of roiling conflict. Whether the issue has been desegregation, finance reform, accountability, student rights, handicapped or bilingual education, teacher power, or curriculum, school districts have found that this fragmented set of conflicts becomes focused on the school board, superintendents, and principals. These currents of conflict are captured in the model of Figure 2.1 earlier. How have these changes influenced local policymaking, the next concept in our dynamic model of superintendents and social change?

THE ARENAS OF POLICYMAKING

The way that local governance is organized affects which groups will get access and services. Accordingly, variations in policymaking arenas act as mediating variables between the forces of external change and the superintendent's environment.

Regular Players of the Game: Different Lineups and Scores

In urban politics, interest groups, legislatures, bureaucracies, and executives constitute *regular players* in the local policy game.[25] How these actors manage conflict can exert an independent influence on decision making, a point we expand on later. Superintendents face conflict within their own organizations, either downward with their staff or outward with community groups. Amid this array of actors who affect conflict management, the central question is how change systematically affects the actors and superintendents.

The reaction to change moves superintendents in stages from

- *reflexive resistance* (i.e., if change were needed, we would have already done it);
- to *damage control* (i.e., let's reduce the effects of external change);
- to *intense conflict* (i.e., they can't do that!);
- to a final *conflict resolution* and *acceptance of changes* within the educational system (i.e., we can live with this).

Also, it is not clear how large a part of the superintendents' actions involve both episodic and routine conflict. If conflict is extensive (i.e., like being pecked to death by ducks), superintendents' time for professional matters, such as planning and oversight, is reduced. In short, the superintendent exists in a political web of relationships with the local actors, all coping with external changes that create conflict locally.

The Structure of Policy Arenas: Different Fields and Games

The organizing of the field on which such conflict is played out can influence the process. An axiom of social science is that organization is not value free, that different forms of organization reflect different values. Early in this century reformers understood this axiom when their middle-class zeal overthrew the party-dominated forms of nominations and elections. The proposition was put precisely a quarter-century ago by political scientist E. E. Schattschneider:

All forms of political organization have a bias in favor of the exploitation of some kinds of conflict and the suppression of others because organization is the mobilization of bias. Some issues are organized into politics while others are organized out.[26]

Consequently, reformed governments featuring nonpartisan election on a city-wide basis show striking policy differences from partisan governments. For example, the reformed governments spend less for many services and give civil rights groups less favorable policies than do the second type. The unreformed types facilitate access to voting and representation by working and lower classes— and racial minorities—while the reformed types do the same for the middle class.[27] This is the meaning of the "mobilization of bias."

Superintendents usually preside over a policy arena of reformed governments, which are more open to middle-class interests— just as Progressive reformers early in this century had in mind. Against this middle-class context, in the 1960s new challenges appeared to that class from federal policies that supported the interests of poor, working-class, and some middle-class groups. Thus the bias of local structure confronted the bias of external policies. In the process, superintendents' conflict management was influenced by different structures of governance. But by the 1980s new efforts by the states to improve the quality of curriculum and teaching generated new pressures on superintendents to these mandates.

SUPERINTENDENT ROLES AND CONFLICT MANAGEMENT

Differences in roles and styles among superintendents provide another way of understanding conflict management. One review of the research expressed some of the dilemmas this way:

A job that self-report surveys discover to be increasingly tension-filled and declining in attractiveness nevertheless finds its role incumbents expressing confidence in their abilities, with a sense that they are very much "up" to their job challenges. A role that is growing in reputation as a high-conflict part of public officialdom is simultaneously described as much less burdened by conflict than the comparable job of city manager. A position known for its visibility and beck and call responsiveness to school board and community is nevertheless described as a position that at its core is more heavily focused *inward* toward management of the school district and its professionals.[28]

The Significance of Role

At the center of any social structure is the individual perform-
ing functions, or roles, learned through socialization. *Role* refers
to expectations of one's behavior by significant others within the
social structure. Professional schools socialize to the roles expected of instructional leaders by the community. Of course, roles
have changed throughout this century from neutral technician,
or manager, to a power-sharing, active advocate of programs.

Role also implies behavior in the pursuit of significant values;
one problem in much writing about superintendents is the unstated
assumption that they pursue all values with equal strength. Can
they strive equally for quality, equity, efficiency, or citizen choice?
That seems unlikely in practice because personal resources are
finite. But certain values are so vital to the administrator that
she or he would expend more resources on these than on others. In those important values, the administrator will fight harder,
even when faced with adverse community pressure. Moreover,
not all superintendent ties with the community are conflictual,
so the degree of conflict provides another variable in studying
the superintendent in community conflict. In short, superintendents will pursue their values differently given different degrees
of community conflict.

We can structure this micropolitics of superintendent values
and community conflict by typologizing them into potential role
models. Table 7.2 ranges degrees of community conflict against
degrees of superintendent value intensity; from this we can infer different role behaviors. We estimate from the research literature that there are many occasions where the Beseiged role
behavior takes place, and there are many occasions for the Overseer
of Routines role; in the other two cases the frequency is in-
determinant. Included in the Overseer of Routines role are the
tasks of routine management and intraorganizational conflict
noted earlier. Much professional training takes place in this area,
but much less training is provided for conflict management.[29]

What role behavior is likely when community conflict is high?
When the superintendent's values are intensely engaged—the
Beseiged case—he or she will have at least one of four orientations
to conflict management: competing, accommodating, collaborating,
or compromising.[30]

Table 7.2

A Typology of Community Conflict and Superintendent Values

Superintendent Value Intensity	Community Conflict	
	High	*Low*
High:	BESEIGED PROFESSIONAL	DOMINANT PROFESSIONAL
Outcome	Win or lose	Win
Frequency	Limited	Unknown
Low:	COMPLIANT IMPLEMENTER	OVERSEER OF ROUTINES
Outcome	Win	Win
Frequency	Unknown	Extensive

Again in Table 7.2, when community conflict is low and superintendent value intensity is high, the model of the Dominant Professional arises. Here, the superintendent dominates policy-making out of a professional orientation of "managing" the service provided to citizens. This role type characterizes the long period before recent challenge and conflict.[31] But when the community is highly conflictual and superintendent values are not intense, the latter can play another role. Assisting the community to devise and administer a program, this Compliant Implementer role behavior implies that no major challenge to professional standards or no fear of job security exists.

Viewing the professional in this micropolitical fashion provides a fuller understanding of role behavior. The typology also makes the point that no role is dominant; rather a number of roles exist that the superintendent may select as conditions warrant. Further, this view prompts us to look at different policy contexts where conflict may or may not exist. The point is that these roles are like a collection of hats; the superintendent may choose one to fit the situation. Of course, the typology does not provide a precise measure of these two qualities of superintendent value and community conflict. But it encourages thinking in patterned terms about the administrative environment when conflict exists.

SUPERINTENDENT STYLES AND CONFLICT MANAGEMENT

Another personal aspect of the superintendent is *style,* or the quality of one's individuality expressed in action. It is distinguished from role because it is a matter of choice rooted in individual emotions and judgments, while role is more narrowly confined to actions to which one was socialized in professional training and experience. Style is little studied in the scholarship of professionals of any kind, although significant anecdotes imply how different styles do operate. Yet studying style is important because the different roles noted in Table 7.2 permit individualization within each.

A Typology of Conflict Styles

Conflict styles are few because individuals in conflict tend to fit into a few patterns of behavior. Different styles are all versions of the classic "fight-flight" or "exit-voice-apathy" characterization of how individuals act when confronted by threatening situations. That is, when confronted one may actively oppose others, leave the scene, or loyally stay but not act. In Table 7.3 we label these three styles in the face of conflict Avoid, Mediate, and Fight. Mediation style can involve such strategies as accommodation, collaboration, and compromise. A comparison of city managers and school superintendents found that superintendents experience less conflict but feel more politically beleaguered because they expect to make decisions based on their expertise rather than on political negotiation.[32]

How does this range of styles interact with a range of intensity in community conflict? If the characteristic style of conflict management is Avoid, then when high community conflict occurs, the superintendent will seek only to preside over, but not to direct or oppose, the conflict. This includes not taking stands, assuring that rules of procedure are followed, and, in effect, deflecting the decision to the authoritative action of the school board. But when conflict is low, the Avoid style will delegate authority to other professionals within the organization and later approve their decisions.

Table 7.3
A Typology of Community Conflict and Superintendent Styles

Superintendent Style	Community Conflict	
	High	*Low*
Avoid	Presider	Delegator
Mediate	Compromiser	Facilitator
Fight	Assertive	Professional

If the superintendent's style is more inclined to Mediate, conflict produces two different roles. One may seek conflict resolution through compromise; note that this style enables one's own policy values to be incorporated into the final result to some degree. When conflict is low, however, the Mediate style may act as facilitator, a "first among equals" style of assisting other professionals to do their job while assuring that the general direction of the organization is maintained.

The Fight style of conflict management is the most dramatic, the subject of "war stories" about "beleagured" professionals whose norms have been challenged. This is most evident when community conflict is high, and the superintendent style becomes assertive, mobilizing group support and building coalitions to deal with problems of change. By competing with other groups, but accommodating where politically feasible, assertive styles differ dramatically from the presider style. When conflict is low, though, the Fight style involves the kind of administrative leadership that training schools and textbooks urge, the style that has created the modern service bureaucracies. This includes thinking in terms of the "one best system."[33]

REFLECTIONS ON CONFLICT BEHAVIOR IN URBAN PROFESSIONS

Research into these diverse superintendent styles and roles operating amid a shifting world of conflict has enriched our conceptualizations. Which role or style the person selects may well involve cost-benefit calculations about getting the job done, advancing professional goals, and enhancing one's career.

The growing fragmentation of the managerial, political, and educational tasks that superintendents perform is implied in these styles and roles. The distinction between administrator and leader that runs through them has been reinforced by superintendents' training and experience. A leading text in educational administration draws the distinction that typically applies to all superintendents:

> In sum, the professional administrator is likely to view his or her role as that of one who finds out what consumers want from the schools and who delivers educational services accordingly. The educational leader, by contrast, is very much concerned with the issues of purpose and direction.[34]

The administrative function exists in all but the Beseiged role of Table 7.2 and the presider and delegator styles of Table 7.3. All other roles and styles in these tables describe the leader. The latter is usually characterized by strong professional values and proactive behavior; the former is portrayed as having uncertain attachment to professional values and a reactive stance amid conflict. The implications for this style within schools will be reviewed later in studying principals who are leaders when their superintendents are.

Research Prospects

Though we can apply broad questions to these role and style concepts that need empirical evaluation, we can only raise general questions here. Many of the following questions are answered on an anecdotal basis by stories in the profession's journals. What are the conditions under which shift will occur in role and style? What does "success" or "failure" mean in these contexts? What are the skills most useful in both behaviors? Do these skills include articulating professional goals, brokering them amid group pressures including those from political masters, strategizing plans drawn from valid concepts of the political territory, using professional knowledge, and so on? Finally, does the professionals' training in the universities provide as relevant skills and styles of micropolitics as they do for other professional roles?

We leave such research questions with the understanding noted earlier that the superintendent is not a pure type because individuals vary and the context of conflict is not static. We see these administrators driven by professional values amid a turbulent administrative environment that is roiled by currents of change arising from outside the organization's boundaries. Often he or she is struggling to do more than simply manage routines–that is, to lead within a context of increasing power-sharing.

NOTES

1. William L. Boyd, "The Public, the Professionals, and Educational Policy-Making: Who Governs?" *Teachers College Record* 77 (1976): 556–58.

2. Based on several censuses of administrators conducted by Paul Salmon, American Association of School Administrators, Washington, D.C., mimeographed.

3. The sources, in order, are: Norman D. Kerr, "The School Board as an Agency of Legitimation," *Sociology of Education* 38 (1964): 34–59; Michael P. Smith, "Elite Theory and Policy Analysis: The Politics of Education in Suburbia," *Journal of Politics* 36 (1974): 1006–32; Peter J. Cistone, "The Socialization of School Board Members," *Educational Administration Quarterly* 13, no. 2 (1977): 19–33.

4. L. Harmon Zeigler and M. Kent Jennings, *Governing American Schools* (North Scituate, Mass.: Duxbury, 1974), pp. 39–42, Pt. III.

5. Leigh Seltzer, "Institutionalizing Conflict Response: The Case of Schoolboards," *Social Science Quarterly* 55, no. 2 (1974).

6. Boyd, "The Public, the Professionals, and Educational Policymaking."

7. M. Kent Jennings, "Parental Grievances and School Politics," *Public Opinion Quarterly* 32 (1968): 363–78.

8. Roland L. Warren, S. M. Rose, and A. F. Bergunder, *The Structure of Urban Reform* (Lexington, Mass.: Heath, 1974).

9. David Rogers, *110 Livingston Street* (New York: Random House, 1968).

10. Frederick M. Wirt, "Professionalism and Political Conflict: A Developmental Model," *Journal of Public Policy* 1 (1981): 83–112.

11. For example, Thomas J. Sergiovanni, Martin Burlingame, Fred Coombs, and Paul Thurston, *Educational Governance and Administration* (Englewood Cliffs, N. J.: Prentice-Hall, 1980). The school of education role in recent decades is seen in Geraldine Clifford and James Guthrie, *Ed School* (Chicago: University of Chicago Press, 1988), Part 3.

12. Larry Cuban, *Urban School Chiefs Under Fire* (Chicago: University of Chicago Press, 1976).

13. Jesse J. McCorry, *Marcus Foster and the Oakland Public Schools* (Berkeley: University of California Press, 1978).

14. Larry Cuban, "Transforming the Frog into a Prince: Effective Schools Research, Policy, and Practice at the District Level." *Harvard Education Review*

54 (1984): 129–51. The study of principals is in Martin Burlingame, "Using a Political Model to Examine Principals' Work," *Peabody Journal of Education* 63, no. 1 (Fall 1986): 120–29.

15. Larry Cuban, "Conflict and Leadership in the Superintendency," *Phi Delta Kappan* 67, no. 1 (1985): 28–30.

16. Jack Brimm, "What Stresses School Administrators," *Theory into Practice* 22 (1983): 64–69.

17. Cited in Brimm, "What Stresses School Administrators." Boyd, "Afterword: The Management and Consequences of Decline," *Education and Urban Society* 15 (1983): 256–57.

18. Gordon Cawelti, "Guess What? Big City Superintendents Say Their School Boards Are Splendid," *American School Board Journal* 169 (1982): 33–35; James Cibulka, "Explaining the Problem: A Comparison of Closings in Ten U.S. Cities," *Education and Urban Society* 15 (1983): 165–74.

19. See sources in notes 15 through 17.

20. Frederick Wirt, Benjamin Walter, Francine Rabinovitz, and Deborah Hensler, *On the City's Rim* (Lexington, Mass.: Heath, 1972). James Guthrie, "The United States of America: The Educational Policy Consequences of an Economically Uncertain Future," in *Education, Recession and the World Village*, edited by F. Wirt and G. Harman (Philadelphia: Falmer, 1986).

21. Stuart Langton, ed., *Citizen Participation in America* (Lexington, Mass.: Lexington, 1978).

22. Rufus Browning, Dale Marshall, and David Tabb, *Protest Is Not Enough* (Berkeley: University of California Press, 1984).

23. Harmon Zeigler, Ellen Kehoe, and Jane Reisman, *City Managers and School Superintendents* (New York: Praeger, 1985).

24. Cuban, *Urban School Chiefs.*

25. Dennis Judd and Paul Kantor, *Enduring Tensions in Urban Politics* (New York: Macmillan, 1992), Part II.

26. E. E. Schattschneider, *The Semisovereign People* (New York: Holt, Rinehart and Winston, 1960), p. 71.

27. This rich literature is reviewed in Charles Jones, *Governing Urban America* (Boston: Little, Brown, 1983), pp. 256–60.

28. Robert Crowson and Van Cleave Morris, "Administrative Control in Large City School Systems," *Educational Administrative Quarterly* 21, no. 4 (Fall 1985): 51-70.

29. Zeigler et al., *City Managers.*

30. Kenneth Thomas and Ralph Kilmann, *Conflict Mode Instrument* (Tuxedo, N. Y.: Xicom, 1974). Zeigler et al., *City Managers*, pp. 121–26.

31. The stages of profession-laity conflict are explored in Frederick Wirt, "Professionalism and Political Conflict."

32. Zeigler et al., *City Managers.*

33. David Tyack, *The One Best System* (Cambridge: Harvard University Press, 1974).

34. Sergiovanni et al., *Educational Governance*, p. 17.

8

The Micropolitics within Schools

A recent focus in the politics of education has been on politics *within* the local schools rather than between schools and other "external" systems such as state or federal government. Clearly, the boundary between the local and the external is not that sharp in reality, but the focus of micropolitics is on "the overt and covert processes through which actors (individuals and groups) in an organization's immediate environment acquire and exercise power to promote and protect their interests."[1] More specifically, micropolitics directs attention to the public and private transactions through which local education "authorities" and "partisans" manage conflict and meld consensus regarding the distribution of scarce but prized material and symbolic resources.[2] Since schools are a democratic political system, they are open to conflicting demands of both authorities and partisans debating the use of resources and values. We begin with an exploration of micropolitical conflicts between professionals and citizens concerning schooling decisions. But note that professionals and citizens also agree in many areas on what schooling should be.

THE TYPES OF MICROPOLITICAL CONFLICT

The micropolitics of education features *local actors with their resources seeking to accomplish distinctive goals within a context where conflict regularly prevails.* Understanding who these actors are is the key to understanding local politics and agendas. Table 8.1 shows how the professional, citizen, principal, teacher, and other actors relate to one another. Different politics exist for the:

- different stakes involved,
- dominant patterns of interaction among actors,
- strategies that each actor employs, actors' styles of playing, and
- policy outcomes.

Table 8.1 further notes in the cells (alphabet), formed by the intersection of these actors and their agendas that are objects of further research, all the interactions that generate the multifaceted nature of local schools that is termed "micropolitics."

The Professional–Citizen Linkage

The micropolitical relationship between the professional and the citizens is shown in the first column of Table 8.1.[3] The *formal* relationship includes how professional educators interact with citizen groups like advisory councils or school boards. Formally, the *stakes* (A in Table 8.1) differ over school activities. For some time, superintendents' values have defined the nature of these activities. However, when citizens think that their schools are very unresponsive to their values (e.g., desegregation or dropping student scores), they challenge professional influence. The *dominant pattern* of professional–citizen interaction (G in Table 8.1) is normally characterized by civility, especially through citizen boards. The main pattern, however, is professional domination, with limited parent influence at the school-site level. *Strategies* (M in Table 8.1) stress professionals' socializing citizens to accept their professional views of schooling. Tactics include screening out citizen critics, co-opting newcomers, soliciting citizens, and so on.

Recent efforts to decentralize school decisions, often supported by parents, represent an alternative *style of play* (S in Table 8.1).

Table 8.1
Interactions Between School Actors and Research Agendas

	Professional–Citizen		Principal–Teacher		Other Actors	
	Formal	*Informal*	*Formal*	*Informal*	*Formal*	*Informal*
Research Agendas						
Stakes	A	B	C	D	E	F
Dominant patterns	G	H	I	J	K	L
Strategy	M	N	O	P	Q	R
Styles of play	S	T	U	V	W	X
Outcomes	Y	Z	AA	BB	CC	DD

Source: Abstracted from Betty Malen, "The Micropolitics of Education: Mapping the Multiple Dimensions of Power Relations in School Polities," in *The Study of Educational Politics*, Jay Scribner and Donald Layton, eds. (Washington: Falmer, *Politics of Education Yearbook, 1995*).

The superintendent may be persuaded to foster this reform, and the principal may work within a new arrangement whereby teachers and parents have influence over budget, curriculum, and so on.[4]

An example of formal *outcomes* (Y in Table 8.1) is the Chicago experience with citizen site-based management that created new kinds of linkages between professionals and citizens, such as adversarial and democratic patterns of governance. But the prevailing pattern in hundreds of local Chicago councils is the familiar outcome—principals maintain or consolidate power.[5] While the basic professional–citizen relationship has seemed to change little, Chicago parents still like the school-site reform, and professionals welcome parental support for their efforts. Unfortunately, these governance changes have done little to improve student outcomes.[6] The weight of organizational history creates inertial forces that undergird an ongoing steady state.

MICROPOLITICS AND ORGANIZATIONAL POLITICS

While standard management theories often stress elements of formal structures of authority, micropolitics emphasizes self-interest and bargaining among actors. In other words, a micropolitical analysis of formal bargaining will take into account various informal agendas. A micropolitical approach also allows us to consider individual and group interests, whether these are professional (e.g., the preparation of curriculum) or personal (improving one's own status or work conditions). Micropolitics differentiates between visible or formal interests and their parallel informal interests advanced in the process of bargaining. Such interests may reflect diverse values held by members of different generations within a school, as in the case of "young Turks" challenging the authority of an "old guard." Interests may also be based on attitudes toward policy change, gender concerns, or networks of friendship. Finally, and most important, micropolitics focuses on the concept of power and its uses. In formal organizational analysis, authority and hierarchy are the bases for power, but in the arena of micropolitics, power rests on the personal ability to mobilize influence and affect decision making. It is important to understand that the contrasting concepts of organizational science and micropolitics, displayed in Table 8.2, are "ideal types," representing a range of possibilities.

Different theories can be used to interpret micropolitical interactions.[7] Exchange theory assumes that actors engage in activities by trading benefits and rewards. Bargaining theories involve a "bargaining zone" of individuals or groups that attempts to establish collective agreements incrementally through influence and bargaining. Other ways of interpreting micropolitics include formal theories of organizational politics, game theories, and even interactionist analysis.[8] In "loosely coupled" schools, for example, principals have authority but may not regularly use it. Teachers in such schools have much autonomy in instructional matters, and this may lead them to challenge the principals' authority. So in order to exercise control, principals must rely on using concepts like exchanges and bargaining.

The interaction between principals and teachers over decision making becomes particularly important in efforts to create governance reforms like site-based management. Here, much of the authority previously held by districts and state agencies is devolved to the school site, which then has greater authority to formulate and manage local policy. Principals and teachers enter into a new set of negotiations about how this increased site

Table 8.2
Conceptual Contrasts of
Organizational and Micropolitical Theories

Micropolitical Theory	Organizational Theory
Power	Authority
Goal diversity	Goal adherence
Ideological disputation	Ideological neutrality
Conflict	Consensus
Interests	Motivation
Political activity	Decision making
Control	Consent

Source: Stephen Ball, *The Micro-Politics of the School* (London: Methuen, 1987), p. 8.

Table 8.3
Resources of Principal and Teachers
in Local Influence Patterns

Principal vis-à-vis Teachers	Teachers vis-à-vis Principal
Material resources	Esteem
Promotion	Support
Esteem	Opinion leadership
Autonomy	Conformity
Lax rule enforcement	Reputation

Source: Eric Hoyle, *The Politics of School Management* (London: Hodder and Stoughton, 1986), pp. 1336–37.

authority should be shared to achieve often diverse goals. As can be seen in Table 8.3, both sides have resources or "goods" that can be traded in order to reach understandings on policies and regulations.

Each actor uses strategies to influence the others. Such influence constitutes a system of exchanges that are not necessarily reflected in the formal organizational system of authority. It is often this informal interweaving of strategies, goals, and influence that many professionals deride as "political." Yet such informal politics is to be expected in any organization where people pursue limited resources for a variety of goals.

THE PRINCIPAL AS MANAGER OR LEADER

A principal can be either a supporter of the status quo or an agent of change. Much of the research on educational administration has found that the primary role of the principal is as maintainer of the system, a role suggested by the designation of a principal as "manager." But when principals want to lead, other research suggests that real change can result. How do these officers operate?

The Principal as Focus of Pressures

From a micropolitical perspective, the principal is the focus of a set of consistent pressures at the local site:

- The central office and the superintendent impose major policy directives, rules, and procedures that limit the autonomy of the principal.
- Community neighborhoods impose an often vague—but sometimes vocal—sense of goals. These can include, for example, demands to improve sports programs or to increase discipline for students.
- The faculty have private interests (about salaries or work conditions) and professional concerns (about improvement of their teaching or of the curriculum).
- The profession of school administration holds standards related to goal setting, and a principal's own views about what constitutes good education motivate him or her to take action.

All of these pressures create problems for school administrators. Groups generating these pressures may have divergent views, for example, about what measures should be taken to enforce student discipline. Principals have certain responsibilities that cannot be escaped (e.g., student attendance reports), even though they may believe that their time might be more productively spent attending to other matters. Principals are often forced to modify their own approaches to goals in order to compromise with an array of pressure groups.

Coping Strategies Employed by Principals

Whether promoting reform or defending the existing system, how does the principal influence others to achieve his or her objectives? To put it another way, how does the principal seek to manipulate the micropolitical environment?[9] Following an ancient political tradition, the principal can divide the opposition in order to rule. Rivals can also be co-opted in order to weaken opposition. New issues can be advanced in order to deflect teacher and parental concerns about other matters, that is, by focusing on "red herrings"—relatively innocuous issues that can distract attention from real problem areas. Further, information can be controlled by deciding who gets certain information or how that information is presented. This strategy changes the ancient Greek concept of knowledge as "virtue" into a more modern formulation: Knowledge is "power"—a good that can be employed to influence outcomes.

By incorporating some or all of these strategies, principals can manipulate the outcomes of meetings and conferences to meet their goals. Such tactics can involve the arrangement of agenda items; "losing" or diverting opposing recommendations; recruiting neutral or indifferent staff to one's side; reinterpreting arguments in such a way that a false consensus is created; and even "massaging" the minutes of meetings. As an example of the last strategy, an apocryphal exchange has one school board member gloating, "You didn't get your own way today," while the administrator replies, "You haven't read the minutes yet!"

Faced with a variety of current challenges to decision making, what are the responses of principals, and how important is the principal in either rejecting or accommodating challenges?

Differing Responses to Change

Principals respond to challenges in several ways: remain within the existing channels of the organization; exercise leadership in instruction; or react to challenge with "burnout."

The Principal as Organizational Man or Woman. This type of principal focuses on following all rules and regulations, commonly referred to as operating "by the book." By adopting the familiar role of system maintenance—not "rocking the boat"—such principals follow all requirements handed down from the central office or outside government agencies. On the other hand, this type of principal will do little to respond flexibly to current challenges or to promote change at the school site because to do so entails stepping out of the organization's channels and upsetting routines.

Underlying this maintenance response may be an invisible contract with teachers based on relations of mutual exchange. The principal combines her authority with "influence strategies." An example of the use of such influence is getting teachers to do their basic job in the classroom, but without causing an uproar among parents or community that could create problems for the principal (or extend beyond the school). This strategy generates support among teachers for the principal's policies. By way of an exchange for the teachers, such a principal may help in furthering their private and professional goals. In this scenario, a principal may respond to new challenges by first fulfilling some of the externally imposed duties, but he may not adapt these requirements to his own school's needs by not exerting internal leadership.

In short, this is the *model of the organizational man or woman,* whose primary purpose is to defend the existing allocation of values and resources. By using her influence to exchange "goods" with teachers and by not exerting the leadership needed to adopt new goals, the principal may shelter herself from criticism from other actors at the local site. Of course the disadvantage of reform from such a strategy is also clear—the principal deflects or blocks changes to the existing system imposed from outside.

The Principal as Leader.   Some principals shape their environment, work within the pressures, but still define a new mission for their schools. The role described here is "leader," defined classically as one who moves others to adopt his or her values and thereby change the organization's goals.[10]

While writings on principals describe both manager and leader types, the latter is the source of much mystery. The observer can see a principal and know from others' behaviors that this is indeed a leader. But it is impossible to predict who will be a leader or to train persons to have these motivations and skills. How do these two types of principals—manager and leader—approach their main tasks?

Recent research has sought to distinguish between these two roles, noting that both relate to five dimensions of action, about which principals hold mental pictures termed "constructs."[11] These five dimensions are:

- defining the school's mission,
- promoting the instructional climate,
- managing the curriculum and instruction,
- supervising teaching, and
- monitoring student progress.

The research purpose of a national poll of principals was to determine whether leaders more likely favored some dimensions (e.g., defining mission) while managers favored others (e.g., supervising teaching). Many attitudinal questions about these missions were used to determine principals' personal constructs on the dimensions.

But the principals' constructs might well be a mask for more basic factors in their lives that shape these attitudes, termed "contexts of operations." Five of these contexts, composed of sets of variables, were devised to explain attitudinal differences about leadership. These were teacher bargaining units, system qualities of schools, and degree of community consensus. These contexts and construct variables are noted in more detail in Figure 8.1, which describes the logic of analysis that involved regressions to sort out differences. Each of these contexts suggests that it might explain principals' attitudes—for example, differences in types of schools (i.e., elementary versus high school) or in kinds of students (i.e., wealthy or poor, ethnic or Caucasian).

To summarize the findings[12] of the regression analysis, many of these context variables had little explanatory power except for three. *Leaders spent many hours at work* or with parents, they *had faculty support,* and—most significantly—they *worked with superintendents* who held professional expectations, supervised their enforcement, and supported principals in pursuing them. Surprisingly, there was little significance in principals' personal status

Figure 8.1
Model of Context-Cognitive Interaction

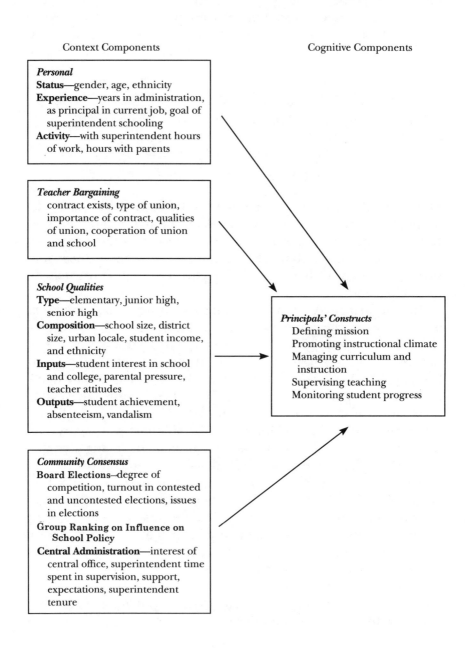

or in local school politics. *Rather, it was this professional network of goal setting by superintendent, hard work by principals, and support by faculty that helped make the principal a leader rather than a manager.*

The Burned-Out Principal.   Another way principals respond to challenges is by making all the required reforms at the site. But when only limited results occur time after time, these principals may become increasingly frustrated. In this case the principal tries to do everything and is vitiated by the effort. Even in the absence of school-based pressures, this principal soon becomes overwhelmed by the proliferation of district- or state-level mandates. The principal finds herself obliged to engage in extensive micropolitics such as exchanges with teachers or dealing with recently "empowered" parents. But student outcomes may not improve despite all the changes and new involvement of adults.

Many principals lack the training or experience in micropolitics to deal effectively with recent challenges, so they often face criticism that grows larger and more intense. These principals soon feel crushed when faced with community indifference or opposition, and they sense a lack of control over schooling. Returning home from a long day at work, they feel like they have been "pecked to death by ducks." Eventually, these principals may become burned out, even to the extent of withdrawing from school life and the profession. As with principals who respond to challenge within organizational channels, this response by principals— characterized by reform, frustration, and eventual burnout—also represents a failure of educational leadership.

THE TEACHER AS A POLITICAL ACTOR

No group has increased its influence on education policy in recent decades as much as have teachers. The timid rabbits of thirty years ago are today's ravening tigers in the jungle of school systems. Unionism has produced this change and consequently has made teachers into major political actors. One study of city schools made a strong argument that a total system transformation in who rules local schools occurred as a result of teacher unions. Those schools were first governed by a political machine rule, then by an administrative reform rule (which meant a professional education bureaucracy); they are now governed by union rule. These three models differ in structure, process, and actors. However, contemporary union rule is characterized by a crucial political quality—lack of control by elected officials. Thus, a continuing question of the democratic polity is whether union rule can be considered an enduring form of urban government.[13]

Certainly their size alone (2,740,000 belonging to a teachers' union in the mid-1990s) enables organized teachers to be a local pressure group that regularly confronts the district board and superintendent. Every autumn, threats of teacher strikes in major cities become a staple news item along with the closing days of the baseball season. Nor are these features found only in big cities. As collective bargaining became ever more authorized by state laws, medium and small communities experienced the unprecedented—a teachers' strike. The results can dramatically rearrange traditional power within the school system. This militancy was not always the case, because as recently as the mid-1960s a majority of teachers opposed collective bargaining or the endorsement of political candidates. Note that two-thirds of our teachers are women who at one time were successfully discouraged from union or political activities by male administrators. Also, some teachers believed that collective bargaining and political campaign activities were "unprofessional."

As of 1996, however, thirty-seven states had some form of collective bargaining statute covering teachers. Even states without such laws have some locals with long-standing collective bargaining agreements (e.g., Texas and Mississippi). As a result, by 1996, 90 percent of all full-time professionals belonged to the American Federation of Teachers (AFT) or the National Education Association (NEA). In short, collective bargaining is now an accepted part of school governance, and covers 56 percent of all teachers.

We can attribute much of the rapid increase in collective bargaining beginning in the mid-1960s to the rivalry for members between the NEA and the AFT (discussed in Chapter 4). Initially, neither the NEA nor the AFT would endorse strikes; it took until 1973 for the strike to become official NEA policy. Recently, the incidence of strikes has been declining from a high of 218 strikes in 1975 to 12 strikes at the beginning of school in 1993.[14]

The recent decline in strikes is in part caused by the large increases in teacher salaries galvanized by the post-1983 education reform movement and by lack of an economic recession since 1982. When teacher salaries are rising, then less need or incentive to strike exists. But the 1994 elections produced more Republicans in legislatures and governorships who proceeded to introduce legislation to curtail strikes, limit tenure, and restrict the scope of collective bargaining in Michigan, California, Illinois, Indiana, Pennsylvania, and Wisconsin. Michigan passed a law that challenged all these teacher prerogatives as well as permitted charter schools that are not covered by prior teacher contracts.

The Impact of Teacher Contracts

The outcome of collective bargaining is a written and time-bound agreement covering wages, conditions of employment, and many other topics. Large district union contracts are over three hundred pages. As well as involving the specifics of the contract, major disputes can occur over the scope of bargaining and grievance procedures.[15] The negotiated contract, however, does not affect teachers until it is implemented in the work setting. At the school site, the board's contract language must be interpreted to apply to specific circumstances. This means that the site principal, teachers, and union building representatives must become very familiar with the contract's terms. Yet even such familiarity does not forestall many disputes about a specific teaching arrangement. These disputes can lead to teacher grievances whose settlement can clarify the contract.

Thus teacher influence varies by district *and* site. Teachers at school sites sometimes permit exceptions to the district contract if they believe specific school conditions warrant them.[16] Teacher unions have had the most difficulty enforcing such contract provisions as pupil discipline, building maintenance, and security because teacher grievance procedures are less effective. On the other hand, seniority and teacher transfer clauses were the most highly implemented because of grievance use.[17] Unions' influence, however, may come more from influencing decisions at state and federal levels that can then percolate down to the local school system in the form of mandates. There is a major potential for rearranging traditional school governance by teachers lobbying in state capitals to specify local operations. For example, California's state education code is over four thousand pages, many of which arose from teacher groups, that affect what happens in the smallest school districts. Of the two groups, the NEA has a much stronger presence at the state level as the AFT has fewer members, primarily from big cities.

What happens to administrative authority, particularly among principals, when contracts filter down through the loosely coupled school system? While some provisions tightly limit administrative freedom of action, as noted, others get redefined to fit the requirements at the site level. The principal has to balance such factors as teacher interests, educational consequences, administrative leadership, and staff allegiance. How he or she works with the contract also affects teachers' respect for him or her. Teachers want the contract respected, but the contract also allows for the principal's interpretation if she or he is seen as seeking a good school, whether authoritarian or democratic in leadership style. In short, having standards and expecting much of teachers earns principals a tolerance and even respect from teachers in interpreting the contract; for teachers, a good school is more important than union membership, close observance of a contract, or running the schools. This is because, as one administrator observed, "Teachers like to be part of a winning team."

Yet the ultimate effects of collective bargaining may not be as great as was once thought. Those effects are deep and pervasive but not so extreme or uniform as critics often suggest:

> Collective bargaining has not been shown to have increased teachers' commitment to their work or enhanced their standing as professionals, but neither has it destroyed the schools. Caricatures of strait-jacketed principals, Kafkaesque school bureaucracies, or schools under siege by militant teachers scarcely represent the experiences of these sample districts. Overall, the organizational effects of collective bargaining appear to be both

moderate and manageable. This is not to suggest, though, that labor relations practices look the same in all districts of all schools. In fact, negotiations, contract language, and administrative practices are remarkably diverse.[18]

Understanding these consequences is confused by the diverse practices that have emerged in local systems. No single factor accounts for this diversity in local labor practices, but certain important variables in those practices include the history of local labor practices, the local political culture, and—most important—the people at the center of negotiations and contract management. In California, the same districts regularly have strikes or acrimonious labor disputes near the expiration of every contract. Some of this is caused by personalities, styles, and relationships, and some is caused by a long and bitter history of labor-management relations. However, in other districts, both sides prefer cooperation over a long period of time. No simple predictive model can account for these factors, and the diverse outcomes are similar to the range in outcomes from federal grant programs.

It is clear that collective bargaining has increased the complexity of the principal's job because he or she cannot apply the contract in a routine and standard manner. Moreover, there are some overall impacts of bargaining:

1. The breakdown of the unitary command structure and its replacement by a multilateral bargaining system, or, in some cases, by a bilateral system.
2. The introduction of new participants into school decision making, including labor professionals (both advocates and neutral third parties), organized and unorganized citizens, and elected officials outside of education.
3. The movement of the locus of decision making to central offices within school systems and to locations outside of school systems, including legislatures, courts, and public administrative agencies.
4. The broadening scope of issues that fall into the labor relations arena—both issues raised during formal negotiations and those joined to the collective bargaining process during the administration of contracts.

5. The changing nature of managerial work, since there is evidence that school administrators face different types of issues, new constituents, different managerial roles, and new criteria for success in their jobs.[19]

These constraints on the principal's role, in light of what happens to the contract at the site level reviewed earlier, suggest a complex concept of this professional's tasks. The constraints also point to a centralization of decision making within the total school system. But local development of contract implementation points to a decentralization of interpretation by the principal. Both developments in collective bargaining mean that the professional at this level, as well as at higher levels, must increasingly work within a power-sharing context. Educational leadership is still possible here but under much more complex requirements involving special issues.

Issues in Collective Bargaining

In the 1970s a major issue arose in direct citizen participation in the bargaining process. Educators have adopted the private industry model for bargaining, but several groups assert that this is inappropriate. In private industry only two parties, labor and management, are at the bargaining table. However, parent advocates pushed for bargaining in open meetings with public observers or even a place for parents at the bargaining table. Nine states have enacted public participation with the hope that it would dampen expenditure increases for salaries and personnel. Whatever the philosophical merits of these arguments, the public has not shown much interest.

Despite the significant effect of collective bargaining on school costs and tax rates, the general public shows little sustained interest in teacher bargaining except during times of crisis. Citizens may simply assume that their elected representatives on school boards take an active part in negotiations, but we have seen that this rarely happens. In any case, community participation advocates appear to lead a phantom army. However, general public attitudes toward organized labor and collective bargaining do affect the very broad parameters of contracts, probably through election of sympathetic board members who then appoint like-minded school executives.[20]

Another improvement in collective bargaining might be accomplished through the issue of a merger of two rival unions. It is alleged that their rivalry leads to increased and unnecessary union truculence. But despite frequent attempts by top union leadership to merge, no visible progress has occurred except in a handful of large cities. The NEA still has a huge numerical majority over the AFT (2.2 million to 875,000, which include teachers at all levels of education) and sees little need to compromise, particularly when its tactics are virtually indistinguishable from the AFT's. The NEA claims that it provides militant collective bargaining while being untainted from affiliation with "unprofessional" unions in the AFL-CIO.

A major new issue fueled by the educational excellence movement is the control of teacher certification. Teachers are certified by the states, but the Carnegie Corporation has advocated a national professional standards board.[21] Originally the concept was to have the national board recognize experienced teachers who could meet unusually high standards. Recently, discussion of national certification of new teachers has increased. Teacher unions' reactions to such reform can be inferred from their work with states. Unions have sought control of state certification boards for years and have succeeded in several states. They have also cut back the influence of the universities and administrators by achieving more teacher members on these state licensing boards. The unions believe a true profession must control the entry of its own members and not cede this prerogative to others, such as universities. Moreover, union contributions to state legislators have given them influence that universities cannot match. The AFT has supported a national certification board while NEA locals have been more cautious.

The Carnegie task force also proposed "lead teachers" who would share some of the principal's responsibilities in the instructional and teacher evaluation areas. This enlarged role in administration for teachers has engendered resistance from some administrator and school board groups. A crucial issue during the 1990s has been whether the private bargaining model would be modified and adapted to the particular circumstances of public education. None of the alternative concepts has engendered much support, and consequently, private sector labor-management bargaining techniques seem embedded in the American public school culture.

By the late 1990s teacher shortages had appeared in several parts of the nation due to greater enrollments and large-scale retirements. This change helped trigger a rethinking of the professional basis for a teaching career. Maybe more control could be exercised; professionals like lawyers and doctors have more control over all aspects of their careers than teachers. Older models of control continue in education. The legacy of the turn-of-the-century reformers was the industrial model with male administrators presiding over a largely transient female labor force. But later, a model involving collective bargaining was a first step in changing this power relationship. It is uncertain whether any more major shifts in teacher power will take place soon. But more recent efforts at teacher empowerment at the site level (e.g., site-based management or restructuring) do suggest a newer model of control over curriculum and other matters.

Teachers as Political Brokers in the Classroom

There is a different way to view the teacher's micropolitical role, and this occurs when we turn from their outward relationship with school authorities to their inward relationship with their students. One aspect of this relationship is the teachers' role in political learning by students. Teachers help transmit the American civic culture and shape children's values about it. But even in such a seemingly value-free subject as elementary-level mathematics, the teacher is not simply an implementer of educational policy. As scholars presenting a political perspective concluded:

> In this semi-autonomous role, teachers are better understood as political brokers than as implementers. They enjoy considerable discretion, being influenced by their own notions of what schooling ought to be as well as persuaded by external pressures. . . . This view represents a middle ground in the classic sociological contrast between professional autonomy and bureaucratic subordination. It pictures teachers as more or less rational decision-makers who take higher-level policies and other pressures into consideration in their calculation of benefits and costs.[22]

In a real sense—by allocating public resources in such matters as choosing which students get what kind of curriculum content—the teacher takes on a political role. This action parallels the similar political role of board and administrative decisions. Thus decisions in elementary math about what will be taught, to whom, and for how long are matters that teachers usually decide. For example, learning about the concept of percent rests on cases of earning interest by investment; in the former U.S.S.R., the cases rested on production goal improvements. Some pressures, however, also come from students (e.g., what has worked with them in the past predisposes its re-use) and from external sources. Teachers receive different messages about what to teach from state, professional, and local sources. Externally, a varied urban environment with its ambiguous messages about instruction is much more likely to free the teacher to make such decisions compared to those found in a small, homogeneous rural setting. Centralized versus decentralized state requirements—for example, statewide text adoption by the state board—are another kind of external factor affecting teacher discretion. But even within the school organization there are factors of organizational rigidity or receptivity that create expectations in teachers about how they use power.[23]

Much of the preceding suggests an organizational structure for schooling that is characterized by "loose coupling." This is the tendency of educational organizations to disconnect policies from outcomes, means from ends, and structure or rules from actual activity.[24] Such a nonstructure puts the teacher's behavior beyond the control of the central office and principal, who themselves have no chain of command with straight lines and precise directions for teaching policy. Within such disjointed relationships, one would not expect program innovations originating outside the local unit to have much impact. A survey of the history of classroom reforms finds there are lasting results only if the changes are structural, create a new clientele, and are easily monitored. Vocational education and driver training are good examples of this. But attempts to change classroom pedagogy have largely been unsuccessful because they lack these essential characteristics.[25]

Much of this political quality is typified in the current education reform policies that present particularly difficult dilemmas for teachers and their unions. Many policymakers have been adamant about linking additional benefits to teachers by the creation of a more performance-based profession. Several state governors, for example, propose new methods, like testing new teachers and using student tests in evaluating teachers, uniform accountability reporting systems, and performance-based compensation. But most teachers would be uncomfortable with a system that does not allocate benefits uniformly on the basis of seniority and educational attainment. Consequently, if teacher unions embrace the reform movement, they may lose the support of rank-and-file members. But if the teacher unions oppose "reform" and "professionalism," they will lose public support and alienate many top policymakers.[26] Gradually, the NEA unions have moved from opposing certain key reform proposals to accommodating and modifying them. The AFT has been quicker to lead in shaping the initial version of the reforms. However, both teacher unions oppose most forms of charter school legislation that remove schools from collective bargaining contracts and state education code restrictions. These charter schools, authorized by the mid-1990s in over twenty states, thereby become independent from local central offices for most functions. Teacher unions envisage that charter schools may lead to vouchers.

Ironically, a national study of local teacher organizations concluded that reform policies were quite peripheral to their local mission and interests.[27] Consequently, opposition to reform was typical, and there was little need to depart from the traditional collective bargaining model. The rank-and-file teachers expect unions to obtain material benefits such as higher salaries and better working conditions, but they are not particularly interested in such "professional" strategies as teacher participation in school-site decision making or performance-based compensation. This rank-and-file viewpoint is particularly troublesome for union leaders who endorse reforms such as site-based management, because for the next few years there are few major improvements likely in teachers' working conditions. Given this lack of progress on "bread-and-butter" items, the grass-roots endorsement of teacher reforms at the building level is highly problematic.[28]

Thus the role of teachers in local governance is much more than just trade-union politics. We need more knowledge of the classroom as a significant screen between external influences and the student. The teacher as a political agent, allocating subject matter time within the classroom, is confronting external efforts by states and central offices to shape curriculum to meet the public's wishes. In the micropolitics of the local site, principal and teacher interact continuously as they contend with other stakeholders for limited resources to meet their goals.

NOTES

1. Laurence Iannaconne, "Micropolitics of Education: What and Why," *Education and Urban Society* 23 (1991): 465–71.

2. Betty Malen, "The Micropolitics of Education," in *Education and Urban Society* 23, no. 4 (1991). See related articles in same colloquium, edited by Catherine Marshall and Jay Scribner.

3. This review follows the judgments of the literature found in Malen, "The Micropolitics of Education."

4. On theory and experience, see Daniel Brown, *Decentralization and School-Based Management* (New York: Falmer, 1990); Joseph Murphy, *Restructuring Schools* (New York: Teachers College, 1990); Joseph Murphy and Philip Hallinger, eds., *Restructuring Schooling* (Newbury Park, Calif.: Corwin, 1993).

5. Sharon Rollow and Anthony Bryk, *Grounding a Theory of School Micro-Politics: Lessons from Chicago School Reform* (Chicago: Center for School Improvement, University of Chicago, 1993).

6. A survey of student effects elsewhere in the nation was equally discouraging; see Betty Malen, B. Ogawa, and J. Kranz, "What Do We Know about Site-Based Management? A Case Study of the Literature—A Call for Research," in *Choice and Control in American Education*, vol. 2, W. Clone and J. Witten, eds. (New York: Falmer, 1990).

7. These concepts are further elaborated in Stephen Ball, *The Micro Politics of School Management* (London: Methuen, 1987), and Joseph Blase and Gary Anderson, *The Micropolitics of Educational Leadership* (New York: Teachers College Press, 1995).

8. For a more detailed explanation of these theories see Eric Hoyle, *The Politics of School Management* (London: Hodder and Stoughton, 1986).

9. From Hoyle, *Politics*, pp. 140–48.

10. The distinction is set out in the prize-winning James Macgregor Burns, *Leadership* (New York: Harper & Row, 1978).

11. The following is based on preliminary testing by Martin Maehr, University of Michigan, and Samuel Krug, MetriTech, Inc., and a national poll conducted of 1,200 principals in the late 1980s by Krug and Frederick Wirt, under auspices of the National Center for Educational Leadership, University of Illinois, under a federal grant.

12. Frederick Wirt and Samuel Krug, "A Cognitive Theory of Leadership," American Political Science Convention, 1993; "From Behavior to Cognition," American Education Research convention, 1994.

13. William J. Grimshaw, *Union Rule in the Schools* (Lexington, Mass.: Lexington Books, 1979).

14. *Education Week* (September 15, 1993): 5.

15. James Guthrie and Patricia Craig, *Teachers and Politics* (Bloomington, Ind.: Phi Delta Kappa, 1973).

16. Susan Moore Johnson, *Teacher Unions in Schools* (Philadelphia: Temple University Press), pp. 162–63.

17. Ibid., p. 163.

18. Ibid., pp. 164–65.

19. Anthony M. Cresswell and Michael Murphy, *Teachers, Unions, and Collective Bargaining in Public Education* (Berkeley: McCutchan, 1980), pp. 386–87.

20. Lorraine McDonnell and Anthony Pascal, *Organized Teachers in American Schools* (Santa Monica, Calif.: The Rand Corp., 1979), pp. 87–88. For the role of the department chair see Leslie Siskin, *Realms of Knowledge: Academic Departments in Secondary Schools* (Washington, D.C.: Falmer, 1994).

21. Carnegie Corporation, *A Nation Prepared: Teachers for the 21st Century* (New York: Carnegie, 1986).

22. John Schwille et al., "Teachers as Policy Brokers in the Content of Elementary School Mathematics" (paper prepared for the NIE Conference on Teaching and Educational Policy, February 1981), p. r, and John Schwille, Andrew Porter, and Michael Gant, "Content Decision-Making and the Politics of Education," *Educational Administrative Quarterly* 16 (1980): 21–40.

23. Robert L. Crowson, William Lowe Boyd, and Hanne B. Mawhinney, *The Politics of Education and the New Institutionalism* (New York: Falmer, 1996); D.C. Lortie, "The Balance of Control and Autonomy in Elementary School Teaching," in *The Semi-Professions and Their Organization,* Amitai Etzioni, ed. (New York: Free Press, 1969); and Alan Peshkin, *Growing Up American* (Chicago: University of Chicago Press, 1979).

24. Karl Weick, "Educational Organizations as Loosely Coupled Systems," *Administrative Science Quarterly* 21 (1976): 1–19.

25. Michael Kirst and Gail Meister, "Turbulence in American Secondary Schools: What Reforms Last?" *Curriculum Inquiry* 15, no.1 (Spring 1985): 1969–86.

26. Lorraine McDonnell and Anthony Pascal, *Teacher Unions and Education Reform* (Santa Monica: The Rand Corp., 1987), p. 3. See also Julia Koppich and Charles Herchner, *The United Mind Worker* (San Francisco: Jossey Bass, 1997).

27. McDonnell and Pascal, *Teacher Unions,* p. 5.

28. McDonnell and Pascal, *Teacher Unions,* pp. 6–8.

Part III

STATE, FEDERAL, AND JUDICIAL POLITICS

9

The History and Evolution of the State Role in Education Policy

Under the United States Constitution, education is a power reserved to the states. In turn, state constitutions charge the state legislatures with responsibility for establishing and maintaining a system of free public schools that are locally operated. Local control has been a hallmark of American education, distinguishing us from most other Western nations. But an unprecedented growth of state influence over local education has taken place since the 1960s.

States show different historical patterns of control over local policies such as curriculum, personnel, finances, and teaching, but all states established minimum standards for local school operations. Presumably the state's requirement to provide for the general welfare sought a basic educational opportunity for all children. Consequently, states require a minimum number of days at school, certain courses of study, and standards for teacher certification. Most states also require localities to levy a minimum tax and to guarantee a base level of expenditures. There has been an urban-rural distinction to this state role. Earlier in this century, states began upgrading the standards of the very many rural schools, while the cities received less attention because

195

their expenditures and property wealth were already the highest in the state. Indeed, Chicago, New York, and Philadelphia had special statutes that exempted them from major areas of state control. Decades later, in the 1970s, state school finance reforms created special provisions for the core cities, but then the rationale was based on high fiscal stress.

A principal reason for state intervention is that only the state can ensure equity and standardization of instruction and resources. This rationale is contested by local control advocates, who contend that flexibility is needed to adjust to diverse circumstances and local preferences. Local control advocates stress that no proven educational technology is optimal for all conditions. This dispute over state versus local control really centers on two values–central equity and local choice. The traditional compromise has been to provide state minimums with local options to exceed the minimums. But this compromise is challenged by school finance reformers because state minimums are either inadequate or are exceeded by localities with extraordinary taxable property.

SOME CAUSES FOR THE GROWTH OF STATE INFLUENCE

Some of the major policy areas that show the dramatic increase of state influence in the last two decades are state administration of federal categorical grants, the state role in education finance, state requirements for educational accountability, state specifications and programs for children with special needs, and state efforts to increase academic standards. Substantive changes have become possible in large part due to an increase in the institutional capacity of states to intervene in local affairs. Thus most state legislatures have added staff and research capacity, and they also now meet annually or for more extended sessions than in earlier years. Legislative staff increased by 130 percent between 1968 and 1974.[1] In the decades since, the states also diversified their tax sources and expanded their fiscal capacities.

The capacity of state education agencies (SEAs) to intercede in local school policy has also mushroomed in the last twenty years. Ironically, the federal government created the impetus for this expansion. The Elementary and Secondary Education Act (ESEA) of 1965 and its subsequent amendments required state agencies to approve local projects for federal funds in such areas as education for disadvantaged, handicapped, bilingual, and migrant children and for educational innovation. In each of these federal programs, 1 percent of the funds were earmarked for state administration. Moreover, Title V of ESEA provided general support for state administrative resources, with some priority given to state planning and evaluation. By 1972 three-fourths of the SEA staffs had been in their jobs for less than three years. All the expansion in California's SEA from 1964 to 1970 was financed by federal funds. A quarter century later, in 1995, the federal General Accounting Office found that the federal share of SEA funding ranged from 71 percent in Iowa to 11 percent in South Carolina.[2] New staff capacity was available for SEA administrators or state boards that wanted to take a more activist role in local education.[3] The 1983 academic reform era galvanized a significant increase in state testing and curricular experts. State staff has increased to implement new teacher policies, including career ladders.

Another factor is the increased confusion among, and decreased respect for, traditional supporters of local control. Thus local control advocates—such as teachers' unions, school boards, and school administrator associations—feud among themselves and thereby provide a vacuum that state control activists can exploit. As we have seen, these education groups cannot agree on common policies with their old allies such as parent organizations. The loss of public confidence in professional educators and the debatable decline of achievement scores also cause many legislators to feel that local school employees should no longer be given so much discretion. However, a local control reaction occurred in the 1990s. Some state legislatures acted to forbid mandates without funding for local districts, which was a local concern against "big government," part of the larger challenge in school politics.

In addition to all this, a key structural change occurred in the growth and diversification of state tax sources. From 1960 to 1979, eleven states adopted a personal income tax, nine a corporate income tax, and ten a general sales tax. Thirty-seven states used all three of these revenue sources in 1979 compared with just nineteen in 1960. State income taxes provided 35 percent of all tax revenue in 1978 compared to 19 percent in 1969. This diversification of the revenue systems provided the states with a capacity to increase services that was further enhanced by numerous tax increases to fund reforms after 1983. The favorite tax to increase was the sales tax, either through rate increases or extension of the sales tax base to services. By 1994 this state control had increased to the point where a backlash developed, featuring Republican advocacy for pruning state education codes, cuts in SEA staff, and policy devolution to the local education agencies (LEAs).

VARIETY AND INDIVIDUALISM

If variety is the spice of life, educational decision making in the fifty American states is a veritable spice cabinet. The situation is reminiscent of Kipling's aphorism that there are a thousand ways to worship God, and they are all correct. This variety is the key to understanding much about the basic value of individualism in the American system. We need not rely merely on assertions about this variety. Figure 9.1 sets forth the patterns of selecting and staffing administrative positions for education in the fifty states. Not only are there differences between the state board and chief administrator in such matters, but also within either office. Moreover, the ranges are impressive in board members' terms, size, and employees. The trend in the last thirty years has been to decrease the number of elected chief state school officers (CSSOs) to the 1996 level of fifteen. The most common method of appointing CSSOs is through the board of education—twenty-six states use this method.

Such variety reflects a pluralism of views on how to express the taproot value of individualism. That value has been reflected through a prism of diverse historical experiences (the impact of losing versus winning the Civil War), different natural resources (the poverty of the South versus the richness of the North), demographic mixes (rural homogeneity versus urban heterogeneity), and so on. Through this tangle of past and present, the

Figure 9.1

Chief State School Officer (CSSO) and State Board of Education (SBE) Selection Patterns and Possibilities.

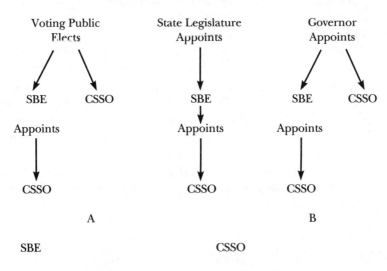

SBE

1) Appointed by governor
2) Elected by public
   either (a) partisan or
   (b) nonpartisan
3) Appointed by legislature

CSSO

1) Selected by SBE
2) Elected by public
   either (a) partisan or
   (b) nonpartisan
3) Appointed by governor

The only combination which presently does not exist is A3/B3. In 1996 state boards of education were elected in thirteen states and appointed in thirty-six states. The CSSO was elected in fifteen states.

Source: From James W. Guthrie and Rodney Reed, *Educational Administration and Policy* (Englewood Cliffs, N.J.: Prentice-Hall, 1986), p. 36. Copyright © 1986. Reprinted/adapted by permission of Allyn & Bacon.

creation of institutions had to take various forms. The very basis of democratic life—the political institutions of party, pressure group, and voting—took different forms from region to region as a result of these combinations of events, resources, and population.[4] We should not be surprised, then, that the evolution of educational institutions took different forms as well. For one thing, ideas about how to organize and provide schooling were affected by varied historical experiences. The New England states' violent

opposition to George III instilled in them a fear of state-central-
ized services, including schools, which remains today. On the
other hand, the states of the Confederacy were so devastated by
the Union troops' destruction that financing by county institutions was wiped out. State control and moneys had to be provided in large amounts, then and ever since.

Even the precise meaning of something that all states agreed
to in principle—compulsory schooling—was affected by an inter-
vening individualism. Massachusetts was the first state requiring
school attendance in 1852. By 1900 thirty-five states had so acted,
but the last state, Mississippi, did not adopt such legislation until 1918.[5] In short, it took two-thirds of a century to institution-
alize acceptance of even an idea that had wide popular support.
Today, though, it is not clear what the meaning of this requirement is; differing political, economic, sociological, and organizational explanations abound.[6]

SOCIOECONOMIC DIMENSIONS OF VARIETY

Multiple Responses to Systematic Problems

Understanding a state's politics of education requires a grasp
of its societal background. In the case of the fifty American states,
such a demonstration quickly overloads even eager students in
the field because of the varied and many dimensions for categorizing or evaluating units of government. The fifty states and
their fourteen thousand LEAs vary along all the traditional dimensions of demography—age composition; size of school-age
population; parents' education, occupation, and income; economic
resources; and so on to form an almost endless list. Districts run
from the behemoth, with a million students in New York City, to
a rural hamlet with a dozen in the graduating class. Economics
range from extremely wealthy suburbs to poor farm villages. Their
resources vary just as much, from a multiple-building high school
in a California suburb to a one-room schoolhouse on the Nebraska prairie.

This variety means that the total school system will adjust differently to impinging nationwide events. No such thing as state

Table 9.1
Number of Reforms Adopted by State Legislatures

Number Adopted	Number of States	States
0–4	17	Alaska, Ga., Md., Mass., Mont., Nev., N.H., N.M., N.Dak., Ohio, Oreg., Pa., R.I., S.Dak., Utah, Vt., Wyo.
5–9	16	Ala., Colo., Del., Hawaii, Ind., Ill., Iowa, Kans., Mich., Minn., Mo., N.J., N.Y., Va., W.Va., Wisc.
10–14	9	Ariz., Conn., Ky., La., Maine, Nebr., Okla., Tex., Wash.,
15–19	6	Ark., Calif., Ind., Miss., N.C., Tenn.
20 or more	2	Fla., S.C.

Source: Doh Shinn and Jack Van Der Slik, "Legislative Efforts to Improve the Quality of Public Education in The American States: A Comparative Analysis" (paper presented to the annual convention of the American Political Science Assn., New Orleans, 1985), p. 36.

education policy exists; what does exist are differential state responses to common external and internal events working on the local political system. The state reaction to the 1983 reform movement varied enormously. Some states enacted omnibus bills with extensive state mandates. Other states did little and left what few programs they did enact to local discretion. Table 9.1 shows how many of the forty recommendations in the *A Nation at Risk* report were adopted in the first two years after its publication. The data reflect a heavy response in the South (and California as well), which suggests that those states used the reform publicity to push changes that would move them toward national standards. Three major forces that caused these state reforms were more activist governors (including the later President Clinton), heightened involvement of big business, and the influence of interstate reform networks.[7]

The Dimension of School Finances

School financing is another useful illustration of variety in local implementation, for money plays such a large part in the American politics of education. Schools have traditionally been heavily financed by local taxes, with the states providing only a small share and the federal government the tiny remainder. That commonality aside, though, almost total diversity characterizes school financing. Each state's contribution has varied with its own resources, traditions, and values, as well as with the general economic effects of wars and recessions. While the overall state share has increased between 1900 and 1981 from about 20 to 50 percent, variations among the states are huge. Thus in 1996, Hawaii, rooted in a royal tradition of centralism, provided 92 percent, while New Hampshire provided about 11 percent.

Though greater disparities exist among the LEAs within each state, much stability still shows up in the ways that states react to local needs.[8] Relatively rich and poor states remain very much the same over long periods of time; thus, the amounts of state aid or the patterns of other policies demonstrate little shift exists in these states' *relative* standings on such matters.[9] For example, from 1900 to 1966 state standings are highly correlated on such matters as the proportion of state support (rho = 0.60). In shorter periods even higher stability is disclosed; for example, average teacher salaries between the very dynamic years of 1963 and 1973 showed almost no shift in these states' rankings (rho = 0.90). (The reasons will be explored later.) Thus, the pattern is one of both stability and variety among the American states. No conceivable socioeconomic dimension exists on which the states do not show such variation. Even the constitutional position of education in these states reveals pluralism.

EVOLUTION OF A NEW STATE ROLE

The shift in the state role has been drastic in recent decades, and the rate of involvement has increased dramatically. The original thirteen state constitutions made no mention of education. Today all states refer to education, sometimes briefly (Connecticut's schools rested on three paragraphs until well into this century) and sometimes at length (for example, California with a four-thousand-page code). State involvement started at the end of the last century with school reforms that introduced more professionalism. The authorization of LEAs and the limitation on their taxing appeared everywhere at that time. Consolidation also emerged pervasively around World War I. By 1925 one-third of the states already had state supervision set out in detailed, minimum standards for many matters. These included as local sites, buildings, lighting, heating, outdoor and indoor equipment (including even the size of a globe), academic and professional qualifications of teachers, length and kinds of courses, requirements for hygiene, and community relations programs.[10]

One significant example of this centralizing process is the number of states requiring a university degree to teach, from none in 1900 to all fifty in 1965; a 1986 survey shows growth of the state in many functions.[11] All states do certain things, such as keeping records on pupils, for example, but only a few states do other things, such as guidance and counseling. These regular policies are part of the "system maintenance" capacities that professions use to control the functions they deem most vital.[12] In other words, the *potential* for state intervention in local schools, once remote but always possible, has today become a pervasive reality. This constitutional position does not, however, exhaust the political aspects of schools. We may now turn to more evidence of schools' political nature.

Increasing State Control over the LEA

Just as no political action takes place without different effects on different groups' values, educational policymaking is contentious because some participants win and some lose. Recall that in Chapter 1 we noted that politics is not only conflict over the distribution of resources, but also and more basically over the distribution of group values. This concept leads us to expect that the basic interactions among schools, political system, and society are about who and what is to be valued in the educational process. So schools are caught up in a competition for resources, status, and value satisfaction like other institutions of our society. In previous chapters, we have seen this concept working in the *local* politics of education.

Central to this situation is the value of local control discussed in Chapter 6, a value that permits individualism to take the manifold forms so characteristic of American education. State control—constitutionally given—has worked in tension with this passion for local control.[13] Controls take several forms: service minimums that the LEA cannot fall below; encouragement of LEAs to exceed minimums (for example, by cost-sharing a new goal); organizational requirements; emphasis on efficiency methods, and so on. Such controls assume that the state can provide equality better than the LEA through standardizing instruction and resources. Advocates of local control assert, however, that greater payoffs will flow from a more flexible, hence more decentralized, system of schooling. Indeed, the 1990s saw local pressures causing some states to forbid any mandates without state funding.

Thus the state-local clash has been between two major values—the provision of state equity versus freedom of local choice. More recently, states have introduced a third value—efficiency— by placing more controls over planning, budgeting, evaluation, and so on. Today equity and efficiency are more stressed by state action, but choice has been reduced despite much publicity. We can see this change in the recent dramatic increase of state control in such areas as the state role in education finance, state requirements for accountability, state programs for children with special needs, and state efforts to increase local academic standards.

This capsule account highlights the point generally accepted by students of education, namely, that local control as a value and operational fact has declined.[14] In this process other values have gained prominence. If concern for equity could not be met by independent LEAs pursuing their separate ways, it was thought that state mandating of equal education programs backed by state resources could do so. Reducing racially based educational inequalities beginning in the mid-1950s, restructuring fiscal relations to reduce resource inequities in the late 1960s, providing more for handicapped children in the mid-1970s, increasing academic standards in the 1980s—all involve state and federal governments dictating the meaning of school equity. Also by 1992 concern over academic standards had heightened interest in more efficient schools. Thus state pursuit of quality and efficiency have once more overridden local choice.

CONSENSUS AND DIVERSITY IN STATE POLICY SYSTEMS

The fifty states are not fifty unique laboratories of schooling policy. Rather, distinct clusters of behavior prevail so that state policy is a matter of limited patterns. Indeed, many areas share a common agreement on policy for schooling. It is this mixture of consensus that characterizes other institutions and policies in American federalism. Both these qualities are evident in the education policy systems of the states.

Policy Values Among the States

We start with Easton's view that the function of the political system is to authoritatively allocate values and resources. Consequently, understanding what values are sought in education policy is a first task in grappling with the diversity of American federalism. The important values here are basic instrumental values, those used to pursue an even more fundamental political value. These instrumental values are four—quality, efficiency, equity, and choice—according to a recent analysis of values in education policy in six states by Marshall, Mitchell, and Wirt.[15] (Quality and equity are often also called excellence and equality.) Their explanation sets the background for understanding how policymakers use public resources to realize values. We use these value definitions here, set out briefly in Table 9.2.

These values are not pursued randomly in policymaking within any state; rather, they follow a natural, logical sequence as policy elites try to meet educational challenges. Quality is the first value sought in any era of education policy when the political will arises to improve an educational service for a constituency (student, staff, administrator, etc.). Horace Mann's initial drive for free public education is a classic example, as is raising course requirements for graduation in the 1980s. But to implement these policies it is necessary to devise other policies that are rooted in the value of efficiency, by using resources effectively measured in economic or control terms.

Next in the policy sequence, equity goals arise when experience shows that a gap has developed between desired standards

Table 9.2
Definitions of Basic Policy Values and School Policy Linkages

CHOICE
Legislated options for local constituencies in making decisions.
    Example: Choice of textbooks.
Instrumental to realize basic democratic value of popular sovereignty, that is citizens' legitimate authority over officials' policy actions.

EFFICIENCY
Either:
    Economic mode, minimizing costs while maximizing gains.
    Example: pupil-teacher ratio.
Or:
    Accountability mode, means by which superiors oversee and hence control subordinates' use of power.
    Example: Publicizing stages of budgetary process.
Instrumental to basic organizational value, namely, responsibility of power-wielders to those who authorize it.

EQUITY
Equalizing or redistributing public resources to meet morally and societally defined human needs.
    Example: Compensatory or handicapped education.
Instrumental to basic liberal value, namely, the worth of every individual and society's responsibility to realize that worth.

QUALITY
Use of public resources to match professionally determined standards of excellence proficiency, or ability.
    Example: Certification of teachers.
Instrumental to the basic social value that education is crucial for the future citizen's life chances.

Source: Abstracted from Catherine Marshall, Douglas Mitchell, and Frederick Wirt, *Culture and Education Policy in the American States* (New York: Falmer, 1989), Chap. 4.

and actual conditions for specific groups. This gap generates calls for using additional resources to bring the group up to standards. Finally, one policy value operates at all stages of the process—choice. A democratic nation provides many opportunities for citizens to select options, and the policy area of education is no exception. Citizens may choose quality standards, efficient means of implementation, or gap-closing equity measures. The prevalence of the elected school board is a familiar and pervasive example of this choice value, as are financial referenda and—less evident—local curricular biases and parental advisory councils.

This brief exposition highlights two points often skimped in understanding policymaking. First, policymakers pursue some fundamental political value through selecting other, more instrumental values, as Table 9.2 indicates. Moreover, such instrumental values can be defined in ways that permit scholars a view of their presence and effect. Consequently values are not fragile clouds floating over the policy scene, barely connected to what goes on below. Rather, they are clearly understood (although not always articulated) motivators of citizen and policymaker alike, who seek public resources in policy for the purpose of enhancing their fundamental values.

Policy Preferences Among the States

Some of these qualities are evident among state education policymakers in government and interest groups in a six-state study in the mid-1980s.[16] What were the common and diverse policy elements of such state policy elites?

First, despite differences among the states, much consensus existed about the relative importance of seven basic *domains*, or broad areas of education policy. Finance policy was everywhere seen as most important; then, personnel, student testing, and school program policies followed in importance; the governance and curriculum materials policies were ranked next; and finally, buildings and facilities policies were of least interest. These priorities cascaded in parallel fashion among the states, with minor variations. Second, in the 1980s state policymakers were pushing for greater state action in all domains but especially in personnel, finance, governance, and buildings. Third, much agreement also prevailed about specific *programs* within each policy domain in all but governance, as listed in Table 9.3. Policy elites reported that these programs were receiving the most attention by their legislatures compared to other alternatives. But beyond such commonalities, considerable variation still existed among them in both policy domain and program, especially governance, finance, and testing.

Table 9.3

*High Agreement on Education Policy Programs Among
Policy Elites of Six States, 1982–83*

Domain	Specific Programs
Finance	Equalization
	Establishing overall funding level
Personnel	Preservice certification and training
Student testing	Specifying format or content of required tests
School program	Setting higher standards for graduation
Curricular materials	Specifying scope and sequence of instruction
Buildings and facilities	Remediation of identified architectural problems
Governance	None

Source. Abstracted from Catherine Marshall, Douglas Mitchell, and Frederick Wirt, *Culture and Education Policy in the American States* (New York: Falmer, 1989), Chap. 5.

This snapshot of state policy structure in the mid-1980s may alter over time. The 1960s and 1970s had exhibited a greater policy emphasis among all fifty states on the value of equity, namely, redistributing public resources to close the gap between standards and achievement for the poor and ethnic minorities. In the 1980s, though, as inflation and the Reagan administration's withdrawal from equity programs combined to drive the states to seek greater resources, more policy emphasis shifted from equity to efficiency and quality as end values in education.[17] The emphasis shifted to constraining educational goals and to improving the services provided. In the future, though, with a different economy and political leadership, a restructuring of these value priorities is certain.

In any period, however, a state's policy structure will result from both national and state influences, one example of the confluence of central and peripheral influences within any modern nation. In short, a current of ideas about policy preferences will swirl through America from time to time, generated by new political movements, emerging perceived needs, or changes in the economy. Illustrative of such national reforms in education policy have been the concern for educating the poor after 1965, the crunch on school funding stimulated by the energy crisis after 1973, the Reagan administration's devolution, and the states' curriculum and testing reforms after 1990.

A second component of a state's policy structure stems from influences special to that state, that is, peripheral preferences. We already noted how past events had produced a political cultural outlook on the issue of state versus local control of schooling. This peripheral influence can affect specific education policies as well. It takes only a little knowledge of American education to realize that citizens in California and Mississippi provide different resources, view their leaders' role differently, and expect different qualities of education. Does this cultural explanation affect what state policymakers see and do in their respective worlds?

Political Culture and State Policy Choices

These differing peripheral influences will reflect *political culture*, that is, "the set of acts, beliefs, and sentiments which give order and meaning to a political process and which provide the underlying assumptions and rules that govern behavior in the political system. It encompasses both the political issues and the operating norms...."[18] These "acts, beliefs ... assumptions and rules" are not infinite in number among the fifty states, rather they group into clusters. Daniel Elazar has developed three distinctive state political cultures with consequent differences in state political behavior.[19]

1. *Traditionalistic culture (TPC)*: Government's main function is maintaining traditional patterns, being responsive to a governing elite, with partisanship subordinated to personal ties.
2. *Individualistic culture (IPC)*: Government is a marketplace that responds to demands, favors economic development, and relies on the political party as the vehicle for satisfying individual needs.
3. *Moralistic culture (MPC)*: Government is the means for achieving the good community or commonwealth through positive government action, social and economic regulations are legitimate, parties are downplayed, and bureaucracy is viewed positively as an agent of the people.

Figure 9.2
State Centroids of Political Culture on Two Functions

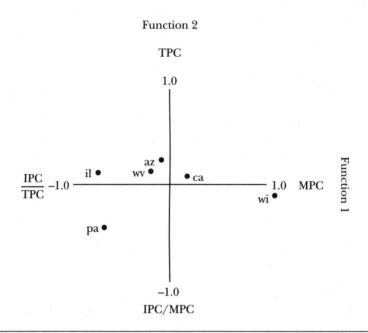

Source: Abstracted from Catherine Marshall, Douglas Mitchell, and Frederick Wirt, *Culture and Education Policy in the American States* (New York: Falmer, 1989), p. 117.

Recent analysis shows that state education policymakers believe that the citizens of their own states possess distinctive "beliefs and sentiments" about the political system.[20] Thus views about government's role, political parties, elections, bureaucracy, and policies—even corporal punishment for students—in one state will cluster out from those held in another state; this occurs in ways that fit the historically based (but still relevant today) designation of the three cultures by Elazar.[21] Figure 9.2 reveals the education policy elites' perceptions in six states of their citizens' political views. Their answers clustered in such a way that Wisconsin anchors one end of the moralistic-individualistic continuum, with Illinois the other end. California and Pennsylvania also fall on the continuum in the direction that their cultural origins would place them. While this dimension accounted for most of the variation in answers (81 percent), another dimension (the vertical axis in Figure 9.2) helped distinguish the traditionalistic culture of Arizona and West Virginia that opposed the other cultural dimension. In short, policy elites perceived their constituents' political culture in the same way that historical evidence had suggested.

But what difference in education policy do these cultural differences make? Because democratic leaders reflect citizen values—no matter how roughly—these elite perceptions of constituencies should be linked to distinctive education policies. The policy domains and programs actually did fit the cultural perceptions of these elites among six states. A statistical analysis of thirty-three program types within the seven policy domains (see Table 9.3) found that predictions were met in twenty-four programs for all three cultures, and another five programs matched the most polar cultures (moralistic versus individualistic); ultimately only four programs failed to fit cultural clusters. Some of the even broader policy domains—defining school programs and preparing curricular materials—demonstrated high, even significant, correlations. Such findings strengthen the belief that political cultures work even amid multiple, detailed program choices characteristic of the American states.

None of this analysis tells us what the best programs are though; that was not its purpose. But we now know that the policies that states use result from both national currents of reform as well as from local historical influences. The latter reflect variations in how policymakers and their constituents think of the political system and want the system to act. History thus shapes contemporary policy actions through socialization to "beliefs and sentiments" that differ among the states and regions, and thus with Whitman, "a nation of nations."

STAGES OF POLICYMAKING AND EDUCATION

Studies of all policymaking employ a chronological sequence of this process, sketched in Chapter 1, even though stages regularly mesh into others. But analytically, we can use this sequence to understand its politics.

Agenda Setting and State Policy

The early phases of public policy are directed toward stimulating government to consider a problem. It is difficult, though, to isolate the subparts or stages of the agenda-setting process as identifiable, onetime, discrete events.[22] We define agenda setting as active, serious consideration of a concrete and specific issue by state policymakers.

To be "on the agenda," an issue must pass through four stages: (1) issue recognition, where legislators notice an issue and believe it to be a topic for potential action; (2) issue adoption, when legislators acknowledge the legitimacy of government responsibility and the possibility that an appropriate response could be found; (3) issue prioritizing so that the existing agenda is reordered to include the new issue; and (4) issue maintenance so that the new issue remains on the agenda after initial consideration.

The agenda spread of numerous standards and state educational reforms during the 1990s was not caused by the traditional role of education interest groups. Consequently, we will explore a variety of other causes.

Influences on the Early Phases of Public Policymaking

Movements and the Media. Public opinion and the news media are often seen as playing important roles in political agenda setting. New ideas can gain ground rapidly if initial events and important influences "surface in the mainstream" and so become issues of public debate or conflict.[23] Social movements and groundswells of public opinion create a broader context within government for decision making; they also allow for greater discretion in the creation and design of new programs.

There is the impact of media and public opinion on traditional special interests or "factions" in agenda setting.[24] The notions of pluralism or elite pluralism do not adequately explain broad social movements such as environmentalism and women's rights. In the cases of large-scale political or social movements, coalitions form with established interest groups and elements of political parties. Elected officials are then quick to follow the trend and so create the bandwagon phenomenon. From this initial coalition, "generations of lobbies" grow in response to the social movements. Television news, in particular, hastens their development or demise.

The news media directly influence members of state legislatures. At one time, party discipline, legislative apprenticeship, and deference to seniority were the most important factors in determining a legislative member's role in political agenda setting. Now the passage of legislation is more and more dependent on "symbolic politics." State policymakers rely heavily on printed and electronic sources "to gain insight into relevant social science findings."[25]

State Political Environment. A second strand of agenda-setting concepts emphasizes policy environment. Of particular value to agenda-setting is the finding that many social and economic factors create a political milieu that seems to affect a state's receptivity to new ideas. One scholar finds that "innovative states are both wealthier and more competitive between political parties than their sister states at the time of adoption of a particular law."[26] The notion is that wealthier states will create more innovative policy agendas, because they have high income, urbanization, industrialization, and education. However, these variables clearly differ in their significance depending on the policy issues being decided.[27] Linkages exist between interest groups and state socioeconomic complexity; for example, states with a few strong interest groups do not have complex economies. These major interest groups (e.g., timber in Oregon) have a very influential role in determining a state's agenda.[28]

In education a six-state study of influence found from a ranking of elites that teachers and other educators were ranked fourth behind formal state agencies–even ahead of governors (in the mid-1980s). But traditionalistic cultures placed these groups much lower in influence.[29]

Intragovernment Factions. Factions within state government can determine the policy agenda, including the "professional-bureaucratic complex" and the "intergovernmental lobby" that form the centers of influence in policymaking. The professional-bureaucratic complex is a "core of officials with scientific training working in close cooperation with legislators and interest groups."[30] The formal organizational structures of bureaucracies allow members to communicate with relative ease and promote the influential role of state bureaucrats as "policy shapers." The "career bureaucrats often 'know best'—in a technical sense how to deal with problems . . . or even to determine whether a particular situation requires a state response."[31]

Policy Issue Networks. Hugh Heclo defines the key concept in our agenda-setting analysis—a policy issue network—at the federal level and distinguishes it from the "iron triangle":

> Issue networks . . . comprise a large number of participants with quite variable degrees of mutual commitment or of dependence on others in their environment; in fact it is almost impossible to say where a network leaves off and its environment begins. Iron triangles and sub-governments suggest a stable set of participants coalesced to control fairly narrow programs which are in the direct economic interest of each part to the alliance. Issue networks are almost the reverse image in each respect. Participants move in and out of the networks constantly. Rather than groups united in dominance over a program, no one, as far as one can tell, is in control of the policies and issues. Any direct or material interest is often secondary to intellectual or emotional commitment. Network members reinforce each other's sense of issues as their interests, rather than (as standard political or economic models would have it) interests defining positions on issues.[32]

A policy issue network differs from a political movement in that movements exhibit great uncertainty about who authentically speaks for those that identify themselves with the cause. Political movements typically create considerable competition among several would-be spokespersons.

A policy network is part of the large policy system and is made up of both those from the larger community outside government and those within it with official decision-making power. Policy networks have vertical—cutting through various layers of government—and horizontal components, tapping into the traditional iron triangle but also extending outside government. The definition we employ views policy issue networks as linked to specific issues rather than attached to general policy areas (e.g., the environment) or to broad interests like teachers. The policy goals of an issue network are more specific than a political movement.

State issue networks are led by policy brokers who play a critical role in translating technical and academic data into "plain English" for other bureaucrats and politicians. The heroes of these subcultures are "policy politicians—experts in using experts, victuallers of knowledge in a world hungry for the right decisions."[33]

Our study of policy issue networks in education points to these conclusions:

1. Policy issue networks are an unnoted concept for understanding the early phases of state policymaking. These networks may be characterized along such internal organization dimensions as membership, central guidance and promotion, conceptual agreement, and information flow. Variability in these dimensions can generate differences in state agenda-setting processes.

2. Networks may also be characterized by the kind of policy solution they advocate. Along this policy dimension, networks vary from a complete, inflexible statute (e.g., scientific creationism) to similarly motivated but highly variable programs and legislation (e.g., minimum competency testing).

3. The content or subject matter of a policy issue network, and the grounds on which the arguments are advanced, may add to how the networks develop, the kinds of policy solutions they advocate, and their designation into distinct types. Ranging from arguments primarily based on philosophy (e.g., creation science) to legal constitutionally based arguments (e.g., school finance) to conventional political bargaining arguments (e.g., collective bargaining for teachers), the network message will help determine variation in the operation and success of policy issue networks. Moreover, centrally driven networks create similar state statutes, as seen in the difference between centrally led collective bargaining and minimum competency testing.

4. Interstate policy issue networks can frequently override political and socioeconomic constraints for state agenda setting. On the whole, network effectiveness—rather than fiscal

capacity, legislative capacity, or state policy centralization—
accounts for certain issues on a state policy agenda. Moreover,
policy issue networks can override the agenda influence of
state-level iron triangles and force them to respond to externally driven issues. Issue networks are not the only means
of agenda setting, but they have been overlooked. In some
states (e.g., Texas), though, the political culture is so hos-
tile to most network issues that they never reach the state
legislative agenda. In the Texas case, this failure occurred
despite persistent network efforts in collective bargaining.

Further research on issue networks within the American states
is needed to test the dimensions, classifications, and assertions
that have emerged from existing cases and to gain an understanding of how issue networks influence state policymaking and
agenda setting. The very rapid diffusion of some agenda items
continues in state education policy. Now that we have analyzed
the broader concepts of state education policy, it is appropriate
to examine next the institutions and actors as they make policy.[34]

NOTES

1. Susan Fuhrman, "Increased State Capacity and Aid to the Disadvantaged" (paper prepared for the U.S. Department of Education, November 1986),
p. 3.
2. U.S. General Accounting Office, *Federal Share of State Education Expenditures* (Washington, D.C.: GAO, 1995).
3. Jerome Murphy, *State Education Agencies and Discretionary Funds* (Lexington,
Mass.: Lexington Books, 1974).
4. An excellent review of this regional variety and its political consequences
is found in Daniel Elazar, *American Federalism: A View from the States* (New York:
Crowell, 1984). For a different view see David C. Nice, *Policy Innovation in
State Government* (Ames: Iowa State University, 1994).
5. George Collins, "Constitutional and Legal Basis for State Action," in
Education in the States: Nationwide Development since 1900, Edgar Fuller and Jim
Pearson, eds. (Wash., D.C.: National Education Association, 1969), pp. 29–30.
6. For a review of five interpretations, see David Tyack, "Ways of Seeing:
An Essay on the History of Compulsory Schooling," *Harvard Educational
Review* 46 (1976): 355–89. Also useful is Michael S. Katz, *A History of Compulsory Education Laws* (Bloomington, Ind.: Phi Delta Kappa Educational Founda-
tion, 1976).

7. Tim Mazzoni, "State Policymaking and School Reform," in *The Study of Educational Politics*, Jay B. Scribner and Donald H. Layton, eds. (London: Falmer, 1995), pp. 53–74.

8. Ellis Katz, *Education Policymaking 1977–1978: A Snapshot from the States* (Washington: Institute for Educational Leadership, 1978).

9. The definitive review of these events, policies, and results is Walter Garms, James Guthrie, and Lawrence Pierce, *School Finance: The Economics and Politics of Federalism* (Englewood Cliffs, N.J.: Prentice-Hall, 1988). For a valuable introduction to current issues, see James Guthrie, ed., *School Finance in the 1980's* (Cambridge, Mass.: Ballinger, 1980).

10. A useful set of essays on many of these developments since 1900 is found in Fuller and Pearson, *Education in the States*. A catalogue of state education requirements for each of the fifty states is found in National Institute of Education, Department of Health, Education and Welfare, *State Legal Standards for the Provision of Public Education* (Washington, D.C.: National Institute of Education, 1978).

11. Margaret Goertz, *State Educational Standards* (Princeton: Educational Testing Service, 1986).

12. Frederick M. Wirt, "State Policy Culture and State Decentralization," in *Politics of Education*, Jay Scribner, ed. (Chicago: Yearbook of the National Society for the Study of Education, 1977), pp. 164–87. A brief statement is in Frederick M. Wirt, "What State Laws Say about Local Control," *Phi Delta Kappan* 59 (1978): 517–20.

13. See Michael Kirst, "The State Role in Regulation of Local School Districts," in *Government in the Classroom*, Mary Williams, ed. (New York: Academy of Political Science, Columbia University, 1979), pp. 45–56.

14. Ibid., p. 11. See William Chance, *The Best of Education* (Chicago: McArthur Foundation, 1987).

15. Catherine Marshall, Douglas Mitchell, and Frederick Wirt, *Culture and Education Policy in the American States* (London: Falmer, 1989).

16. Douglas Mitchell et al., "Building a Taxonomy of State Education Policies," *Peabody Journal of Education* 62, no. 4 (1985): 7–47.

17. David Clark and Terry Astuto, *The Significance and Permanence of Changes in Federal Educational Policy 1980–1988* (Bloomington, Ind.: Policy Studies Center of the University Council for Educational Administration, University of Indiana, 1988).

18. Lucius Pye, "Political Culture," in *International Encyclopedia of the Social Sciences*, Vol. 12 (New York: Crowell, Collier and Macmillan, 1968), p. 218.

19. Daniel Elazar, *American Federalism*.

20. Marshall et al., *Culture and Education Policy*, Chap. 5.

21. For a review of that literature, see Frederick M. Wirt, "'Soft' Concepts and 'Hard' Data: A Research Review of Elazar's Political Culture," *Publius: The Journal of Federalism* 213 (1991): 1–14. One article in this symposium shows culture affects even student discipline; Sue Vandenbosch, "Political Culture and Corporal Punishment in Public Schools," pp. 117–22.

22. Charles O. Jones, *An Introduction to the Study of Public Policy* (Monterey, Calif.: Brooks, 1984).

23. Donald A. Schon, *Beyond the Stable State* (New York: Random House, 1971).

24. Andrew S. McFarland, "Recent Social Movements and Theories of Power in America" (mimeo., 1979). See also James Kingdon, *Agendas, Alternatives, and Public Policies* 2nd ed. (New York: Harper Collins, 1995).

25. Douglas E. Mitchell, "State Legislatures and the Social Sciences" (Stanford, Calif.: Institute for Finance and Governance, Report 81–A10, September 1981).

26. Virginia Gray, "Competition, Emulation, and Policy Innovation," in Lang C. Dodd and C. Jillson (eds.), *New Perspectives on American Politics* (Washington, D.C.: Congressional Quarterly Press, 1994). See also Mazzoni, "State Policymaking."

27. Mitchell, "State Legislatures" p. 29.

28. Harmon Ziegler, "Interest Groups in the States," in *Politics in the American State*, edited by Virginia Gray et al. (Boston: Little, Brown & Co., 1983).

29. Marshall et al., *Culture and Education Policy*, p. 23.

30. Samuel H. Beer, "Political Overload and Federalism," *Polity* 10 (Fall 1977): 12.

31. Richard Elling, "State Bureaucracies," in Gray et al., *Politics*.

32. Hugh Heclo, "Issue Networks and the Executive Establishment," in *The New American Political System*, edited by Anthony King (Washington, D.C.: American Enterprise Institute, 1978), pp. 98–99.

33. Ibid., p. 96. For a different perspective see Frances Berry and William Berry, "State Lottery Adoptions as Policy Innovations," *American Political Science Review* 84 (June 1990): 395–415.

34. See D. Rochefort and R. Cobb, *The Politics of Problem Definition* (Kansas: University of Kansas, 1995). For an overview of network analysis see David Knoke, *Political Networks: The Standard Perspective* (Cambridge, England: Cambridge University Press, 1990).

10 _____

The State Political Process

Policymaking engages representatives of formal government agencies, special interests mobilized as groups, and the public in general. The process is mainly centered around routine decisions, the incremental changes in the vast body of past policy decisions already in existence. But this flow of incremental action is disrupted every so often by the sudden call for innovative policy change, involving new uses of public resources to achieve old educational values of quality, efficiency, equity, and choice. The last quarter-century has known much more innovation on all levels of government, arising from the political turbulence and challenge discussed throughout this book.

Amid such change, how have the state policymakers acted? Is it a case of fifty sets of policymakers doing fifty different things? We find that the process is more patterned because some commonalities are evident in each state. For example, the same set of official actors operate in each state; they have similar influence on policymaking; and all these actors must deal with limited assumptions about policy ventures as they do their job. We turn to review the influence of these actors and their outlook on the policy process for education.

PATTERNS OF INFLUENCE AMONG POLICY ACTORS

A recent six-state study found that educational policy elites
ranked one another's influence with surprising consistency.[1] In
Table 10.1 we see the composite ranking for eighteen types of
policy influentials; the result is a picture of concentric circles of
influence.

The Insiders have constitutional authority in making laws; these
are the powerful legislators or the legislature as a whole. This
finding confirms other research on the central influence of legislators in state policymaking, but imposing term limits may lessen
future legislative influence in some states. Next in influence are
the Near Circle, school professionals (especially teachers) and
specialists in the executive branch (especially the chief state school
officer or CSSO). Next are outer circles more removed from
pervasive influence. The Far Circle is influential but not vital to
policymaking; among these, the state board is most prominent.
Yet other actors have little if any influence. For example, Sometime Players are the pressure groups for local boards and administrators who are sometimes heard on special issues. The
Forgotten Players, like courts, may affect only one state; an example is the powerful impact that West Virginia's supreme court
had in altering local school financing in the state. But in the
policy worlds surveyed here, many of this last cluster did not
even come into view.

The ranking of each type of policy elite varies among the states.
A state board can have no influence if it does not exist (Wisconsin), and the usually high influence of the CSSO was low in Illinois—just before he was replaced. In Arizona the often low-ranking
state board and local board associations rated well; the governor, well-regarded elsewhere for policy influence on education,
was rated poorly here when he had to work with a legislature
controlled by the other party. Illinois and West Virginia had many
differences from the six-state average ranking, although California matched the average ratings quite closely.

Most important in this analysis is the rough agreement among
state policy actors on the crucial importance of the legislative
branch. This finding means that informal influence matches
constitutional authority, a condition that adds to the legitimacy

Table 10.1
Ranking of Policy Influentials: All Six States

Cluster	Six-State Rank	Policy Group
Insiders	1	Individual members of the legislature
	2	Legislators as a whole
	3	Chief state school officer
	4	All education interest groups combined
Near Circle	5	Teacher organizations
	6	Governor and executive staff
	7	Legislators staff
Far Circle	8	State Board of Education*
	9	Others**
Sometime Players	10	School Boards Association
	11	State Administrator Association
	12	Courts
	13	Federal policy mandates
Other Forgotten Players	14	Noneducator interest groups
	15	Lay groups
	16	Education researcher organizations
	17	Referenda
	18	Producers of educational materials

* Based on Arizona, Illinois, West Virginia, and California. Wisconsin has no state board of education.
** "Others" includes, for example, Illinois' School Problems Commission and West Virginia's School Service Personnel Association.

Source: Catherine Marshall, Douglas Mitchell, and Frederick Wirt, *Culture and Education Policy in the American State* (Falmer, 1989), p. 23.

of the policy process. While regularity and differences showed among the rankings, "the regularity speaks to the impact of institutionalizing democratic practices across the nation. The differences speak to the distinctive impact on policy services and decisional systems made by state political cultures and the culture of each state capitol."[2]

RULES OF THE GAME OF POLICYMAKING

Remarkable uniformity prevails in the lawmaking procedure of the fifty states because they are rooted in the British and colonial traditions. But just how that uniform procedure is perceived and conducted depends very much on the different perceptual screens that different actors bring to lawmaking. In the words of Marshall and associates, "These perceptions related to the expected behaviors, rituals, and judgments about feasible policy options. This perceptual screen we term the assumptive worlds of policymakers."[3] No printed manual of these perceptions exists in each state. Rather, these "assumptive" worlds emerge from the words and stories of policymakers when they informally discuss the persons and processes of their world.

This instructive use of qualitative data to build a grounded theory suggests that hidden within the operations of policymakers is a set of questions about their work to which they give answers in experience. How questions are answered often varies, but the basic questions remain the same:

1. Who must, and who has the right to, *initiate policy action?* Experience reveals that actors' answers focus especially on the roles of the legislature (as noted above) and others in the policy elite. In each state the elite easily reveal who has this authority in their anecdotes and responses to influence scales.

2. What are the *unacceptable policy initiatives?* Again, experience shows that they are ideas that trample on group, regional, or big-city interests; lead to refusal of agencies or citizens to obey; clash with existing practices; challenge dominant economic interests; or promote unorthodox values. Even limited inquiry among the elite will provide agreed-on accounts of what policy ideas won't fly.

3. What are the *appropriate policy actions?* Experience again points to such rules as: to get along, go along; carry out informal rituals that will recognize and define the boundaries of power; mobilize everyone who can benefit from a proposed policy; don't let friendship block policy action; utilize policy issue networks within and across the states; and so on.[4]

As a concept, then, assumptive worlds are derived from answers to fundamental questions arising everywhere in policymaking; of course, a particular state culture will contribute a distinctive cast to these answers rooted in its own history. Moreover, these culturally shaped answers are imposed on new actors entering the state's educational policy world, a classic form of political socialization.

These general propositions are illuminated by the assumptions surrounding higher education policy in two states, West Virginia and California. The former has treated this policy passively; indeed, in mid-1987 some of its state colleges had to close early due to reduced state funding. California, on the other hand, prepares this policy the way that other nations go to war—with full resources, vigor, leadership, and high expectations. Consequently, the two sets of policymakers treat the issue differently because their states' assumptions about important policy ideas vary.

Behind these assumptive worlds lie attributes of political culture discussed in the previous chapter. West Virginia's elite-based and traditionalistic culture has consistently constrained the expansion of education, until its own supreme court compelled otherwise. California's open society and moralistic culture has spurred an expansion of school resources in the search for the best education. In either state, though, such attitudes about the acceptable policy ideas have a dual effect; they keep the policy environment predictable, and they help policymakers build group cohesion that can produce policy outputs.

Such aspects of influence and assumptions attending the making of education policy reveal patterns for understanding it, despite the profusion and ambiguity of fifty state arenas. Broad expectations are widespread about which people have policy authority and how they should act amid policy conflict. State variations in these expectations do exist, though, due to varying histories and emphases in education values. Yet the common patterns among states do provide clarity, not confusion, to the policy system of American federalism. And it is the patterns that enable the testing of theory building in social science to thrive.

STATE-LEVEL INTEREST GROUPS

Among the many factors that could influence a state's policy system, major ones are variations in party competition, party cohesion in the legislature, and the socioeconomic context.[5] Scholars have found two basic mixes of these factors among the American states. One pattern consists of strong lobbies, weak legislative parties, and a population that is low on urbanism, income, and industrialism. In the second pattern, lobbies are weak to moderate in influence, parties are competitive, and the economy is urban and industrial.[6]

Patterns of Interest Groups

What emerges from these two concepts is not one pressure pattern among the states but four. The first is an *alliance of dominant groups,* much like the strong-lobby syndrome noted above; the Southern states are a good example of this. Second, a *single dominant interest* pattern emerges in states with undiversified economies, two-party competition, and some legislative cohesion; the roles of a copper corporation in Montana or oil companies in Texas are examples.

Third, a pattern of *conflict between two dominant groups* is visible where a diversified economic base generates differences that the two-party system expresses, for example, auto manufacturers versus auto trade unions in Michigan. Fourth, a *triumph of many interests* appears where lobbies can freely interact in a legislature unbounded by party control; thus in California, a highly diversified economy generates multiple interest and shifting legislative coalitions.[7] Clearly, lobbying overrepresents the business and professional strata of society; about three in five registered state lobbyists act for corporations or trade groups.

The chief lobby for education, though, has been the professional, particularly teachers. Chapter 4 sketched this lobby's evolution in the National Education Association (NEA) as an umbrella organization for teachers, principals, superintendents, school board members, and others.[8] We also noted that, beginning in the 1950s, events led to a more militant teacher movement, climaxing in successful collective bargaining drives in most states. This focus on the interest of only one of its constituents—teachers—weakened the cohesion of the NEA, which then took a more aggressive stance similar to its challenger, the American Federation of Teachers. As competition for shrinking financial resources grew

in the 1970s, the unitary myth, which once bound different kinds
of professionals, had dispersed. No longer did teacher and administrator believe that they shared a unity in the goal of educating the young.

Changes in Lobby Types

What best describes the lobby type that exists in the fifty states?
In research up to the mid-1960s, Iannaccone found that the
statewide monolith was most prevalent. But one study a decade
later of twelve states reported a major shift to the statewide fragmented type in nine of these states.[9] These were the more Northern
industrialized systems, which shared a common history of a col-
lapse of the old NEA umbrella that once had protected the
statewide monolith. Coalitions of schoolpeople had formerly written
education law in their private councils and then issued an agreed
proposal to the legislature, which accepted it because education
was hard to be against and would reap the legislators little reward to oppose it. But in a few decades this pattern had been
broken by growing conflicts of interest in education and by the
increased interest and capacity of legislatures and governors to
initiate their own policies.

What the twelve-state study also revealed was a system more
complex than even Iannaccone's typology suggested. Added complexity came from those centrifugal forces that were making the
school legislatures' policy systems everywhere more pluralistic and
open. Indeed, the nature of the policy process seemed to vary
with the issue in focus. This openness was a major shift from
earlier decades when professionals kept policymaking a closed
shop.[10]

When school lobbies sought success in the legislature, what
were their resources and strategies? They possessed numbers and
money (teachers) and high status (administrators and school
boards). They transformed these resources into power by different means. All used professional staffs, but teachers relied more
on their campaign money and votes, while administrators and
school boards relied more on their information resources and
local legislator contacts. Unlike the other two, teachers were much
more likely to campaign, transforming their prime resource of

size directly into votes. This electoral activity marks a sharp break
with teachers' traditional apolitical stance.

As a result of such uses of power, school lobbies were seen by
their own leaders and legislators as among the most powerful
pressure groups in the state. Legislators gave highest marks to
the teacher associations, while administrators received the worst.
They found: teacher associations generally the more effective of
the school lobbies and administrators the more efficient (obtaining
the most for their fewer numbers and less money); the smaller
teacher federations inconsistent; labor-management relations the
dominant issue of such politics; and former school coalitions
increasingly crippled by splits over the issue. So long as schooling
issues were regarded as "educational," school boards and administrators were more influential because they could rely on their
higher status to be heard. But when teacher groups changed the
criteria for deciding issues from the professional to the "political," the teachers benefited from their greater numbers and money.
But as criticism of student learning grew, teachers' status under-
went decline in popular opinion. It declined also in ranking among
state elites in the late 1980s, as the six-state study seen earlier in
Table 10.1 shows.

Specific State Educational Interest Groups

An alternative tool for differentiating among state-level lobbies is to divide them into "general focus" and "special focus"
groups. [11] The former—typified by teacher, administrator, and
school board organizations—are broad based and must, therefore, represent the full spectrum of educational interests. Given
their size and resources, they are often assumed "to have more
political clout than they actually have." Their resources are scat-
tered over a wide range of issues at the federal, state, and local
levels. Despite formal procedures and often sophisticated state
leadership, power is essentially decentralized. They are "characterized by a strong 'bottom-up' flow of power wherein there is a
continuous and taxing necessity of building coalitions among
significantly autonomous locals." This is especially true of the
management associations, whose independent-minded membership is reluctant to cede authority to state executives. Consistent

with Olson's interest group theory of collective action discussed in Chapter 4, the costs of organizing large-member groups are high, while group cohesion around specific policy goals is low.

In contrast, the small-member group with a single "special focus" finds it easier to reach optimal effectiveness and out-maneuver the larger associations. Special focus groups fall into two kinds. One is functional, such as those representing special education, and the other is geographic, such as the big-city school district. Because of their narrow interests and concentrated power bases, these organizations are becoming increasingly influential in state politics.

The functional type generally pays attention to the source of its special funding, often the federal level and then the state administrative unit that dispenses those funds. A typical arrangement involves only a few governmental officials, as most state policy actors never enter the narrow realm of the special interest. For example, in Michigan the directors of the respective special and compensatory education units within the state department were reported to be among the most powerful individuals in state educational politics. They are able to mobilize the highly motivated and frequently volatile constituents and practitioners who support the causes of handicapped and compensatory education.[12]

The highly effective, geographically based, special interests are even better embodiments of the institutional interest group. Here school districts in a given locale form natural alliances with other local and state government agencies, and they employ other groups to augment their gains in the allocation process. Their greatest resource is their direct link to legislative delegations, which in the case of a large city, such as New York, Chicago, or Los Angeles, can have enormous influence. In a reaction against teacher influence and response to reformers, Illinois in 1988 legislated for Chicago over five hundred school-based management systems with an elected parent presence on the council of each. With these descriptive concepts in mind, we can now delineate individual groups, beginning with the broadly based interests.

The State Teachers Association.   Teachers affiliated with the NEA remain a strong, if not the strongest, group in most states (see Table 10.1). Although weakened by the growth of the rival

AFT and the expulsion of school administrators, local associations possess a powerful resource advantage over other groups. Due to sheer numbers, the money from dues used for political action, and sophisticated staffing, they remain, according to one analysis, "giants by comparison."[13]

This glowing assessment of the associations' influence must be tempered by the fact that we cannot measure power by a simple aggregation of membership, money, and information. Internal cohesion is crucial to effective mobilization of those resources. For example, the Michigan Education Association (MEA), although much larger than many others, is so internally divided over local political strategies that it cannot muster much influence at the state level. MEA's power is thus more apparent than real; local rivalry with the AFT has certainly contributed to this ineffectiveness.

The State Teachers Federation.   Although growing rapidly in most urban areas, the AFT affiliates have a tendency to bypass state-level lobbying in favor of local militancy. This underdeveloped and inconsistent state influence does not apply in California, though. There, the federation's strong labor stances in the 1970s pushed rival NEA locals into more militant postures; the latter no longer characterizes itself as a purely professional association. Between 1965 and the late 1990s the proportion of teachers in the AFT versus the NEA remained stable. NEA controls teachers in 87 percent of the LEAs with over 1,000 students; the AFT controls 13 percent.

Classified School Employees Associations.   The nonprofessionals who work in schools are usually ignored by commentators on state educational interest groups. Classified employees include custodians, secretaries, and food service personnel. That neglect stems from their relatively recent emergence in state politics and their lack of a substantive focus. They are labor unions whose sole objective is the protection of their membership's financial interests. Until the recent increase in state authority, these people have been able to rely on local collective bargaining strength. Their sheer numbers and financial resources give them considerable potential clout at the state level; thus they became a factor in school finance policymaking.

The State School Boards Association.   Members of the State School Boards Association find themselves pitted against the teachers in an effort to hold the lid on salaries. Increasingly, local school boards—confronted with the politically, economically, and legally complex realities of collective bargaining—rely in varying degrees on the data and expertise that the state association could muster. At the state level, policymakers view school board groups as deserving respect and empathy because they represent locally elected officials who, in turn, unselfishly represent the interest of the public.[14] This status and prima facie credibility are augmented by small but generally efficient lobbying staffs funded by the highest membership dues of all the education groups.

The State School Administrators Association.   School administrators often try to be "a bridge over troubled waters" for school principals, business officials, superintendents, personnel managers, and other administrators. Once firmly entrenched at the peak of most state teachers associations, the administrators became exiled by teacher militancy, and administrator groups find themselves allied with the school board groups in order to provide some semblance of balance vis-à-vis the teachers. Legislators accord administrator groups respect as representatives of educational leadership in their districts. In fact, engaging in face-to-face contact with legislators in their home districts is a prevalent political strategy. This reversion, born of necessity, to tradition generates a locally based, disparate, interest-group politics. But this predilection for going it alone can hamper the group's lobbying efforts. The administrators pay high dues, second only to the school board's, and maintain an effective lobbying staff.

Other Groups.   In addition, there are categorical interests and associations of geographically based groups too numerous to mention that can be powerful players in state educational politics. They have their champions in the legislatures, either individuals with pet interests or constituency links or, in the case of programs for the disadvantaged, the black and Hispanic caucuses. Their bureaucratic home bases have a vested interest in sustaining and adding to the programs, and they often have recourse to the threat of judicial intervention. In short, many special focus groups have clout disproportionate to their numbers.

The PTA.   Associations representing nonprofessional or lay persons interested in education, while locally oriented, have both state and national organizations. The National Congress of Parents and Teachers is not only the largest of these groups but also the largest volunteer organization in the United States. Its strength is felt primarily at the local level where it actively pursues solutions to specific problems at specific schools. At the state level, its influence diminishes due to the heterogeneity of its membership and the lack of any method for maintaining internal discipline.

Labeled "good government groups," the PTA and its allies, the League of Women Voters (LWV) and the American Association of University Women (AAUW), are occasionally granted formal representation on advisory committees and asked to join educational coalitions. They generally restrict themselves to monitoring policy developments and providing lay support for professionals' recommendations. The professionals who gain the most from PTA activism are the administrators. Others tend to regard them as useful friends when they agree but not a very bothersome enemy in the event of conflict. As we saw in Chapter 4, though, many participants obtain psychological rewards from their involvement.

The LWV and AAUW exist to promote much broader social improvements. State branches may have a specialist in education, but they tend not to posit controversial views, preferring to provide general support for public education as an ongoing social good.

Business Groups.   State business groups became major state players after the 1981–83 recession, and have continued their strong support for state academic and assessment standards. State business roundtables use their campaign contributions and access to governors to advocate a nine-point plan for systemic reform that includes professional development and technology. Most big business groups have not supported vouchers, but are favorable toward charter schools and supported Chicago's site-based management system in 1988. This positive role toward education is a shift from the tax limitation focus it had in the 1970s.

Business's impact on education policy varied across the states, with Ross Perot playing a major role in Texas and other big business success in Washington and Minnesota. But business support of teaching mathematical problem solving and new science curricula is opposed by traditional Christians and others who want a more basic curriculum. Business-backed proposals for standards were defeated in the early 1990s in Connecticut and Pennsylvania. Governors and legislators reformulated general proposals backed by business, so business is just one of several influential actors at the state level. The larger businesses have not built coalitions with small business groups like the Chamber of Commerce to construct and implement state systemic reform. Such coalitions would be politically effective at the state level and may develop. State business roundtables have not retreated from their stand favoring statewide academic standards and more complex assessments despite pressure from both left- and right-wing state lobbies. Consequently, state business roundtables are usually allied with education groups such as the AFT and school administrators.

Lobbying Strategies

Whatever their type, groups are more than just structures of interests. They appear most clearly as dynamic parts of the policy process, from the emergence of issues through implementation and evaluation. We can see this dynamic quality in case studies of single-issue conflicts, such as that over creationism in textbooks, but little systematic knowledge emerges from this kind of understanding. We can portray the interaction more fully by focusing on the lobbying strategies that education interest groups use.

Both personal experience and research suggest that lobbying strategies in the states parallel those at the national level. Partisanship is risky in competitive two-party situations except where party identification of interests is a given. Thus management and labor tend to support the Republican and Democratic parties, respectively. Timely campaign contributions sprinkled across party lines, however, are an effective means of obtaining access and occasionally influencing a vote. However, individual lawmakers do not want to become obligated or "owned" over the long haul. In general, campaign contributions are of much lower volume in state politics than at the national level, "although a little money goes a longer way at the state level."[15] Volunteers and endorsements in association newsletters are also popular tactics, especially in large membership labor groups. In heavily unionized states, the labor organizations can take on the entire job of running a campaign. The mass public relations pressure tactic, more prevalent in national politics, is usually too expensive and too complicated for state education interest groups.

Direct contact with state legislators is easier, cheaper, and still more effective. Consequently, most education lobbying strategies are fundamentally low key; they emphasize expertise, professionalism, and honesty. Lobbyists prefer to work within the conventional mode; they are, after all, representatives of the dominant social interests and have a corresponding commitment to maintain the status quo. If the moderate approach fails in a particular instance, contributions of money and election workers to specific legislators may help. Another step often adopted before "all-out-war" is cooperative lobbying and coalition building.

State Coalition Concepts

In large part, politics involves fashioning coalitions of influence in an attempt to determine what values government will authoritatively implement. Different individuals and groups bring various interests and objectives to state educational policy forums. Amid this tangle, an essential quality of a state education leader is to build political coalitions.

The coalition view of state decision making envisions any decision is possible if enough support for it exists among interest groups. In order to secure support, various trade-offs are undertaken. Policy proposals are modified to include (or exclude) items of concern to key potential supporters; agreements are made to trade support on other or future state policies for backing on a current issue; and third parties are encouraged to intervene. In short, coalitions are formed by horse trading until an acceptable policy is reached.

Several theories on coalitions can be validated in state education lobbying.[16] Most coalitions take place within a specific institutional context that will contain rules, constraints, and historical events that will influence the coalition. The growth of coalitions depends on the ability of leaders to attract followers by offering "side payments." These include anything that has value for possible coalition members, including money or promises on policy. Sometimes coalition leaders have a stock of side payments in their hands as working capital when they begin negotiations. As they dispense promises, they use this capital, which presumably will be replenished from the future gains of a winning coalition. More typically, in our judgment, education leaders operate on credit; that is, they promise rewards with the understanding that they will honor their promises only if successful.

Leaders and followers are differentiated according to whether they offer or receive side payments. A leader rarely has enough resources to pay everybody. Also, excess members of a winning coalition cost something to acquire, and they lessen the gains. Thus at some point in the process of making side payments, the leader decides that all has been paid out that is worth winning. But as some factions are still left out, the attempts to form a coalition generate opposition that could result in an opposing coalition.

These kinds of side payments can be illustrated from education lobbying.

1. *The threat of reprisal.* This side payment consists of a promise not to carry out the threat, so the follower simply gains an escape from prospective misfortune. For example, a governor can threaten to campaign against an elected state superintendent of schools.
2. *Payment of objects that can be converted to money.* One example is appointing a major financial backer of a key legislator to a position in the state education department.
3. *Promises on policy.* A leader accepts an amendment to her or his bill that brings the support of the state teachers' association, but modifies the policy thrust of the bill.
4. *Promises about subsequent decisions.* The speaker of the assembly can promise to support an agricultural bill if rural interests will vote for an income tax dedicated to education.
5. *Payments of emotional satisfaction.* Some legislators will follow the educational decisions of a charismatic governor.

These strategies involve lobbyists in subtle considerations, for the possibilities in any single policy conflict are numerous. The ways these considerations can be combined in practice are particularly complex. Such analysis requires making judgments and answering strategic questions.

Is there a winning coalition? Is the goal to be achieved by a winning coalition unique? Is anything (for example, a particular legislative provision) clearly excluded? Would the possibilities (for example, more school finance reform) be changed by expanding the coalition slightly? It follows that in some situations several potentially winning coalitions exist. Consequently, there is a role for leadership in constructing a particular coalition and thereby limiting the policy options and goals. It is this matrix of lobbies that the state legislatures face.

State Legislatures

With exceptions, the following characterizes American state legislatures as they have responded to the increased pressure from many sources to address many state and local problems:[17]

1. Primarily political, not value-free, institutions.
2. Recently subject to more demands.
3. Recently taking on a more professional cast, for example, more and better staff.
4. Better apportioned as a result of Supreme Court actions that resulted in an increased voice for urban and suburban interests, an advantage to Democrats, and more responsiveness to new needs.
5. Often recruited to office by political parties, but the turnover rate high and the influence of the party on legislative votes varying widely with state tradition.
6. Electoral competition for seats limited.
7. The general public evaluating them negatively (mostly for wasting time), but they are very responsive ("congruent") to public wishes on controversial issues.
8. Some policies are innovative (usually controversial), but many are incremental (for example, budgets), but, as noted earlier, reforms are adopted in different degrees.
9. Subject to influence from external and internal sources (committees, caucuses, governors, lobbies, experts, and so

on), but the influence of the legislators is still prime.

10. Pressure groups everywhere influential, but one group's influence varies from state to state (most often mentioned: bankers, trade unions, teachers, manufacturers, farmers, doctors, and utilities).

Observers agree that the legislative role in school policymaking has recently changed. Education was once of limited interest to legislators, but since the 1970s they have taken a strong hand in education standards and school violence.[18] In particular, lawmakers are now more involved in the distribution of state revenue, both its proportion and uses. The reasons for this change reflect other changes.[19] That is, because legislatures now are more representative and better staffed, groups can turn to a body ready and willing to act; and as their sessions became longer, they were readier longer. Legislatures are also developing closer ties with other states and exchanging ideas about program possibilities.

Explanation of the legislature's role in school policymaking is confounded by three vigorous research traditions.[20] The *institutional* approach (the oldest) focuses upon the internal structure of the legislature. The *process* approach examines the dynamic interaction between structure and outside environment, for example, correlations among environmental characteristics of states, their policies, and legislative votes. The *behavioral* approach (the most recent) explores legislators' interactions within the body itself. As a consequence of these different approaches, what we know is much like the three blind persons who described an elephant in terms of the particular part each touched. However, great variation in both stable and dynamic elements are found in legislatures from state to state. Education is currently a popular arena for legislators because of its size and visibility. Ideas spread rapidly across states through interstate organizations like the National Conference of State Legislators and the Education Commission of the States, as well as policy issue networks noted in preceding chapters. Most state legislators feel they were elected to "legislate," and education as the largest state function is no exception.

American Governors

Head of state and of party, the American governor has had to weave these two roles together to be effective.[21] But the recent increase in demands on all states has brought this office under greater cross pressures. Service demands continue to increase, but so do demands to stabilize taxes that would pay for the services. The social welfare needs of the central cities are opposed by suburban and nonmetropolitan legislators who are less responsive to those needs. Most observers would agree that beneath the federal level the governor is the most important agent in American policymaking. This fact emerges in many individual studies of policymaking, even though it runs counter to earlier macrolevel analyses that stress the primacy of the state's environment (especially economic factors) rather than the political context.[22]

What is the significance of the governor for education policy? The limited research of this role prior to the 1970s generally found it minimal, "and when it does exist it appeared sporadically, reflecting the idiosyncratic character of particular governors and/or educational crises in specific states."[23] When the first truly comparative analysis of these figures appeared in the early 1970s, it found a much wider range of behavior across the states and the stages of policymaking.[24] As policymaking progresses, the governor's influence declines. Governors are most active in budget control and defining educational issues before their authorization, and least active in having a decisive effect on legislative enactment. But again, the spread expresses the usual American style—a wide range of possibilities. But the academic and teacher quality reforms of the 1980s and 1990s produced a new activism on the part of governors and a greater influence (see Table 10.1).

Strong gubernatorial leadership emerges in particular kinds of states. These are the larger industrialized states with highly effective legislatures and a moralistic political culture that emphasizes policy reform. However, governors from the South were very active in initiating the 1983–87 reforms featuring higher academic standards. The governors of South Carolina, Tennessee, Florida, Virginia, Georgia, Arkansas, Texas, and North Carolina made national news with their comprehensive ideas. One prime leader in the South was Arkansas' governor and later president,

William Clinton. The governor is also most likely to be involved and powerful in certain issues, particularly where a traditional policy climate exists of supporting education by creating much state revenue: North Carolina, Florida, and California.[25] The weaker governors appear in locally oriented policy cultures: Nebraska, Colorado, and New Hampshire. In the 1980s governors in several states have advocated tax increases to improve education, citing the international competition. Further, this office is becoming more politicized over educational policy, as are other agencies of government.

As with interest groups and legislatures, the governor's office fails to provide regular leadership for the development of educational policy in the American states. Some do so, of course, but only on limited issues and episodically. Like Sherlock Holmes' nonbarking dog, the systematic importance of this office is that it does not consistently do the expected. For example, governors from 1992 to 1996 did not provide as much focus on education policy innovation as they did from 1983 to 1992. Some governors, however, maintain strong alliances with big business that are favorable to state education standards. One role of the governor in galvanizing new state policies has increased dramatically when one compares 1996 to 1969.

THE IMPLEMENTERS OF STATE SCHOOL POLICY

The initiation and authorization of major school policy do not complete the policy process, for laws are not self-executing. The implementation stage in state school policy involves three agencies: the state board of education (SBE), the chief state school officer (CSSO), and the state education agency (SEA). The diversity of these authorities has already been suggested earlier in Tables 9.1 and 9.2, so again our focus is on patterns of behavior.[26]

The State Board of Education and Chief State School Officer

School policy implementation has been spread among these three agencies, with the SBE and CSSO responsible for oversight and innovation and the SEA for daily administration. The linkage between the SBE and CSSO is complex because their methods of appointment and authority are so diverse. They may be independent (elected, appointed, or a mix), or the SBE may choose the CSSO. Some SBEs only issue regulations, while others have operating responsibilities (vocational schools, state colleges, or universities). Rarely, however, are such broad responsibilities unified in a single office (except the New York Board of Regents).[27]

SBEs are usually appointed by the governor and the CSSO by the SBE, but the linkage is not ministerial. The selection methods of the SBEs seem to have consequences for their policy behavior. That is, elective bodies are designed to be open to more conflict, while appointed bodies respond to their appointers. That is the case with the SBEs, where 69 percent of those appointed reported little internal disagreement compared with 42 percent of those elected.[28]

Whatever their origins, these actors have differing influence. One observer reported that SBEs are "only marginal policy actors in the legislative arena and are largely overshadowed by the CSSO in state education."[29] Table 10.1 shows this in the late 1980s. Elected SBEs appear to have more influence with the CSSO and legislature, for they can speak with independent power. Few SBEs are elected, and their elections are rarely competitive, visible, or draw many voters; such elections are "nonevents." In the main, then, the SBE is a weak policy actor, especially where the board is unable to hire or remove the CSSO who has major constitutional oversight of state education. The SBE is also usually poorly staffed or organized to operate effectively and often lacks political links to the legislature and governor. SBEs seem to wander about on the fringes while the battle is being fought on a plain somewhere else.

The CSSOs, however, know where the action is and are often in the thick of it (see Table 10.1). SBEs look to them for leadership and information in policy conflict and seldom oppose them. But the CSSO is not a strong office with the legislature unless it is elected, and has a big staff and formal powers. The same office can be used for quite different policy concerns by different occupants. Thus in California in the 1970s, categorical programs for the disadvantaged were a priority, but in 1996 curriculum content in academic subjects became the priority. By 1996 the CSSOs, through better interstate coordination and national networks, were becoming even stronger, even though three states left the national organization representing CSSOs over disputes concerning federal policy, including Goals 2000. However, the impact of state political culture helps shape the role and impact of all state administrators.

> The element of political culture that most affects state policymaking is the strength of local control norms. Both the role SEAs play in state education policy and their capacity to assist local districts largely depend on the support they receive from general government and whether the political culture sanctions an active presence in local jurisdictions. This finding suggests that state political culture, in effect, preordains SEA roles and that SEAs in states with a strong local control ethos will always play a less active role and have less capacity than their counterparts in states where a strong central government is seen as legitimate.[30]

The State Education Agency

The daily job of implementing state policy goals rests in the hands of anonymous bureaucrats in the SEA. When the century opened, these agencies were tiny, but then succeeding waves of school reform policies were left with the SEAs to administer, and so they expanded greatly.

Today, SEAs supervise a vast array of federal and state programs, either through direct administration (for example, state schools for the blind) or through overseeing state guidelines. Their compliance techniques include requiring and reviewing a torrent of reports from the LEAs; enforcing mandated levels of service (for example, curriculum); assisting LEAs in designing and staffing newly required programs; providing continuing career education for professionals; and so on.[31] In a larger perspective, they were given the task of institutionalizing the professional model of the schools that states adopted over the last century. Programs that fell to them sought the "Americanization" of immigrants, vocational training for farm and city work, upgraded language and math training, improved resources for educating disadvantaged and minority children, and on and on in an almost unending list.

Specialists in little niches of expertise, SEAs constitute a complex of daily spear carriers for curriculum, finance and accounting, administration, personnel, and many other matters. Their political influence may be the most subtle, that of inertia defending the status quo. Their role in innovation and its implementation is one of the many unstudied aspects of the educational policy system, but it appears to be increasing because of state initiatives concerning testing, teacher quality, and local academic standards. A fundamental problem for SEAs is that they have been organized around categorical programs like federal Title I, but new standards require cross-cutting implementation that links curriculum and instruction.

The SEAs sometimes find themselves in political disputes with governors and legislators. Recently:

> Even in states where education enjoys the active support of general government, this support does not extend to federal programs for special needs students (administered by the SEAs). . . . Governors and legislators are generally opposed to categorical funding, and except for handicapped students, those representing special needs students command little visibility or political influence. . . . The governor and the state legislature believe that these programs should be subordinated to more general goals, such as increased competency in basic skills for all students.[32]

State Political Parties

In democracies numbers count, as do organizations of voters. The chief organization is the political party, so its role in shaping any public policy must be looked at. After all, the institutions reviewed above are products of electoral impulses diffracted through political parties in times past. And the epitome of individualism is not merely voting for officeholders but speaking directly on policy matters through the initiative and referendum.

A surprisingly little studied aspect of school policymaking is the role of political party. Available reports show that parties differ on school policymaking, although no consistent pattern in this difference emerges. Some of these studies are of single states in which the party is seen as a significant agent affecting policymaking.[33] State legislatures are frequently quite partisan, such as the 1995 California case where a Republican governor preserved his budget through straight party-line votes. An analysis of the link between parties and the adoption of school reforms from the 1983 study entitled *A Nation at Risk* provides a rare chance to trace statistically the influence of parties. Findings show that adoption rates were little associated with the degree of party competition, but adoption had occurred much more often in states where parties had usually not taken policy stands (e.g., the South). In the main, though, party factors were not significant. Yet we still have no fifty-state comparison using such process-oriented studies.[34]

NEW STATE/LOCAL REGULATORY APPROACHES

Policies enacted in 1995 will change major parts of the intergovernmental system. Much of this activity focuses on devolution, deregulation, reorganizing state education agencies, and cutting the capacity of state government to oversee LEAs. In 1995 thirty states considered reorganization or reduction of their SEAs as a part of broad political trends to reduce government. For example, Texas repealed a third of its education code and limited the SEA to six basic functions. Moreover, new categories of school systems were authorized to be freed from state mandates so that "home rule districts" could create their own governance charter. North Carolina cut its SEAs by half and deregulated many laws, but required annual school performance reports. Presumably, these cuts in SEAs will limit the enforcement capacity of state regulators. Many other states, including Michigan and Texas, have major efforts underway to prune the state education code and consolidate categorical programs. In short, these changes reflect a theory of dissatisfaction presented in earlier chapters about local control that became manifest at the state level. These changes reflect one part of the challenge to the earlier steady state of school systems.

For example, Minnesota abolished its Department of Education and merged several functions into a new Department of Children, Families, and Learning. Wisconsin removed virtually all powers from its independently elected school superintendent and created a new agency as part of the governor's cabinet.

Different regulation policy was one of the objectives of new state governance organizations. Moreover, some states are cutting back the scope of union negotiations (Illinois, Michigan), with one objective being increased local flexibility.

While political rationales, such as excessive state control stifling local creativity, are featured in the media, there are implicit theories of local response in these new state regulatory regimes. Since states have chosen different deregulation approaches, researchers need to examine the different local impact of different policy strategies and designs. We do *not* envision local response to be a simple binary relationship between state regulation and consequent uniform local response. Each deregulation policy outcome is influenced by an existing local capacity that helps explain differences in local response. Some LEAs have the staff, resources, and political context that will take advantage of state flexibility. Other LEAs will have a less favorable context to exploit state deregulation opportunities. Consequently, there is an interactive effect between local capacity and state deregulation policies that causes local disparate effects.

Supporters of state deregulation hope there will be positive local response, but not much is known about the impact of these newer approaches. As the nation moves to the next century, new questions require research. For example, does deregulation lower local costs and increase efficiency? What policies do change at the local level, and is deregulation a discernible cause of these changes? Given these local differences, what are the consequences for quality? For equity? The key issues will be the difference deregulation makes on local policies in matters like

- local curricular/assessment policies
- use of categorical programs
- staff development
- student policies such as discipline

The state political context is crucial—deregulation in historically centralized Texas may have more local impact than in more decentralized Michigan. Some states have more enforcement resources and traditions of investigating local compliance, so the effects of deregulation may vary in different state enforcement contexts. But the larger picture remains for scholars in educational politics, how a steady-state system responded to challenges arising over stress that developed in service delivery noted throughout this book.

NOTES

1. Catherine Marshall, Douglas Mitchell, and Frederick Wirt, *Culture and Education Policy in the American State* (New York: Falmer, 1989).

2. Ibid., "Influence, Power, and Policy Making," *Peabody Journal of Education* 62, no. 1 (1985): 88 .

3. Ibid., "Assumptive Worlds of Education Policy Makers," *Peabody Journal of Education* 62, no. 4 (1985): 90–115; citation is at p. 90.

4. Michael Kirst, Gail Meister, and Stephen R. Rowley, "Policy Issue Networks: Their Influence on State Policymaking," *Policy Studies Journal* 13, no. 2 (December 1984): 247–64.

5. The following is drawn from Harmon Zeigler and Henrich van Dalen, "Interest Groups in the States," in *Politics in the American States: A Comparative Analysis,* Herbert Jacob and Kenneth Vines, eds. (Boston: Little, Brown & Co., 1976), Chap. 3.

6. Ibid., p. 134.

7. Ibid., pp. 95–103 characterize and detail these types. For a fuller elaboration based on four states, see Harmon Zeigler and Michael Baer, *Lobbying, Interaction and Influence in American State Legislatures* (Belmont, Calif.: Wadsworth, 1969).

8. For a brief history, see J. Howard Goold, "The Organized Teaching Profession," in *Education in the States: Nationwide Development since 1900,* Edgar Fuller and Jim Pearson, eds. (Washington, D.C.: National Education Association, 1969), Chap. 14; and Lorraine McDonnell and Anthony Pascal, "National Trends in Teaching Collective Bargaining," *Education and Urban Society* 11 (1979): 129-51.

9. J. Alan Aufderheide, "Educational Interest Groups and the State Legislature," in *State Policy Making for the Public Schools: A Comparative Analysis,* Roald Campbell and Tim Mazzoni, Jr., eds. (Berkeley, Calif.: McCutchan, 1976), p. 201.

10. See the review of Iannaccone's typology using twelve-state data in Raphael Nystrand, "State Education Policy Systems," in Campbell and Mazzoni, *State Policy Making,* Chap. 7. Nystrand's analysis may not have fully tested this typology, according to some critics.

11. William Boyd, "Interest Groups and the Changing Environment" (paper presented to the American Education Research Association, Washington, D.C., 1987). The following quotations are from this source.

12. Michael Kirst and Stephen Sommers, "Collective Action Among California

Educational Interest Groups: A Logical Response to Proposition 13," *Education and Urban Society* 13, no. 2 (1981): 235-56.

13. Aufderheide, "Educational Interest Groups," p. 213.

14. Ibid., p. 209

15. Zeigler and van Dalen, "Interest Groups," p. 147

16. William H. Riker, *The Theory of Political Coalitions* (New Haven, Conn.: Yale University Press, 1962); James G. March and Johan P. Olsen, *Democratic Governance* (New York: Free Press, 1995).

17. For a useful introduction to this literature, see Samuel Patterson, "State Legislatures and Public Policy," in *Politics in the American States*, 5th ed., Virginia Gray, Herbert Jacob, and Robert Albritton, eds. (Glenview, Ill.: Scott, Foresman/Little Brown, 1990), Chap. 5.

18. Nicholas Masters, Robert Salisburg, and Thomas Eliot, *State Politics and the Public Schools* (New York: Knopf, 1964); Jerome T. Murphy, "The Paradox of State Government Reform," in *Educational Policymaking*, 1978 Yearbook of the National Society for the Study of Education, Milbrey McLaughlin, ed. (Chicago: University of Chicago Press, 1978).

19. Ellis Katz, *Education Policymaking 1977-1978: A Snapshot from from the States* (Washington, D.C.: Institute for Educational Leadership, 1978), pp. 40–41 .

20. A major review and addition to this scholarship is Douglas E. Mitchell, *Shaping Legislative Decisions: Education Policy and the Social Sciences* (Lexington, Mass.: Lexington Books, 1978).

21. The following draws on Thad L. Beyle, ed., *Governors and Hard Times* (Washington, D.C.: Congressional Quarterly Press, 1992).

22. The seminal work is Thomas Dye, *Politics, Economics, and the Public* (Chicago: Rand McNally, 1966).

23. Iannaccone, *Politics in Education*, p. 44.

24. Edward Hines, "Governors and Educational Policy Making," in Campbell and Mazzoni, *State Policy Making*, Chap. 4.

25. An excellent analysis is Mike Milstein and Robert Jennings, *Educational Policy Making and the State Legislature: The New York Experience* (New York: Praeger, 1973).

26. A full catalogue of these traditional authorities is Sam Harris, *State Departments of Education, State Boards of Education, and Chief State School Officers* (Washington, D.C.: United States Government Printing Office, 1973).

27. For their history and variety, see Lerus Winget, Edgar Fuller, and Terrel Bell, "State Departments of Education," in Fuller and Pearson, *Education in the States*, Chap. 2. For New York, see Milstein and Jennings, *Educational Policy Making*.

28. Fuller and Pearson, "State Departments of Education," *Education in the States*, p. 83.

29. On the "nonevent," see a major challenge to the once-popular notion of the SBE influence, Gerald Sroufe, "State School Board Members and the State Education Policy System," *Planning and Changing* 2 (April 1971): 16–17. For a twelve-state review of the SBE, see Roald Campbell, "The Chief State School Officer as a Policy Actor," in Campbell and Mazzoni, *State Policy Mak-*

ing, Chap. 3. For suggestions on how to improve state boards, see Michael Cohen, "State Boards in an Era of Reform," *Phi Delta Kappan* 69, no. 1 (September 1987): 60-64.

30. Lorraine M. McDonnell and Milbrey W. McLaughlin, *Education Policy and the Role of the States* (Santa Monica, Calif.: Rand, 1982), p. 79.

31. Almost all the comparative chapters of Fuller and Pearson, *Education in the States,* detail these SEA functions. Especially useful for understanding the different kinds of authority under which SEAs operate are Chapters 8, 10, and 13.

32. McDonnell and McLaughlin, *Education Policy,* p. 73.

33. Zeigler and Baer, *Lobbying,* pp. 143, 146, 149.

34. Doh Shinn and Jack Van Der Slik, "Legislative Efforts to Improve the Quality of Public Education in the American States: A Comparative Analysis" (paper presented to the annual conference of the American Political Science Association, New Orleans, 1985). For an overview of state policy innovation, see Frances Berry, "Sizing Up State Policy Innovation Research," *Policy Studies Journal* 22 (1994): 442-456.

11 _____

Federal Aid

Education was a major national issue in the 1996 elections, and the federal role was part of this debate. A nationwide poll conducted by CNN and *USA Today* on January 7, 1996, indicated that 67 percent of participating voters said a candidate's position on the quality of public schools would be a "very high priority" campaign issue in deciding for whom to vote for president. Education as the top-ranked issue was followed by crime (66 percent) and the economy (64 percent), and Republicans, Democrats, and Independents all listed education quality as one of their top two concerns.[1]

This high visibility of education as a federal issue is surprising to some observers, because the federal share of the total spending on education is just 6 percent, having peaked at 9 percent in 1971. Polls suggest that the public exaggerates the scale of federal funding and does not have a good grasp of the current and potential federal role. President Clinton's 1997 State of the Union Address, however, capitalized on this high public concern about school quality by featuring a long list of education proposals ranging from school uniforms to technology. Despite Republican attempts to cut federal aid significantly, Clinton asked

Congress to create a new program of $1,000 university scholarships for top high school students. Meanwhile, the Republican Congress targeted large federal programs for big cuts, including Goals 2000 and Title I. Senator Robert Dole vowed the Congress would hold firm on "unfunding wasteful programs and meddlesome departments."[2] The latter reference is to the attempt by the majority Republican House to abolish the U.S. Department of Education (DOE) that failed passage in 1996. There is no doubt that the 1994 Congressional election began a rancorous partisan debate about the future federal education role. Before analyzing this dispute, it is useful to review the historical evolution of the federal role.

EVOLUTION OF THE FEDERAL ROLE

The federal government has always been a junior partner to state and local agencies in financing and operating American schools.[3] The impact of federal policies on the nation's classrooms, however, continues to fascinate researchers, policymakers, and the public. Interest and concern about this role intensified during the 1960s and 1970s, motivated in part by expanding expenditures as well as by the increasing directiveness of most new federal policies. Through the 1970s the federal role emphasized securing extra services for traditionally underserved students, promoting innovation, and supporting research.

In the 1980s the federal government's spending for elementary and secondary education did not keep pace either with inflation or with state and local support of schools. Relative to state and local spending, the DOE's share of elementary or secondary school expenditures dipped to 6.1 percent by the 1984–85 school year, its lowest share in almost twenty years.[4] Federal expenditures for education increased slightly during the Bush administration to 7 percent of total spending, but did not increase as much from 1994 to 1996. Also, federal regulatory pressures that escalated under Bush have subsided during the Clinton administration.

In 1950, when the U.S. Office of Education (USOE) was transferred from the Interior Department to Health, Education, and

Welfare, it had a staff of three hundred to spend $40 million. By 1963 forty-two departments, agencies, and bureaus of the government were involved in education to some degree. In 1983 the Department of Defense and the Veterans Administration, however, spent more on educational programs than the DOE and the National Science Foundation combined. The Office of Education appointed personnel who were specialists and consultants in such areas as mathematics, libraries, and school buses; these specialists identified primarily with the National Education Association (NEA). Federal grant programs operated through deference to local and state education agency priorities and judgments. State administrators were regarded by USOE as colleagues who should have the maximum decision-making discretion permitted by categorical laws.

The era of 1964–1972 brought dramatic increases in federal activity, but the essential mode of delivering federal services remained the same. This differential funding route sought bigger, bolder categorical and demonstration programs. The delivery system for these categories stressed the need for more precise federal regulations to guide local projects. Indeed, the current collection of overlapping and complex categorical aids evolved as a mode of federal action that a number of otherwise dissenting educational interests could agree on.[5] It was not the result of any rational plan for federal intervention, but rather an outcome of political bargaining and coalition formation. Former DOE head, Harold Howe, expressed its essence this way:

> Whatever its limitations, the categorical aid approach gives the states and local communities a great deal of leeway in designing educational programs to meet various needs. In essence, the federal government says to the states (and cities), "Here is some money to solve this particular program; you figure out how to do it. . . ." But whatever the criticisms which can in justice be leveled against categorical aid to education, I believe that we must stick with it, rather than electing general aid as an alternative. The postwar period has radically altered the demands we place on our schools; a purely local and state viewpoint of education cannot produce an educational system that will serve national interest in addition to more localized concerns.[6]

An incremental shift in the style of DOE administration also came with expanded categories. The traditional provision of specialized consultants and the employment of subject matter specialists were ended in favor of managers and generalists who had public administration rather than professional education backgrounds. As we will see shortly, these newer federal administrators have been more aggressive, creating a political backlash against federal regulation that the Republicans were able to highlight in their 1994 and 1996 campaigns.

Modes of Federal Influence

There have been basically six alternative modes of federal action for public schools:

1. General aid: Provide no-strings aid to state and local education agencies or such minimal earmarks as teacher salaries. A modified form of general aid was proposed by President Reagan in 1981. He consolidated numerous categories into a single bloc grant for local education purposes. No general-aid bill has ever been approved by the Congress.
2. Stimulate through differential funding: Earmark categories of aid, provide financial incentives through matching grants, fund demonstration projects, and purchase specific services. This is the approach of the Elementary and Secondary Education Act (ESEA) and Goals 2000.
3. Regulate: Legally specify behavior, impose standards, certify and license, enforce accountability procedures. The bilingual regulations proposed by the Carter administration (and rescinded by President Reagan) are a good example.
4. Discover knowledge and make it available: Have research performed, gather and make other statistical data available. The National Science Foundation performs the first function and the National Center for Education Statistics the second.
5. Provide services: Furnish technical assistance and consultants in specialized areas or subjects. For example, the Office of Civil Rights will advise school districts that are designing voluntary desegregation plans.
6. Exert moral suasion: Develop vision and question assump-

tions through publications and speeches by top officials. Thus President Reagan's Secretary of Education, William Bennett, advocated three C's—content, character, and choice—in numerous speeches and articles in the popular media. This mode of federal influence is termed "the bully pulpit" by the press.

The Reagan administration endorsed a tuition tax credit to reimburse parents who send their children to private schools. Although various members of Congress have pushed this idea for decades, this was the first time a president had endorsed it. While Reagan was defeated, federal aid to private schools continues to be a major issue in federal aid during the 1990s, although vociferously and unanimously opposed by public education interest groups.

Overall, the Reagan administration promoted five other basic changes in federal educational policy in addition to assisting private schools, moving:

1. from a prime concern with equity to more concern with quality, efficiency, and state and local freedom to choose;
2. from a larger and more influential federal role to a mitigated federal role;
3. from mistrust of the motives and capacity of state and local educators to a renewed faith in governing units outside of Washington;
4. from categorical grants to more unrestricted types of financial aid;
5. from detailed and prescriptive regulations to deregulation.

The Reagan administration made no progress on financial support for private education but was able to implement a major policy shift by diminishing the federal role as the initiator of change. The 1996 Congressional Republican agenda is very similar to Reagan's, so the call for change in 1981–1984 was a harbinger of the future.

For two decades (1960–1980) the equity value, that of promoting equal educational opportunity, had been the most pervasive theme of federal education policy. Indeed, the Reagan administration could not substitute choice or efficiency priorities as the major orientation of federal policy, because the Democrats controlled Congress. The most obvious expression of equity is through numerous categorical grants targeted to students not adequately served by state and local programs (for example, the disadvantaged, handicapped). The Reagan administration attempted to scale back aggressive federal activity in such areas. The interest groups that are the recipients of federal policy resisted and were able to form successful countercoalitions at both the federal and state levels. As one scholar noted:

> The interest groups are also quite typical in their efforts to concentrate as much influence as possible, at the appropriate time, in a variety of policy arenas—the courts, particular state legislatures, the Congress, federal agencies, and so on. The accomplishments of the past decade indicate that they have all acquired a large degree of sophistication in political maneuvering.[7]

The last comment suggests that the objectives of categorical interests such as the handicapped may lose out temporarily at the federal level of government only to succeed at another.

AN OVERVIEW OF FEDERAL STRATEGIES

The federal government provides support to education through numerous agencies including the Departments of Labor, of Health and Human Services, and of Agriculture, and the National Science Foundation. The creation of a Department of Education in 1980 was justified partly on the basis that it would consolidate more education programs in a single accountable department. But many interest groups resisted this change, preferring to stay in separate agencies. Several of the lobby groups with programs outside of DOE did not want their programs controlled by a department that they presumed would be dominated by professional educators. Consequently, school lunch aid is still provided by the Department of Agriculture, and the National Science Foundation provides research and demonstration grants for secondary school science. Head Start is part of the Department of Health and Human Services, even though it is designed to help the transition to public school kindergarten.

The major federal strategy to change local education has been to specify purposes for federal funds (e.g., categorical grants), and then monitor local compliance through federal auditors. Since no one was sure which categorical program would impact local schools, Congress's approach from 1964 to 1976 was to pass almost any politically palatable program. This proliferation of programs led to a condition called "hardening of the categories," whereby each program operated largely in protective insolation. Federal aid began for almost every type of learner—gifted, handicapped, limited-English-speaking, vocational, disadvantaged, preschool, artistic, and so on. There are categories to spur innovation, effective schools, desegregation, and schools near federal military bases.

The use by presidents and secretaries of education of the "bully pulpit" as a major, independent policy strategy has been inadequately examined. There is broad recognition of the widespread public and professional reactions to the publication in 1983 of *A Nation at Risk*, lower college entrance scores, and other moral suasion devices. Still, to date, most commentary on these strategies has little if any empirical base and has been more public-relations filler than systematic assessment. A challenge for researchers of the federal role in elementary and secondary education will be to design and conduct systematic assessments of the origins and impacts of modern use of the bully pulpit strategy. Only through such scholarship, and with the benefit of time's perspective, will the impacts of the Reagan and Clinton administrations' education policies be fully understood.

The past decade has produced a consensus on ways to improve the probability that federal intent will be implemented at the state and local levels. This consensus includes (a) having a precise and feasible objective, (b) securing broad-based state and local political support for the intervention, (c) generating a sense of urgency for achieving the objectives, and (d) concealing the federal government's weaknesses in forcing the state and local units to comply.[8] The federal threat to recover funds by audits is used sparingly because it is difficult to enforce through the courts. Federal administrators can build vertical networks of like-minded administrators in the state and local bureaucracies. This strategy has been successful in vocational education and Title 1 funding.

The key is to bring about a sharing of values within this vertical administrative network. Two scholars of those interactions summarize:

> The central paradox of policy implementation is that policies cannot succeed unless individuals and organizations take responsibility for their success, but if they had assumed that responsibility to begin with it may not have been necessary to have a policy. The paradox is instructive in two ways. It tells us that compliance is a necessary part of any implementation strategy, but that it is hardly ever a sufficient condition for success. Mobilization of the knowledge necessary to make a policy work depends on people accepting responsibility for their actions.[9]

The 1994 congressional election and 1996 presidential campaign changed the dialogue about the federal role. Most Republicans want to eliminate DOE, and to turn most categorical programs over to states with few federal requirements. The difference in spending between the two parties is highlighted by Table 11.1. The 1994 elections in Congress resulted in a major turnover of members on committees concerned with education; often those new members had less legislative experience. For example, the years of congressional experience of members on the House Appropriations Subcommittee for Education declined from an average of 16.6 years to only 5.9 years. Moreover, education committees went from being among the most liberal to right of center. Clinton administration attempts to provide better coherence and more integration of federal categorical programs were greeted by the Republican Congress with little interest. The Republican agenda was to merge most of the categorical funding into a single pot of money and let states or localities decide on spending priorities.

The 1996 budget conflict ended with a 2 percent overall cut in education with specific amounts close to the Senate amount shown in Table 11.1. But the 1997 proposed budget reversed these cuts in part because President Clinton used his bully pulpit to awaken the public to Republican education cuts.

The defenders of the historical federal role are primarily within the Democratic party. This helps to preserve the political and fund-raising alliance between the Democrats and teacher unions as evidenced by Table 11.2.

Table 11.1

Differences Between the Democratic Senate and the
Republican House Concerning Federal Funding, 1996

	FY 1995 enacted	FY 1996 House (Initial)	FY 1996 Senate (Initial)
Goals 2000: Educate America Act	$371,870	$0	$310,000
School-to-Work Opportunities Act	245,000	190,000	245,000
Title I			
Basic Grants	5,968,235	4,949,505	5,266,863
Concentration Grants	663,137	549,945	692,341
Impact Aid	728,000	645,000	677,959
Safe and Drug-Free Schools and			
Communities Act	440,981	200,000	200,000
Bilingual and Immigrant Education	206,700	103,000	172,959
Special Education	3,254,846	3,092,491	3,245,447
Vocational Education	1,110,766	911,067	1,009,497
Eisenhower Professional			
Development Program	598,548	550,000	550,000
Education Research, Statistics			
and Assessment	167,105	182,488	166,818
Education Technology	22,500	25,000	25,000
Charter Schools	6,000	6,000	10,000
Total, Department of Education	32,929,963	27,394,536	28,788,696
Total Discretionary Spending	24,517,164	20,809,845	22,149,145

Sources: House and Senate Appropriations Committees; *Education Week*, March 16, 1996.

NATIONAL STANDARDS AND THE FEDERAL TITLE I PROGRAM FOR THE DISADVANTAGED

The 1995 Republican Congressional majority made Goals 2000 and national standards a major partisan issue. They contended that the federal government should *not* play a role in establishing or approving national curriculum or performance standards. Republicans believe Goals 2000 grants to SEAs and LEAs could lead to excessive federal control.

While the national standards debate proceeded, the largest federal education program ($7.4 billion), Title I, continued to rely on low-level standardized tests and a curriculum that was not acceptable to the national standards alliance. How could

Table 11.2
Congressional Campaign Contributions
by the NEA and the AFT
in Recent Two-Year Election Cycles

NEA	1993–94	1991–92	1989–90
Democratic candidates receiving contributions	365	375	329
Total contributed to Democrats	$2,230,050	$2,228,447	$2,168,000
Republican candidates receiving contributions	13	32	45
Total contributed to Republicans	$25,800	$82,175	$14,910
AFT	1993–94	1991–92	1989–90
Democratic candidates receiving contributions	243	246	234
Total contributed to Democrats	$1,278,690	$1,077,400	$999,350
Republican candidates receiving contributions	6	14	18
Total contributed to Republicans	$11,000	$23,850	$25,050

Source: Federal Election Commission, 1993.

Title I be so deeply rooted in past practice and seemingly so inattentive to present developments? A bit of history is in order.

Throughout their history, Title I programs have been directed primarily toward elementary reading and math and have emphasized remedial approaches.[10] When enacted in 1965, the program was the centerpiece of an equal opportunity policy and assumed that state and local educators could not be trusted to target scarce federal dollars to disadvantaged students. The federal management approach reflected a fear that local political concerns would divert Title I funds to less needy children. Therefore, the principal delivery mode relied on detailed federal financial flow regulation reinforced by field audits. There was little federal concern about curriculum content, but a great deal of attention was given to which schools and students received federal money.

There evolved a deep fear, lasting from 1965 to 1986, that Title I money might spill over to non-Title I students in the school or classroom. Consequently, a separate administrative apparatus was created and sustained, composed of state and local Title I coordinators whose allegiance was different from, and sometimes counter to, that of supporters of a districtwide or statewide core curriculum. These Title I coordinators created their own professional association and often met separately from regular classroom teachers at state and national education conventions. Technical assistance and provision of services, such as curricular models, was abandoned by the late 1960s. From then until now, program managers and auditors have been the key federal Title I players, and curriculum or teaching experts have been shunted to other federal divisions. Federal research efforts have concentrated on program regulation and fiscal compliance, with scant attention to the commonplaces of education—teaching, curriculum, and learning strategies. In effect, Title I developed an accounting, rather than an instructional, mentality as it grew from $1 billion in 1965 to $7.4 billion in 1997.

This regulatory focus and distinctly identifiable federal role in categorical programs has long been reinforced by a view that Title I is effective and, thus, it would be unwise and risky to alter it. It was assumed that acceptable levels of compliance with Title I financial targeting and special service requirements were linked to achievement gains in the early grades among Southern blacks. Indeed, a careful administrator could listen carefully to the federal rhetoric surrounding Title I in the 1970–1985 period and hear almost nothing about curricular content or how to teach. There was an assumption that something educationally different needed to be done through Title I, but the federal government transmitted no clear message about what or how.

Instructional issues began to surface in the debate about the 1988 congressional reauthorization of Title I. Education experts in the 1980s returned to a concern about instruction. The DOE commissioned a series of papers from education researchers. One asserted, "Tracking, pullout programs, and reliance on paraprofessionals [in Title I] to monitor remedial learning serve as barriers rather than facilitators to improving the curriculum of literacy for youngsters at risk."[11] Reformers contended that Title I should be aimed at improving whole schools as education organizations instead of focusing on programs targeted to individual students within schools. For instance, low-income students receive Title I services that differ from the regular curriculum and are less likely to promote literacy. Title I reading teachers stress decoding at the expense of comprehension and rarely require expository essays.

There are weak links between the remedial reading specialists who tutor Title I students and regular classroom teachers. This does not mean that all pullout programs are bad or that such a strategy cannot be improved. Until regular classroom teachers are retrained, there may remain a need for pullout remedial strategies. The Clinton administration's point is that both pullout and regular teachers need a new vision of Title I's curriculum content and improved instructional techniques based on national standards.

Bill Honig, California's former chief state school officer, expressed the federal administrative issues surrounding this reconceptualized learning approach as follows:

> Chapter I is often operated as a separate remedial program, substituting a narrow, repetitious curriculum for a well-balanced core curriculum. There is a need for some development work in this area to train teachers to help eligible students to master the base curriculum and to provide integrated learning experiences.[12]

A CLOSER EXAMINATION OF TITLE I POLITICS

The advent of the Clinton administration placed in power a number of Democrats and Republicans critical of Title I policies and results. Much current thinking about instruction reflects the 1989 education summit and the 1994 Congressional statement of national goals. National content standards in Goals 2000 are merged with the current administration's thinking on "systemic reform." The key themes of this new amalgam are policy coherence, alignment, and linkage to high content standards.[13]

Categorical programs, such as Title I, bilingual education, and special education, have come to be viewed as major contributors to incoherent policy. Current Title I programs rely on low-level standardized tests to demonstrate accountability because federal legislation requires that national norms be used to judge local

Title I programs. This approach, in turn, encourages schools and teachers to use a "pullout drill-and-kill workbook curriculum."

In 1993 the Clinton administration proposed ESEA and Goals 2000 legislation to link Title I to a new instructional approach. States would be expected to develop content standards and submit them for certification by a federal unit, the National Education School Improvement Council. A state's student performance assessment practices are to be revised and aligned with these nationally approved content standards. Local Title I programs would then be based on these state content standards and assessments. In 1993 the U.S. Department of Education proposed:

> The Clinton Administration would replace all current testing requirements in Chapter I which, evidence suggests, have held back efforts to enrich the curriculum with more challenging material. In their place would be a state-level set of high-quality, yearly student assessments. These assessments would be comprised of multiple, up-to-date measures of student performance, and be used as the primary means of determining whether LEAs [local education agencies] and schools are, in fact, making adequate yearly progress.[14]

The Clinton Administration was successful in its bill to deregulate the instructional approaches used to meet high content standards. This means more use of schoolwide approaches and fewer fiscal incentives to use pullout programs. The new legislation, however, eliminated all references to national curriculum standards and tests because of Republican concern about the potential loss of state and local control.

Incentives to meet state content standards were included. Presumably, the administration will audit SEAs to make sure that local Title I programs are based on state content standards and assessments that are more challenging than commercial standardized tests. Since opportunity-to-learn standards were *not* set at the national level, federal oversight of Title I on this issue will be minimal.[15]

Advocates for state standards are quickly realizing that such standards offer leverage for upgrading the education of historically neglected or low-achieving groups of students. Indeed, such standards might provide far more powerful legal leverage to ensure better education for such students than any prior Title I compliance standards focusing on inputs. However, state standards opponents may also try to dilute or water down state standards for Title I, bilingual, and handicapped pupils. Johnny, no matter how poorly he performs, may still meet the standard if the "bar" is set low enough.

Political Inertia

Many national, state, and local educators and government officials have a strong vested interest in maintaining Title I as it is now and has been for a long time. More is at stake than simply having to learn new rules. Title I currently pays the salaries of thousands of school district, state, and federal employees. State content and assessment standards imply an entirely different set of skills that emphasize problem solving and curriculum knowledge rather than input compliance monitoring. It may be that many current Title I employees will be quite capable of acquiring the new skills, but certainly many will not. Moreover, even those who can may not be eager to expend the effort necessary. Consequently, there is substantial inertia that may block any transition to state standards.[16]

Why is this? Title I politics are dominated by Title I employees.[17] The Bush administration backed off its 1988 efforts to radically alter Title I through the use of a modified voucher system. Former President Reagan proposed that Title I should offer grants to pupils rather than to schools. An early 1981 Reagan proposal attempted to combine Title I with many other already existing authorities into a huge federal bloc grant program. It did not take Reagan administration officials long to see that the entire plan was jeopardized by the inclusion of Title I. All the other vested interests could be overcome and finessed. Indeed, they eventually were and the current version of ESEA Title II is a massive bloc grant program. However, Title I was withdrawn as a proposed component simply because its political defenders were too strong to overcome without the expenditure of more presidential energy than appeared justified. It is unclear whether the Clinton administration will be successful in reorienting Title I to meet more challenging education standards.

LOOKING AHEAD

The future of federal aid appears to be policy incrementalism. President Clinton featured education in his 1996 campaign, but the Republicans retained control of both houses of Congress. Most Republicans discovered that their stance to eliminate the U.S. Department of Education and cut federal education funds was not popular with local voters. Election polls demonstrated that female voters were very concerned about education, which was one cause of females voting for Clinton in a higher percentage than males. Consequently, the 1997 Congress began with Republication rhetoric about reaching compromise with Democrats, and adding slightly to the federal education budget. But there are no dramatic new proposals emanating from either President Clinton or Congressional leaders to expand the federal role substantially. Balancing the budget remains the priority, so symbolic federal initiatives such as urging local mandates for pupils to wear school uniforms are proposed. Politicians are focusing on middle-class voters, rather than the disadvantaged groups targeted by large federal programs from the 1965–1975 era. Consequently, federal aid for college attendance may increase significantly, but through tax policy rather than federal categorical programs that entail large federal administrative operations.

NOTES

1. *School Board News*, "Education is Top Concern of Voters," January 13, 1996, p. 1.
2. Robert C. Johnston, "Clinton Speech Issues Education Challenges," *Education Week*, January 31, 1996, p. 18.
3. For an overview, see Michael Timpane, ed., *The Federal Interest in Financing Education* (Cambridge, Mass.: Ballinger, 1979).
4. U.S. Department of Education, *The Fiscal Year 1987 Budget* (Washington, D.C.: U.S. Department of Education, 1986).
5. James Sundquist, *Politics and Policy* (Washington, D.C.: Brookings Institution, 1968), pp. 155–221.
6. Harold Howe, "National Policy for American Education" (speech to the Seventy-First Annual Convention of the National Congress of Parents and Teachers, Minneapolis, Minn., May 22, 1967.
7. Edith Mosher, Anne Hastings, and Jennings Wagoner, "Beyond the

Breaking Point," *Educational Evaluation and Policy Analysis* 3, no. 1 (1981): 47.

8. Lorraine M. McDonnell and Milbrey McLaughlin, *Education Policy and the Role of the State* (Santa Monica, Calif.: Rand, 1982).

9. Richard Elmore and Milbrey McLaughlin, "Strategic Choice in Federal Education Policy: The Compliance-Assistance Trade Off," in *Policymaking in Education,* Ann Lieberman and Milbrey McLaughlin, eds. (Chicago: University of Chicago Press, 1982), p. 175.

10. Marshall Smith and Jennifer O'Day, "Systemic School Reform." In *The Politics of Curriculum and Testing,* Susan Fuhrman and Betty Malen, eds. (New York: Falmer, 1991), pp. 233–68.

11. Robert Calfee, "Reinventing Chapter I." In *Designs for Compensatory Education,* B. I. Williams, ed. (Washington, D.C.: ERIC 293901, 1986), p. 250.

12. Bill Honig, 1986. Letter to Secretary of Education, William Bennett. August 5.

13. Smith and O'Day, "Systemic School Reform."

14. U.S. Department of Education, *Improving American Schools Act of 1993.* (Washington, D.C.: U.S. Department of Education, 1993).

15. Elmore and McLaughlin, "Strategic Choice."

16. Michael W. Kirst, "The Federal Role and Chapter I." In *Federal Aid to the Disadvantaged,* Dennis Doyle and Bruce Cooper, eds. (Philadelphia: Falmer, 1988), pp. 97–118. See also David Tyack and Larry Cuban, *Tinkering Toward Utopia* (Cambridge: Harvard, 1995).

17. Kirst, "The Federal Role."

18. Tyack and Cuban, *Tinkering Toward Utopia.*

12

Court Functions amid Conflict over Change

Anyone who has participated in a ball game among youth without an umpire or referee knows how poorly the game progresses. Amid conflicts of interest, there are cries of "Safe!" and "Out!" and nothing much gets done. Americans' values and interests are diverse, and they often—but not always—conflict. When they do, the need for conflict resolution by a third or disinterested party is clearly necessary. That central function inheres in all courts in the nation when people and units of government fall into dispute, and someone must call somebody "out" or "safe."

We will start with placing courts within the systems analysis framework, then view their role in policy innovation and set out their primary functions. Special attention is given to how courts have been used to channel current challenge to the established system. In democracies, after all, any policy arena is open to resolving challenge in the use of power, and courts are not different in this function. For at least forty years schools have known this process of challenge and defense that is fought out within formal judicial channels. But within the states, courts have also had major functions of legalizing established policies and often defending them. Not surprisingly, then, courts have served as another arena in the current challenge to the steady-state qualities of American schools.

COURTS AS A NEW POLICY AGENCY

The enlarged role that state and federal governments play in the local schools comes in part from the judicial branch. Group after group, frustrated by school policies, have turned to the state and federal courts for relief. The courts became involved not merely in settling disputes, but in initiating policy solutions to school problems and then overseeing their implementation. This chapter surveys this dual judicial role of innovation and implementation that has affected all school districts in some ways.

At first thought, courts seem an unlikely adjunct of schools and an unlikely partner in policies. Yet the history of education has been shaped by important court decisions on the duties and responsibilities of school officials; though trivial, the right of students not to have their hair cut is just one of the latest of many such contributions. At a more significant level, the United States Supreme Court has been directly involved in the question of religion in our schools, considering Bible reading, required prayers, flag salutes, the transportation and other expenses of parochial students, the teaching of evolution, and "secular humanism" in textbooks. Court involvement can be as narrow as whether school lockers can be searched (they can) or as extensive as whether schools can be segregated by race (once no, but in the 1990s, probably). School officials may react by massive noncompliance, as with the Bible and prayer decisions, but they find that being indifferent is very difficult.

Court involvement in such matters surprises only those who view the bench as a political eunuch. Contemporary analysts of the judiciary look not only at its behavior but also at the values that this behavior reflects. Judges are political because they must choose between competing values brought before them in a real conflict. As early as 1840, Alexis de Tocqueville was noting that "scarcely any political question arises in the United States that is not resolved, sooner or later, into a judicial question." The reason for this is that when citizens differ in the political arena, the arena for resolution may be not in politics but in court. The form and rules of judicial contests may differ from those in other arenas, but they remain essentially political. That is because contenders are seeking the authority of the political system to command the distribution of resources—such as rights and property—that each wants. The allocation of resources to citizens that follows from a court mandate is just as effective as legislation.

What, then, are the relationships between the judiciary—part of the political system of the state—and the political system of the school? What are the constraints and strengths in this relationship? What are the accommodations and conflicts in the system aspects of the political process here? How does federalism filter the outcome? What values are reflected among participants?

THE FEDERAL JUDICIARY AS A SUBSYSTEM

Viewed holistically, the judiciary is only one system of the larger political system. Like other subsystems, its environment faces demands that become outputs and outcomes, so that no distinct boundaries separate the judicial subsystem from the others. Instead, it interacts with other subsystems continuously, as well as with private systems in the social environment.

The environment of judges marches constantly into their chambers, sometimes unobtrusively and sometimes loudly, seeking the protection or enhancement of certain values. Earlier, we saw in state law the four basic educational values of quality, equity, choice, and efficiency. However, the judge is not free to make such value choices alone. A constitution imposes certain constraints, shaping a judge in what he or she does. Professional canons have additional effects on who is selected or even considered to judge; institutional traditions also require procedures that shape the pace and division of labor. Further, the partisanship of extramural party life has affected a judge's recruitment and deliberations in our past, and carries influence even today.[1]

Finally, changes in the social order outside the judicial chambers often bring conflict inside to the courts' domain where certain functions must be met. The value conflict thrust into the court seeks authoritative allocation of resources to implement those values. Consequently, federal courts have a *manifest* function of resolving conflict within our federal system in accordance with special rules. Such decisions have an impact—not always favorable—on all branches of the national government and at all levels of government. This function means that federal courts affect the values underlying the conflict. Consequently, the Supreme Court legitimizes national policies and the values they reflect and, conversely, illegitimizes others. Illustrative are the reinforcement given to desegregation and special education by favorable Court decisions in recent decades. The difficulty, of course, is for the Court to do this in such a way that support for the courts as an institution does not decrease, while their decisions are complied with. This is why the forefathers thought this branch the weakest, as it lacks legitimation through election.

Further, courts must maintain some kind of balance with other national subsystems to reduce conflict among them. In its own processes the judiciary provides signals to litigants, the general public, and other political actors (including their own local courts) as to the outputs that it will reinforce. Issuing such signals is not the same as their acceptance by others, however. Throughout its history, the Court has had to balance itself carefully at key intersections of a nationally separated government, a federally divided nation, and a diverse population.

Yet its policymaking has shown more consistency than one might expect because regular processes are at work. Thus, there is initiation of controversies, accommodation among contestants via out-of-court settlement, persuasion of judge or jury, decision making, implementation of decisions, and so on. Indeed, the nature of justice has always been determined by such procedures. The courts reflect environmental demands, but their form and presentation differ here from other institutions. The lobbyist gives way to the lawyer, buttonholing takes the form of law review articles; and publicity campaigns appear as litigants' briefs.[2] The demands on a court are presented formally, dealing with matters of logic and legal precedent; however, research has stressed the independent role of a judge's values in the decisional process. So, the outputs of courts result from the interplay of judicial values within the court procedures, with resulting political consequences for the environment.[3]

However such decisions are derived, they constitute outputs

for society. They instruct a wide circle of citizens as to the value norms that the courts seek to impose on the environment. But what if no one notices or, if noticing, defies them or, if obeying, misinterprets them? When the Supreme Court confirms widely accepted social values, as with its nineteenth-century opposition to polygamy, then output and outcome are similar—compliance is very high. When, however, courts innovate in a direction contrary to accepted norms, some gap between output and outcome is to be expected, and compliance will be less. Despite the popular notion of a powerful Supreme Court, the conditions under which it can innovate are highly limited. Successful innovation could occur when a majority of justices favor a change, a national majority is also in agreement, and the decision would not hurt the court in other areas of government. If the Supreme Court moves when conditions do not permit, though, considerable opposition can arise from other subsystems.

JUDICIAL FUNCTIONS IN SCHOOL POLICY

Courts have been an arena for the recently increased political challenge to the system of schools by introducing new substance and rules. Two functions of the court have been sought in new school policy—legalization and regulation. *Legalization* involves "establishing a system of decision making committed to rules, trafficking in rights rather than preferences or interests, and justifying outcomes with reasons." *Regulation* involves "efforts of one level of government to control the behavior of another level."[4] These activities of courts, legislatures, and bureaucracies have promoted educational programs such as desegregation and compensatory, special, and bilingual education. Such efforts, however, have been subjected to heavy criticism from school professionals and lower governmental officials who must live under these mandates. It is important to remember that this top-down policy movement pursues the value of equity in distributing school resources; opponents claim, however, that other values are being lost in the process, such as quality or choice.

Two central legal concepts justified this legalization, namely, substantive and procedural rights. *Substantive rights* are advocated because students, educationally disadvantaged by the prevailing distribution of resources, had suffered a wrong inflicted on their constitutional rights. These rights were linked to the federal Constitution, particularly the equal protection clause of the Fourteenth Amendment. This process first appeared in *Brown* v. *The Board of Education of Topeka* in 1954, which evoked the right of equity for black segregated students. But such a right could also be applied—and later was—to equity for handicapped, Hispanic, poor, and female students. Court decisions often stimulated major congressional action embodying equity rights with application to all school districts nationwide.[5] For example, a 1988 act of Congress said that discrimination in the use of federal funds in one part of an institution—say, a university—could bar such funds for all other parts.

A second aspect of rights in legalization was the emerging concept of *due process in schooling*. That is, students were held to have protections about how school policies were made and implemented; these procedures became fixed in federal law as a result of this judicial stimulus. This was a case of adult legal requirements that were applied to the young. An ancient concept, due process arose from protection in criminal law, rooted as far back as the Magna Carta of 1215 A.D. and in our own Fourteenth Amendment. The procedural protection was spread by litigation in the 1960s to welfare and public employment and in 1975 to education in the Supreme Court decision of *Goss* v. *Lopez*. Congressional statutes then provided education for handicapped children with explicit procedural protections in the individual education programs' required meetings, hearings, and appeals. Court-based protections against arbitrary suspensions and dismissals have also created elaborate procedural safeguards that school administrators must follow. For example, in many schools today there are many rules for expelling a student. In short, new judicial rules from higher courts that rested on student rights had built a new structure for defining schooling. This challenge of the 1960s and 1970s built a new system that was in turn challenged later within the courts of the last two decades, especially the case for desegregation, as noted later.

As the new legalization in education arose, implementing them meant issuing more and more regulations. Officials in Washington and state capitals sought compliance by coercion through detailed regulatory oversight, reports, and threats of withdrawing funds. Behind this implementation was the potential citizen threat of litigation if particular children were treated inequitably. Also, many states subsequently incorporated these programs into their own statutes (sometimes under federal stimulus) and thus sought compliance on their own by issuing even more regulations that thrust one more layer of mandates to local officials. Education was not the only policy area where this centralization occurred; in fact, it was impacted less than other areas. Analysis of the origins of mandates for twelve policy areas in the late 1970s found that states were issuing far more regulations than were "the feds." The ratio of state to federal mandates was higher in seven of these twelve areas than in education, with two state actions for every federal one.[6] Even critics of the excesses of legalization and regulation recognize its success. As one scholar notes,

> It bears remarking that the promise of legalization has been greatly fulfilled. The history of America generally and of the public schools in particular may be told as a tale of progressive inclusion in the polity, and in that telling the forms and values of law have a central place.[7]

If the interests of certain groups have been advanced in the name of equity, the interests of yet others have not. Certainly the claim of educational professionals that they provide quality has been challenged, as we have noted throughout this book. Further, the failure of states and local school boards to provide certain groups with access to decision making and district resources also brings into question their commitment to the democratic value of choice. Moreover, the costs—economic or otherwise—of regulations for the system of schooling have not been calculated against their alleged benefits. That is, the value of efficiency in various legal actions has not been much addressed. That charge of the costs of a heavy bureaucracy enforcing legalization became a central argument in reformers urging "choice" schools in the late 1980s. They argued that to create a "market" solution to school ills, parents should be free to choose, via voucher payments, schools that would better educate their children. This, they proposed, would eliminate much of the hand of bureaucracy.[8]

This call for reform came at the end of a decade of the Reagan administration trying to overturn many national regulations. "Deregulation" meant federal education budgets being cut, and thirty small categorical grants were combined into a bloc grant with few regulations. But many of the regulations for bigger categorical programs still remained (e.g., compensatory, handicapped, and bilingual education). Also, while the Reagan administration withdrew from the plaintiff's side in desegregation cases, those cases continued nevertheless, and the Supreme Court continued its support until the early 1990s when Reagan's appointees changed the Court's emphasis. However, the Reagan-sponsored voucher system of school funding got nowhere in Congress, and the U.S. Department of Education was not abolished. But its secretaries reduced some regulations, and its Office of Civil Rights stopped requiring reports on the amount of desegregation. Finally, the attempt of the Office of Management and the Budget to apply cost-benefit measurements to regulations in the area of handicapped education was stalled.

In short, the tenacity of regulation in education often blocked reform. Also, networks of pressure groups defended special programs before often friendly legislative committees, and the courts were always available, too, as an option for asserting rights against unresponsive local administrators. Nor has federal deregulation down to local districts had much success at the state level, where state groups have closer contact and often greater strength with the formal agencies of state government.

Federal and state courts thus remain arenas for making decisions that may implement earlier legislation—or even overturn it. Notice the cross-currents of legalization's growth and challenge after 1980. Reagan administration attempts not to enforce earlier laws granting rights or entitlements were blocked by uncooperative federal courts. But parallel reform efforts in the states in this decade—the "top-down" addition of more course requirements—added even more regulations for local schooling. Under the Bush and Clinton presidencies, efforts began to centralize once again with the effort to get professionals to set national schooling standards. The Supreme Court decided in the 1990s to forego desegregation unless there was evidence of official intention to remain segregated, in effect overturning the *Brown* v.

Topeka decision of almost forty years earlier. After the 1994 congressional election, successful Republicans offered a "Contract with America" that sought to overturn national centralization by abolishing the Department of Education and sending funds back to the states. Two years later that had not been done.

This quick sketch focuses again on the role of the judiciary as a policy arena and on its interactions not only with other federal and state agencies, but with the social environment of ideas about education. We next examine two large-scale examples of this political process to flesh out the forces of change and stasis. Desegregation and finance reform policies are appropriate.

THE DESEGREGATION EXPERIENCE

As noted earlier, the Supreme Court initiated and concluded a forty-year experiment in desegregating schools. Experiences in the South and North demonstrate some different results, but the role of the judiciary was a constant in attempting to enforce this policy.

The Southern Experience

The Court in 1954 in *Brown* v. *Board of Education of Topeka* overturned an historic Southern practice of legal discrimination of the races in schooling. Moreover, this case was a dramatic departure from the Court's sixty-year-old decisions that "separate but equal" education was constitutionally acceptable.[9] The new decision called for "all deliberate speed" to desegregate, but that was taken by Southern opponents as a signal for delay (although justices later said that "deliberate" had meant "thought out"). Almost forty years later in *Freeman* v. *Pitts* (1992), the Court reversed itself, saying that a court may determine that it will not order further remedies in the area of student assignments where racial imbalance is not traceable, in even a proximate way, to constitutional violations.

Earlier with the *Topeka* case but with no specific guidelines, the Southern states resisted for a decade or more by adopting evasive practices, especially "freedom of choice" plans that desegregated very little.[10] So the Court began to insist on changes that would bring the two races together in schools, and a key was the busing of students to achieve that goal. Meanwhile, the administration of President Lyndon Johnson secured a new law providing federal aid to poor schools, but with a requirement that such funds were not available to segregated institutions. Both the judicial and legislative push put local districts between a rock and a hard place. Southerners could continue segregating but would lose much needed federal money; or they could attempt desegregation and get funds but must endure local and vocal opposition.

Reluctantly, the South chose the latter course, while indignant white Southerners—if they could afford it—fled public schools to new "Christian academies." As early as 1972, the percentage of black students in formerly white schools had risen to 44 percent from 18 percent before desegregation. But in the 1970s this increase leveled off and held constant through the 1980s. The results were that the percentage of

- black students in mostly minority schools dropped from 81 to 57 percent,
- black students in heavily black schools dropped from 78 to 23 percent, and
- predominantly white schools fell to 43 percent of all schools.[11]

There was considerable variation among states, with the most desegregation in Kentucky and Florida but the least in Mississippi. The percentage of white students attending schools with blacks points to variation among Southern cities: 61 to 66 percent in Tampa, Louisville, and Greenville, but only 16 to 19 percent in Miami, Atlanta, New Orleans, Memphis, and Houston. And no change in these numbers since the 1980s indicates a lack of national leadership to improve conditions. But at the local level, a "New South" emerged in which there was much more desegregation than in the past.[12]

What was occurring in these decades was the growing opposition of national institutions—presidents of both parties, majorities of Congress, and a new Supreme Court majority. In both regions a majority opinion of whites resisted further efforts to improve increasingly black schools and backed it up by increased "white flight" to the suburbs. Lacking political will by leaders and citizens, the reform went quite far but no further. By the time of the Supreme Court's 1992 opinion that if demography caused segregation, there was no constitutional barrier to its continuation. In that case, an *amicus curiae* brief by fifty-eight scholars of this field petitioned that research had found that desegregation was no failure, as critics alleged—but the Court ignored it. Thereafter, many school districts—including Topeka—successfully sought to cast off earlier desegregation orders.

THE COURTS AND FINANCE REFORM

Earlier in this book we pointed out that a major aspect of the new school turbulence is found in efforts to reform the basis of school financing. As with desegregation, the judiciary played a key role in stimulating this effort by formulating a general constitutional wrong and by calling for a change in school policy. Unlike desegregation, though, most of this effort has been a product of the *states'* highest court. By a narrow five to four majority in 1974, the Supreme Court refused to claim a constitutional safeguard against finance schemes that discriminated between rich and poor school districts. But note that school finances engage three of the four major education values—equity, quality, and efficiency. And if public school critics got their way with school vouchers, there would also be a choice value. Finance is also the issue that most engages legislators every year because it is the largest single expenditure in the state budget. The finance issue is always current, controversial, and relevant to almost everything that schools do.

School finance reform began in California as a result of the stimulus of the state policy issue network cited in Chapter 9. That state's supreme court declared a new principle, in *Serrano* v. *Priest*, that the "quality of public education may not be a function of the wealth of . . . a pupil's parents and neighbors." Financing schemes had to possess "fiscal neutrality," and because California's did not, it offended the equal protection clause of the state constitution and so would have to undergo reform. This constitutional approach spread as over half of the states legislatures faced similar challenges. By 1996 several dozen states had made changes, some minor but others major, to meet this new equity standard.

More inequities than just those traceable to taxable wealth were under attack. Complex state financial support formulas were introduced to adjust for adequacy, city cost overburdens, and special kinds of educational needs of handicapped and vocational programs and of other educationally needy children.[13] The degree of technicality now contemplated in the work of the courts generates serious problems. The courts are involved in areas that scholars know less about—how to measure educational adequacy and how to relate finance to pupil attainment. It was much easier when the task was only to devise formulas so that equal property tax effort resulted in equal amounts of local school revenue. Such changes also require more state funds for low-wealth districts. Political limitations also emerge out of the effort to sustain a reform coalition when each partner worries about getting its own slice of limited resources.[14]

The initiative of the state courts thus generated a flurry of legislative actions, and both court and legislature were further stimulated by an elite of scholars and educational reformers. The reformers met with much success in many states, providing authorities with new knowledge and policy options, as noted earlier. If success is measured by the number of states addressing the problem of resource inequity, then the reform did well—over half of the states made changes. But if success is measured by how much money actually got redistributed to improve the poor's schooling, the evidence is less certain. Certainly, reforms created school finance specialists, possessed of inventive minds, knowledge, and other resources needed to continue fighting. But their source lay in the stimulus of state courts.

A second generation of lawsuits later arose claiming that state governments had not met the court requirements imposed from the 1970s. In New Jersey, for example, plaintiffs in 1995 were successful in asserting that the low-property-wealth districts, or big cities, have not received state aid sufficient to close the spending gap with wealthy suburbs and thereby to neutralize the predominant effect of local property wealth on school spending. The

Serrano case in California, initiated in 1969, was finally settled in 1993 on yet another appeal based on the same reasoning as the 1969 case. The plaintiffs in California and New Jersey acknowledge that each state has made some improvements in its finance formula; but claimants charged that they have not met the standards set by the initial court orders. While finance equity was not a highly publicized issue, it played a role in orienting how the states distributed the large increases voted to enhance academic "excellence."

The debate can never be completely resolved until the courts have heard arguments based on all major educational values. To date, plaintiffs have featured equity as their key goal through the method of equalized, per-pupil spending. Often the state defendants have countered with arguments based on quality and efficiency. For example, state defendants claim that no strong correlation exists between per-pupil expenditures and education achievement, that marginal increases in per-pupil spending are not strong determinants of educational outcomes. Also, defendants assert that waste and inefficiency occur in school spending, with too much money allocated to overhead costs that do not help teachers in the classroom. Voucher proponents contend, on the other hand, that choice should be the priority value by giving money directly to parents rather than school districts. Parents could then choose which school they wanted, rather than being assigned a school by a public authority. These differing viewpoints will never be fully reconciled, and the courts will be just one of the arenas that the contestants will use to advance their specific values.

ROLE OF THE JUDICIARY IN TRADITIONAL AND REFORM LITIGATION

These accounts of two major educational reforms in which the judiciary played a major part do not exhaust either the impact of this process or the reforms; the latter are much too extensive for any but the most superficial review. Rather, we now turn to the meaning of the courts in the political process when they deal with public policy.

Judicial and Legislative Policy Functions Compared

It would help to understand first that far more similarities exist between what courts and legislatures do than is popularly known. Formal litigation seems different from the sweaty legislative committee rooms or boisterous chambers, but the differences are only matters of form. Also, some analysts have argued that reform litigation differs basically from traditional litigation, partaking more of the nature of legislation than do court decisions.

The distinctions emerge clearly between, on the one hand, traditional litigation and, on the other, public law litigation and legislation.[15] The first deals with only two interests of antagonists, it looks backward for experience, it provides relief for a sharply defined violation and, finally, it involves a judge who is passively unpartisan in the matter. But public litigation and legislation possess quite different qualities. They deal with multiple interests and look to future experiences for a "solution" that will work; the relief sought must be modifiable and involve many others; and the judge and legislators are partisan in the sense of being policy advocates.

The implementation of decisions requires different behavior by courts and legislators but both also take on other similarities. Table 12.1 sets out different tasks that both undertake when they seek to reform an institution, as was demonstrated in desegregation and finance noted above. Implementation breaks down any time even one of these tasks is not done. Note the problems that arise in just one task, for example, "setting intelligible standards" of compliance. In both policy cases the highest courts— federal and state—failed in this task in their initial decrees. When there was no supportive coalition to seek fuller compliance in the state legislatures—as with desegregation—contending parties then had to go back to the courts to set standards drawn out of specific cases. Yet where there was support for the court decision, as with financial reform, parties in each state still had to work their way through the legislative labyrinth, in which each member was vitally interested in the outcome for his or her district. But in the finance case, despite its complexity, a more precise set of standards—such as various formulas of tax reform—resulted in the early stages than was the case with desegregation.

Table 12.1

Structural Aspects of Traditional Litigation, Public Law Litigation, and Legislation

Structural Aspect	Traditional Litigation	Public Law Litigation	Legislation
Parties	Two, with mutually exclusive interests	Many with diverse interests—for example, amici in *Robinson v. Cahill*	Intervention by multiple interest groups is the rule
Fact-Finding	Retrospective and adjudicative (what happened, and so on)	Prospective and "functional"—what will work	Problem-solving approach is the norm
Relief	Coextensive with violation—nature of violation determines relief	Violation tells little about relief. New factors, like cost, enter in	Total pragmatism
	Relief closes transaction	Continuing jurisdiction, relief modifiable	Corrective amendments common
	Relief "nonintrusive," especially damages	Relief often entails running local governments	More detailed plans common
	Relief imposed and adjudicated (defendant has no role)	Formulation of decree involves negotiation, compromise	Social reform usually accommodates opposing interests
Decision Maker's Role	Judge is passive as to fact-finding, uninvolved with relief, no public identity	Judge must form court's position on facts, work out relief, and become identified with cause	Legislative fact-finding committees, work on specifics of bill, legislator identification with bill.

Source: William H. Clune with Robert E. Lindquist, "Understanding and Researching the Implementation of Education Laws: The Essential Characteristics of Implementation," Law, Governance, and Education Seminar, Institute for Research on Educational Finance and Governance, Stanford, February 1980, p. 31.

Part of the problem is that actors in both arenas are necessarily vague in their pronouncements in court order or law. Why, then, should they be so vague? There are some major strategic advantages to ambiguity under some circumstances. One scholar noted about the Supreme Court on the early desegregation cases:

> Ambiguity may be, in part, a tactic to minimize the anger caused by the opinion. An unclear opinion leaves people puzzled and, consequently, less angry. Ambiguity also leaves the Court more room to maneuver in the future, to change directions as practical requirements arise which recommended such a change. Finally, ambiguity might be marked up to judicial uncertainty regarding its proper role without scheme of government... When doctrine is less clear, this leaves more room for the political process to have its way [as] choices can be left to the discretion of others.[16]

If there are policy change agents who are willing to seize on one aspect of the ambiguous goal that the court sets, as with finance reform, then the political process can be carried out. But what if judicial vagueness has no decisive public support so that the normal political processes are blocked? That actually occurred in the South for a decade after the *Brown* decision and thereafter in the North as Congress and presidents backed off from enforcing both court orders and national law.[17]

Then the other tasks of implementation noted in Table 12.2— monitoring, dispute resolution, enforcement—fell into the laps of the judges. In this process, the highest court at first seeks to provide only broad guidelines, but these get more narrowly defined as more and more specific situations are brought to it on appeal. This means that the lower-level judges become increasingly embroiled in the implementation of desegregation. As a close study of the Boston case reveals, the monitoring judge can get involved in the innumerable minor details of school administration—boundary changes, personnel replacements, and so on— because the local school system ignores or resists the original order to desegregate.[18] As judges become increasingly faced by noncompliance with what for them is a constitutionally based order, they are compelled by their institutional responsibility to take on more of the implementation usually associated with administrative oversight.

Table 12.2
Judicial and Legislative Implementation Tasks

Courts	Legislatures
Decree formulation: negotiations between plaintiffs and defendants, use of experts, concern with such factors as fiscal burden and personnel resentment, setting intelligible standards.	*Formation of legislation:* input from interested parties, expert testimony, budgetary role, setting intelligible standards.
Monitoring retention of jurisdiction and compliance reports, need for master or special experts to serve as unbiased ally of courts.	*Administrative monitoring:* compliance data, field offices, inspections, and so on.
Dispute resolution: application of standards to new facts, differing interpretations of standards.	*Administrative dispute resolution:* negotiation when standards are unreasonable, appeal to administrative law judge, and so forth.
Enforcement: use of contempt power, brinkmanship, clarification of responsibilities, obtaining new resources, graduated sanctions.	*Enforcement:* continuum of harassment (extra reports, inspections), threatened fund cut-offs, actual cutoffs, and so on.

Source: Note, "Implementation Problems in Institutional Reform Litigation," *Harvard Law Review* 91 (December 1977): 428-63. Copyright © 1977 by the Harvard Law Review Association.

An Evaluation of Judicial Action

Clearly, there are limits to what judges can do. Nor is it the case that judges should do nothing because no political support exists for correcting an unconstitutional situation. If this were the case, we could leave the interpretation of every law up to each citizen, an excellent formula for social anarchy and a major reason why we have rules of law in the first place. But in over four decades of judicial involvement in major policy reform and institutional changes, courts have been able to do some things better than others. While one may worry about the limits of legalism, the federal government can indeed provide national standards of service and behavior with the funds to implement them; however, settlement of the details is better attained by political agencies at all levels of government.[19] Yet, as desegregation demonstrates, what if those agencies not only do not act but even obstruct the national standard?

Judicial Activism and Its Effects

What are the consequences of judicial activism? Besides having direct effects on groups of citizens (e.g., the Brown child in the *Topeka* case or Rodriguez in the *San Antonio* case), it can affect other governmental institutions as well. In desegregation, there is a "ratcheting" effect, in which one court's determination that a particular school practice is discriminatory becomes an input to federal agencies; they then incorporate it into their regulations, which can later be used in other courts as litigation arises. Or courts may affect one another more directly. State supreme courts have been found to influence one another mutually in public policy initiatives, a form of "horizontal federalism," found in school finance reform.[20]

For example, complicated events in New Jersey over financial reform brought the state supreme court into conflict with the state legislature.[21] The latter's lack of guidelines for policy direction, as well as its mandate to correct the unconstitutional financing law, threw the politics of that state into greater conflict in 1996. However, the results did establish standards that in turn set off challenges to such laws in other states, just as the California decision in the *Serrano* case in the late 1960s set off a round of challenges. A close analysis of the New Jersey controversy concluded that the results demonstrated that the judiciary's main role must be "agenda setting," not "decision making." That is, courts do their utmost when they raise policy issues that other government agencies must resolve but without the courts designating the actual process of solution.

Others have noted the broader policy roles of *state* supreme courts in our history. They have innovated in policymaking, complemented state legislative goals, elaborated the meaning of Supreme Court opinions (but also restricted the latter's opinions to protect their state's laws from invalidation), and lobbied in legislatures to maintain and develop their own institutions.[22] All of these court actions have consequences for public policy—causing

new policy issues to emerge, stimulating discussion of policy alternatives, authoritatively deciding the direction of new policies,
and overseeing policy administration.

Judicial capacities are impressive because when undertaking
implementation the judiciary possesses considerable authority,
trust, and information. A judge is thus in a strategic position in
policy conflict to assure that decisions are emphatically enforced.
This presence changes the power quotient of the plaintiffs when
court sanctions and information can be added to their side. Policy
goals thus can more easily be put into effect. However, courts
can also lag in such matters because they can also misconceive
and misapply knowledge. As critics of regulation insist, courts
can use sanctions that are too clumsy and actually counterpro-
ductive.[23] Then, as is true of other governmental agencies who
fail in their political tasks, the policy results will not meet plaintiffs' needs and so may generate distrust of the courts.[24]

The Judiciary in the World of School Policy

The judiciary has made its role much more evident in the
arena of educational policies in the last four decades. When it
does not act to define problems and needs, other agencies do so.
When it *does* act, new distributions of resources and values usually emerge as educational policy. If both judicial inaction and
action have policy consequences, then either condition makes
the courts into policy actors. When the Supreme Court sidesteps
a decision on the equity value in the finance reform case, then
other levels of government feel free to seek their own solutions.
However, when that same Court voids legal segregation or later
accepts demographic segregation, it sets the scene for actions
that effectively alter the practice. If, however, the Court is evasive
in defining Northern segregation problems, then lower federal
courts take on a much more active and determinative role.

The judiciary, however, cannot do everything, as the initial
Southern rejection of the *Brown* decision demonstrated. Inter-
vening between what the court seeks (outputs) and what eventu-
ates (outcomes) are certain barriers. These are raised by group
resistance based on other values, by popular ignorance, by communication failure, by information overload, and by other con-
founding aspects of social and policy conflict. A court mandate

does not bring total or quick acceptance, does not provide sufficient resources for the resourceless, and does not teach us how to resolve conflict or to live with ambiguity. Other persons and events must perform these tasks, even with a supportive judiciary. While the judiciary has been a major stimulus for educational innovation in the last four decades, it has also met with obstruction, misunderstanding, and uncertainty. The court is thus in the position that Shakespeare described in *Henry IV*, when one character proclaims, "I can call spirits from the vasty deeps," and Hotspur responds, "Why, so can I, or so can any man, but will they come when you do call for them?"

The supreme courts of state and nation have been called for from their "vasty deeps" by citizens afflicted by racial and fiscal discrimination. Despite some reservations about how much courts can do in policy innovation, both judicial friend and foe would agree that little would have been changed without positive judicial response to such calls. That agreement marks the significant potential that inheres in these judicial "spirits." Even on its own, the judiciary can at least create a national dialogue about the standards of education that we will provide our children. In this way, the unthinkable of yesterday becomes the convention of today. Creating this flexibility of mind is a function that the judiciary and good teachers share equally.

NOTES

1. Even by 1987 differences between federal judges appointed by Presidents Jimmy Carter and Ronald Reagan were clearly evident.

2. Clement R. Vose, *Caucasians Only* (Berkeley: University of California Press, 1959); and "Litigation as a Form of Pressure Group Activity," *Annals of the American Academy of Political and Social Science* 319 (1958): 22–25.

3. The behavioral school embodying this concept of values is illustrated in Glendon Schubert, *Constitutional Politics* (New York: Holt, Rinehart & Winston, 1960); and Glendon Schubert, ed., *Judicial Decision-Making* (New York: Free Press, 1963).

4. David Kirp, "Introduction: The Fourth R: Reading, Writing, 'Rithmetic— and Rules," in *School Days, Rule Days*, David Kirp and Donald Jensen, eds. (Philadelphia: Falmer, 1986), p. 12. This book is a thorough, often critical, view of these developments but with a balanced sense of what they have produced that is beneficial.

5. For a full review of these leading decisions, see David Kirp and Mark Yudof, *Educational Policy and the Law* (Berkeley: McCutchan, 1982).

6. Catherine Lovell and Charles Tobin, "The Mandating Issue," *Public Administration Review* 41 (1981): 321.

7. Kirp, "Introduction," p. 6.

8. John Chubb and Terry Moe, *Politics, Markets, and America's Schools* (Washington, D.C.: Brookings, 1990).

9. Robert Kluger, *Simple Justice* (New York: Knopf, 1975) is an exhaustive account of this drama.

10. For a thorough coverage of the 1960s, see Gary Orfield, *The Reconstruction of Southern Education* (New York: Wiley, 1969). For the most comprehensive analysis of all phases of desegregation up to 1978, see Gary Orfield, *Must We Bus? Segregated Schools and National Policy* (Washington: Brookings Institution, 1978).

11. Data below from Gary Orfield, *Public School Desegregation in the United States, 1968–1980* (Washington, D.C.: Janet Carter for Political Studies, 1987).

12. For a detailed review of how that happened in one Mississippi country, over a quarter century, see Frederick Wirt, *"I Ain't What I Was"* (Durham, N.C.: Duke University Press, 1997).

13. A thorough examination is found in Walter Garms, James Guthrie, and Lawrence Pierce, *School Finance: The Economics and Politics of Education* (Englewood Cliffs, N.J.: Prentice-Hall, 1987) and successive editions.

14. Michael W. Kirst, "Coalition Building for School Finance Reform: The Case of California," *Journal of Education Finance* 4 (Summer 1978): 29–45; Joel S. Berke, *Answers to Inequity: An Analysis of New School Finance* (Berkeley: McCutchan, 1974).

15. William Clune with Robert Lindquist, "Understanding and Researching for the Implementation of Education Laws: The Essential Characteristics of Implementation," (Stanford, Calif.: Law, Governance, and Education Seminar, February 1980).

16. Tyll van Geel, "Racist Discrimination from Little Rock to Harvard," *Education Administration Quarterly* 168 (1980).

17. Orfield, *Must We Bus?*, Pt. two.

18. See the details in Emmett H. Buell, Jr., *School Desegregation and Defended Neighborhoods: The Boston Controversy* (Lexington, Mass.: Lexington Books, 1981).

19. David L. Kirp, *Just Schools: The Idea of Racial Equality in American Education* (Berkeley: University of California Press, 1982); Donald L. Horowitz, *The Courts and Social Policy* (Washington: Brookings Institution, 1977).

20. In G. Alan Tarr and Mary C. Porter, "State Supreme Court Policymaking and Federalism" (paper presented to the American Political Science Convention, August 1980).

21. Richard Lehne, *The Quest for Justice* (New York: Longman, 1978).

22. Tarr and Porter, "State Supreme Court Policymaking."

23. For education, see Kirp and Jensen, *School Days*.

24. Compare the judge's role with that of the "fixer" in administration in Eugene Bardach, *The Implementation Game* (Berkeley: University of California Press, 1977). A review of experience with this and other policies delineating this distinction is in Paul Peterson, *The Price of Federalism* (Washington, D.C.: Brookings Institution, 1995).

Part IV

CURRENT POLITICAL CONTROVERSIES

13

Regulation and Intergovernmental Relations in Education Policy

The history of intergovernmental relations in education policy has been dominated by regulations, categorical programs, and technical assistance by higher levels of government to stimulate or require lower levels to make changes in policy and practice.[1] There have been many metaphors to depict education policy within intergovernmental relations, including "marble cake" or a "picket fence." The marble cake recognizes that the federal, state, and local levels are not distinct, and policy spills over from one level to another. The picket-fence metaphor is based on categorical programs like Title I or special education, noted in the previous chapter, whereby the federal and state levels interact to mandate or stimulate specific local programs. Each picket in the fence includes administrators (e.g., of vocational education) at all levels of government, and auditors to ensure that federal/state funds are spent within a separate picket (or policy sphere).

Intergovernmental policies have more to do with legitimating change or with structure than with the nature of teaching or classroom practice. A useful metaphor is that of an "ecology of games" that are largely separate, but do interact and provide inputs to each intergovernmental unit. For example, there is a state legislative game, a state administrative game, a district and school administration game, and a teaching game.[2] Each game has separate players, rewards, inputs to other games, and provides outcomes to other games. Programs from higher levels are just one of many influences on the local school district and classroom game. State programs interact with local demands, local taxes, and needs of local board members, local employees, and community groups.

Winning the local game for some players focuses on obtaining state categorical and general aid to create more local programs. But many local administrators are not particularly rewarded in the intergovernmental game, so they tend to tune out signals from the state or federal levels. Teachers see their successes in terms of student learning or just getting through the day. The publicity surrounding the passage of an omnibus state or federal reform package is not central to teachers' lives. Consequently, intergovernmental policy has limited influence on classroom practice.

This ecology of games of education policy is one appropriate concept for attempts by higher levels of government to leverage and change lower levels. It is easier to use state regulatory policies to influence administrators at the local level rather than to change classroom teaching. Some state policies employ mandates that outrun the state's existing technology and capacity at local classroom levels. For example, attempts to "tinker" (e.g., business-oriented budget systems, like Program Planning and Management by Objectives) have left scant residue at the local level.[3] In sum, each governmental level tries to maximize its sphere of influence by seizing opportunities or rejecting higher-level policies. It is in this larger political context that stasis and challenge interact in American education today within a complex intergovernmental system.

GENERAL FINDINGS FROM A DECADE OF RESEARCH ON INTERGOVERNMENTAL RELATIONS

Over the last ten years, researchers have reached general conclusions about intergovernmental relations, of which four have major implications.

Not a Zero-Sum Game

Power and influence in education intergovernmental relations is *not* a zero-sum game whereby one level gains and another level loses the ability to influence policy.[4] Rather, the result may be an increased volume of policy at *all* levels. For example, state curricular frameworks can galvanize more local curriculum policymaking and leadership at the local level, so that the policymaking impact of all governance levels can increase simultaneously. For instance, state graduation standards in the 1980s became a required floor beyond which many local education agencies (LEAs) added courses. The dominant concept, then, is mutual influence among education policy levels, not zero-sum.

The interaction may take the form of state mandates; for example, requiring a semester of economics for high school students is strongly directive of local behavior. But mandates and rules have not been the main strategy for states to guide or influence local curricular content. California curricular policies in science and social studies, for example, are not mandates but provide a framework rather than prescribe a detailed list of content to be taught. Moreover, many local districts use the state curricular framework as a springboard for their solution to a particular local context. Much state policy is characterized by low enforcement, imprecise policy directives, and local initiatives. Many local districts not only complied with California's 1983 reform law (SB 813), but also were building on the state-based mandates to add new policies of their own.[5] In their study of six states (including California), researchers at the Consortium for Policy Research in Education found that:

> Local activism in reform has been noted in several studies of the reform movement. . . . This local activism takes a variety of forms: staying ahead of

the state and of peers by enacting policies in anticipation of higher state policies to meet specific needs, and using state policies as a catalyst for achieving district objectives.[6]

Limited Impact of Deregulation

Deregulation per se (perhaps even including abolishing state codes) does *not* result in widespread significant local policy change.[7] Additional policies and capacity building actually are needed to utilize the flexibility and creativity that deregulation may stimulate. This result implies that elimination of state code sections should be supplemented with other policies such as technical assistance. Changes in state or federal regulatory policy interact with wide variations in local capacity and context. The impact of deregulation will vary depending on many local factors, and there may be no central tendency of local responses.

Different policy designs, however, can alter local responses. For example, blanket waivers of state regulations have more potential impact than rule-by-rule waivers. Blanket waivers broaden the local horizon for change.[8] Often, LEAs are unaware that some desired local changes do not require a state waiver. In South Carolina, for example, one half of the changes undertaken in the wake of a flexibility program could have been implemented prior to deregulation.[9] However, automatic sweeping deregulation may stimulate change because it broadens the horizon for planning change, and removes constraints more thoroughly than rule-by-rule waivers.

States use differential regulatory strategies whereby some districts are granted more or less regulation depending on performance indicators and fiscal problems. The consequences of state differential treatment strategies are highly dependent on their designs and the local context. The less successful schools may be the most in need of deregulation, but some states restrict waivers only to high-performing schools.[10] The takeover of low-performing local districts by states has had little direct impact on schools.[11] The consequences of state takeover depend in part on the capacity of the state agency, and whether it can assist or broker meaningful help. State takeover of local school districts, like Jersey City, New Jersey, does provide better fiscal control and solvency in LEAs that have been near bankruptcy or using questionable fiscal practices. But unless the intervention is specifically designed to focus on instruction, the state presence is typically not felt beyond the central office. In sum, deregulation supporters assume particular types of local responses, but not much is known about the impact of large-scale bloc grants or massive repeal of state codes.

Sanctions, Incentives, and Knowledge Creep

Several states and localities have attempted to use sanctions and incentives to stimulate desired change or performance. But incentive systems are still in the trial-and-error stage. It is very difficult to obtain sufficient political support for sanctions on teachers or schools, such as decreasing teacher pay or removing categorical funds. Using state assessment systems for rewards or sanctions at the school level has raised serious questions about their reliability and validity for such purposes.[12] Teacher salary schedules have not changed in decades and continue to include academic credits beyond the B.A. and years of service. In sum, intergovernmental incentive systems are exceedingly complex to design if policymakers desire to have consistent effects on schools and students.[13]

Many recent curricular reforms (e.g., National Council of Teachers of Mathematics standards) are not clearly specified in terms of expected LEA and school implementation. State standards and frameworks have been promulgated in general terms with considerable local latitude (for example, see the standards statements under U.S. Department of Education grants). Though teachers may complain that such general policies fail to give sufficient guidance for instruction,[14] they still may have an effect on practice by shaping attitudes about content and performance. For example, state curricular policies can change the local discussion and inject new concepts and thinking into local policies. This is another example of how intergovernmental relations need *not* be a zero-sum game.

State policies can provide knowledge that creeps into local *practice* over time, such as the use of student portfolios in Vermont.[15] Curricular reform networks that are started and supported by government but not part of government have changed class-room practice.[16] These reform networks, such as the California Science Improvement Network (CSIN), can build teacher capac-ity, reorient staff development, and seep into the classroom.[17] Policymakers get more impact by using "push" factors, like as-sessments and frameworks, *in conjunction* with "pull" factors, like incentives and demonstrations. Some package of these policies has more potential than stand-alone policies to help classroom practice.

The context of teachers is very different in reality from how many policymakers view intergovernmental impact on classroom practice.[18] Consequently, policy needs to be designed from a view inside the classroom looking outward rather than a view from top-down intergovernmental leaders. This classroom context-prac-tice view indicates that capacity-building policies such as staff de-velopment are crucial if they provide teachers with coaching, follow up, and professional communities for mutual assistance.[19]

Organizational Capacity

State and local education agencies are slow to adapt to new policy goals. State education agencies (SEAs) are not well struc-tured or well prepared to help implement and sustain systemic reform.[20] SEAs are organized primarily along categorical or special-purpose units that inhibit alignment among an array of policies and comprehensive approaches. These segmented organizations need to be recast into shared understandings, roles, and tasks that flatten the hierarchy. Comprehensive reform requires policy coherence and treatment of holistic problems, which means SEA teamwork and collaboration are crucial. Because even aligned state policies cannot be expected to have consistent local effects, adjustments will be needed for diverse local contexts.

Most local central offices suffer from the same fragmented struc-tural and operational problems as SEAs.[21] Until the effective schools movement in the 1970s, local central offices paid scant attention to curriculum and instruction. District structures resemble geo-logical accretions over many years and are not monolithic.[22] State policy is just one of many influences, while LEA central subunits react differentially to policies from higher levels. In some LEAs,

Title I central units are leading new practices, but in others they inhibit attention to new state assessments or curricular frameworks. Some central offices are strong in science standards leadership, but weak in math or some other subject.

Districts in the 1990s find it difficult to work intensively on all subject matter areas at once. Moreover, districts are beginning to reduce reliance on staff development if it is not aligned with subject matter reforms. Districts report more interaction with intrastate and interstate teaching and subject matter networks such as the Urban Math Collaborative.[23] Some SEAs have utilized their support of these networks as a way to amplify their impact and compensate for a lack of highly qualified SEA employees. These teacher networks have considerable promise for changing classroom practice, but they often need sustenance from federal or state funds. For instance, California Science Improvement Network (CSIN) was started by the California State Department of Education and is now nurtured by the University of California. This network helps elementary teachers improve their science instruction with coaching and follow up among local teacher colleagues as well as from science experts from around the state.

CURRENT INTERGOVERNMENTAL ISSUES

Much current debate, particularly at the federal level, focuses on replacing categorical grants for special purposes (e.g., vocational education) with bloc grants that state and local authorities could use for any purpose. As noted, categoricals developed largely in isolation of each other, which rapidly led to a local and state disease called "hardening of the categories." Most of the categoricals initially were not directed at the core classroom technology for curriculum and instruction. Special education and Title I, for example, relied significantly on "pull-out" programs that were not integrated well with core subject instruction.[24]

Some states in the 1970s followed the 1965–1970 federal categorical growth by creating many of their own. SEAs became more regulation oriented as they enforced the federal and their own categoricals. Categorical policymakers and administrators became adept over time in finding enforcement and influence techniques that helped federal/state grants come closer to their intended local purposes.[25] Such techniques included federal/state field audits; lawsuits; socialization of state and local administrators hired with categorical funds; and gradual infusion of categorical purposes within the standard operating procedures of schools. There developed suddenly a proliferation of regulations, rules, monitoring, and auditing. This trend periodically resulted in agitation for deregulation, waivers, and bloc grants as evidenced in the Reagan education program.

As this categorical enforcement "success" was becoming more evident, concern shifted to the alleged negative, cumulative, and aggregative impact of the totality of categorical grants. But studies by Stanford Research Institute and others indicated that LEAs had become "accustomed" to handling the numerous federal categories and were not overburdened by regulations.[26] The Reagan administration attempted to consolidate most federal categoricals, but was rebuffed by the Democratic Congress, and ended up with only minor consolidations.[27]

Categorical issues and regulation then began to recede from the spotlight of intergovernmental concern around 1983 when state reforms turned to higher academic standards for all pupils, and the core curriculum. Later in the 1980s categorical programs became a concern because they were not well integrated or aligned with high academic standards and systemic reform. Their restructuring and deregulation were a major focus of the 1994 ESEA reauthorization, and currently is being discussed by Republican Congressional leaders for bloc grant legislation.

The Clinton administration has tried to link and align categoricals with national academic standards. For example, Title I achievement gains are to be measured using more challenging state assessments rather than nationally normed basic skills tests. But national Republican leaders have emphasized eliminating categoricals altogether through flexible bloc grants to states or localities. The current pro/con arguments about categorical programs are many sided. Supporters contend that categorical grants protect client groups that states and localities tend to neglect, and decategorization has historically been linked with funding cuts because there are few special interests that support untied funding. Opponents stress that categorical grants fragment the approach to cross-cutting problems like education standards, prevent the reallocation of funds from ineffective programs, involve excess overhead costs, and lead to excessive federal and state intrusion in local decisions.

What enlightenment can research provide this political and conceptual debate? Categorical grants can have a lasting impact on local schools.[28] For example, policies can promote change in organizational structure including added personnel layers (e.g., vocational specialists or aides) or "pull-out" teaching structures under Title I. These instructional methods or organizational changes require a new layer of specialists that can be organized into a constituency for maintenance of the "program." Categorical grants also have a strong influence on pupil classification and the definition of specialties in teaching. For instance, certificates for teaching remedial reading or bilingual education differentiate the specialist from the regular classroom teacher. They are necessary to assure that federal funds are used for special programs and constituencies.

On the other extreme, categorical programs have little influence on the extent and nature of curricular coverage of specific topics or on teaching methods or strategies—such as individualization of instruction or inquiry methods. A study found that new math concepts and science inquiry methods promoted by the federal government in the 1960s have vanished from the vast majority of schools a decade later.[29] Teachers initiate most classroom talk and orchestrate classroom interaction around brief factual questions.[30]

These probable low-impact areas are the most difficult for federal and state governments to monitor or create political constituencies for program maintenance. Some tinkering such as federally sponsored in-service training could have some impact or leave a residue, but have been small scale since NSF programs in the mid-1960s.

The school-level impact of bloc grants is more difficult to discern because unrestricted dollars cannot be easily identified. They become part of the general support base of an organization and will free up dollars for other purposes. In 1981 the Reagan Administration succeeded in consolidating twenty-eight federal categorical programs into a Chapter 2 ESEA bloc grant. Field studies indicate that Chapter 2 was used for nonrecurring expenditures like computers that were not part of an articulated school improvement effort.[31] This small bloc grant ($800 million) did reduce local administrative burden, but local parents had less influence on spending decisions than under categorical grants, and the classroom impact is unknown. Recent studies suggest that increased local flexibility over small amounts of money not accompanied by local capacity building is unlikely to have much school or classroom impact. Larger bloc grants may have more potential for changing practice, but there are no data to support either a positive or negative case.

CONCLUSION

It is a long way from a federal or state grant to thousands of classrooms. Policies create a skeleton or shell within which classroom practice can change, but much more than policy is needed to alter instruction for most classes. Moreover, policies need to be much more robust and sophisticated than most traditional approaches that stress solely either regulation or deregulation and bloc grants. Policymakers must also not lose sight of the realities and context of the classroom teacher. Intergovernmental policies can help establish favorable conditions for teachers who are operating in their own varied contexts, but policy is only one of many influences on how teachers respond to students in their classrooms. What are the political factors that do improve educational standards? In the next chapter we turn to that question.

NOTES

1. Michael W. Kirst and Robert Jung, "Beyond Mutual Adaptation, into the Bully Pulpit," *Educational Administration Quarterly* (1986): 17–33.

2. William A. Firestone, "Education Policy as an Ecology of Games," *Educational Researcher* 18, no. 7 (1989): 18–24.

3. David Tyack and Larry Cuban, *Tinkering Toward Utopia* (Cambridge: Harvard, 1995).

4. Richard F. Elmore and Susan H. Fuhrman, "Understanding Local Control in Wake of State Education Reform," *Educational Evaluation and Policy Analysis* 12 (1990): 82–96.

5. Michael W. Kirst and Gary Yee, "An Examination of the Evolution of California State Education Reform, 1983–1993," in *Ten Years of State Education Reform*, Diane Massell and Susan H. Fuhrman, eds. (New Brunswick, N.J.: Rutgers, Eagleton Institute of Politics: Consortium for Policy Research in Education, 1994), pp. 158–171.

6. Susan H. Fuhrman and Richard F. Elmore, "Understanding Local Control in the Wake of State Education Reform," *Educational Evaluation and Policy Analysis* 12 (1990): 82–96.

7. Susan H. Fuhrman and Richard F. Elmore, *Ruling Out Rules: The Evolution of Deregulation in State Education Policy* (New Brunswick, N.J.: Rutgers, Eagleton Institute of Politics: Consortium for Policy Research in Education, 1994).

8. Susan H. Fuhrman and Richard F. Elmore, *Takeover and Deregulation* (New Brunswick, N.J.: Rutgers, Eagleton Institute of Politics: Consortium for Policy Research in Education, 1992).

9. Consortium for Policy Research in Education, "Ten Lessons About Regulation and Schooling," *CPRE Policy Briefs* (New Brunswick, N.J.: Rutgers, Eagleton Institute of Politics, 1992).

10. Ibid.

11. Fuhrman and Elmore, *Takeover and Deregulation*.

12. Richard F. Elmore, Charles H. Abelmann, and Susan H. Fuhrman, "The New Accountability in State Education Policy," in *Holding Schools Accountable*, H. Ladd, ed. (Washington, D.C.: The Brookings Institution, 1996).

13. Consortium, "Ten Lessons."

14. Elmore, Abelmann, and Fuhrmann, "The New Accountability."

15. David K. Cohen and James P. Spillane, "Policy and Practice: The Relations Between Governance and Instruction," in *Designing Coherent Education Policy: Improving the System*, Susan H. Fuhrman, ed. (San Francisco: Jossey-Bass, 1993).

16. Robert E. Floden, "Portfolios for Capacity Building: Systemic Reform in Vermont," in *Studies of Education Reform: Systemic Reform*, Margaret E. Goertz, Robert E. Floden, and Jennifer O'Day, eds. (New Brunswick, N.J.: Rutgers, Eagleton Institute of Politics: Consortium for Policy Research in Education, 1995); Jennifer O'Day, "Systemic Reform in California," in Goertz, Floden, and O'Day, *Studies of Education Reform*; Richard Murnane, "Teaching to New Standards," in *Rewards and Reform: Creating Educational Incentives that Work*, Susan H. Fuhrman and Jennifer O'Day, eds. (San Francisco: Jossey-Bass, forthcoming).

17. Consortium, "Ten Lessons"; Richard F. Elmore and Susan H. Fuhrman, eds., *The Governance of Curriculum* (Alexandria, Va.: Association for Supervision and Curriculum, 1994).

18. Milbrey McLaughlin and Joan Talbert, *Contexts that Matter for Teaching* (Stanford, Calif: Center for Research on the Context of Secondary School Teaching, 1993).

19. Ibid.

20. Susan Lusi, *Systemic Reform: Challenges Faced by State Departments of Education* (Washington, D.C.: ASCD Yearbook, 1994).

21. Richard F. Elmore, *The Role of Local School Districts in Instructional Improvement* (New Brunswick, N.J.: Rutgers, Eagleton Institute of Politics: Consortium for Policy Research in Education, 1991).

22. David Cohen, "Policy and Organization," *Harvard Education Review* 52, no. 4 (1982): 474–499.

23. Floden, "Portfolios for Capacity Building."

24. Dennis Doyle and Bruce Cooper, *Federal Aid to the Disadvantaged* (New York: Falmer, 1988).

25. Kirst and Jung, "Beyond Mutual Adaptation." A similar pattern emerged in other national policies; see Paul Peterson, *When Federalism Works* (Washington, D.C.: Brookings Institution, 1986).

26. Michael Knapp, *Cumulative Effects of Federal Education Policies on Schools and Districts* (Menlo Park, Calif.: SRI International, 1983).

27. Chester Finn, Jr., "Reflections on the 'Disassembly of the Federal Educational Role,'" *Education and Urban Society* 15, no. 3 (1983): 389–396.

28. Michael W. Kirst, "Teaching Policy and Federal Categorical Programs," *Handbook of Teaching and Policy*, Lee Shulman and Gary Sykes, eds. (New York: Longman, 1983), pp. 426–448; Richard F. Elmore and Susan H. Fuhrman, "The National Interest and Federal Role in Education," *Publius* 20(1990): 149–163; Fuhrman and Elmore, "Understanding Local Control."

29. Robert Stake and James Easley, *Case Studies in Science Education* (Washington, D.C.: National Science Foundation, 1978).

30. John Goodlad, *A Place Called School* (New York: McGraw Hill, 1984).

31. Kirst and Jung, "Beyond Mutual Adaptation."

14

The Politics of Education Standards

THE POLITICS OF APPROVING CURRICULUM CONTENT STANDARDS*

As the national standards debate demonstrates, curriculum policymaking is essentially a political as well as a technical process. What decision rules will state and local standards bodies use to choose among competing alternatives? As noted politics is the authoritative allocation of competing values. Disputes such as AIDS education and creation science highlight the values conflict embedded in curriculum disputes.[1] Proposals to increase curricular scope have reached their logical (and absurd) conclusion when elementary teachers are expected to teach reading, writing, several varieties of arithmetic, geography, spelling, science, economics, music, art, foreign languages, and history. At the same time they are helping children to develop physically, morally, intellectu-

*This section adapted from Michael Kirst, "The Politics of Nationalizing Curricular Content," *American Journal of Education* 102 (August 1994): 388-392. Copyright © 1994 by the University of Chicago Press.

ally, and be molded into good citizens. If the school were to take advantage of the millions of dollars invested in national curriculum development, each of these matters should be treated independently with specially trained teachers. Things are hardly less chaotic in secondary schools.

The oldest and simplest solution to this problem is to endow an individual or small group with the authority to make these decisions by exercising professional, and presumably expert, judgment. This decision-making body (e.g., a state school board or a national subject matter association) is linked to the community that gives it authority and power. This linkage provides the decision makers with a degree of autonomy that ranges from absolute responsiveness to virtual independence.

But this only pushes our search one step further. What sort of decision procedures do curricular decision makers follow? In the past, this can best be described by a strategy of *disjointed incrementalism,* that is, a strategy that simplifies complex problems.[2] The major features of disjointed incrementalism are (1) acceptance of the broad outlines of the existing situation with only marginal changes contemplated, (2) consideration of only a restricted variety of policy alternatives, excluding those entailing radical change, (3) consideration of only a restricted number of consequences for any given policy, (4) adjustment of objectives to politics as well as vice versa, (5) willingness to reformulate the problem as data become available, and (6) serial analysis and piecemeal alteration rather than a single comprehensive attack.

So, many curricular decision makers use pragmatic methods of decision making that result in minimal changes at the margin. Conflict can be avoided by using vague language concerning standards and covering so many topics that no major interest group feels left out. Content priority is sacrificed to the political necessity of breadth in coverage.

The push for national standards, however, proposes to change this disjointed incrementalism to a nonincremental and complete overhaul of subject matter standards and exams. Examples cited by national standards advocates include recent efforts by the National Council of Teachers of Mathematics (NCTM) and the California History/Social Science State Framework. The politics of these efforts are complex, as one observer of the NCTM noted,

> Twin needs propelled the development of NCTM's standards for schools mathematics: the need to gain consensus and the need to promote change. On the one hand, if these standards were to stand as the banners of the community, then they had to reflect shared values and commitment. On the other hand, if change was desired, then these standards had to do more than reflect current practice. New ideas were needed, ideas that departed from extant assumptions and practices.[3]

Others prepared curriculum formulation case studies of NCTM, California and New York social studies, science curriculum reform in the 1960s, and the College Board's Advanced Placement Program.[4]

Some political dilemmas confronting policymakers based on these cases are presented below. The list is written from the vantage point of the decisions that will be faced by a state or local standards group when they consider certification of national content standards.

1. Who must be involved in the process to feel it is inclusive? Students? Business? If you exclude groups, this will lead to charges of bias. If you include every group that is suggested, this will lead to a cumbersome and slow process.
2. If you chose standards that achieve a broad consensus in the field, then the "leading edge thinkers" will object. You will be accused of certifying "what is" rather than "what ought."
3. If you chose a standard that achieves consensus in a field you will *not* be able to satisfy demands for "less is more"— consensus expands topics rather than cutting them.
4. If you chose a standard that reflects current content consensus, this will lead to criticism that you have not sufficiently stressed interdisciplinary content. There is limited interdisciplinary content in any of the subject matter organizations like NCTM.
5. If you approve standards that are too general, or do not contain pedagogy, you will be criticized that there is insufficient instructional guidance for teachers, and the content gaps will be filled by tests or assessment. If you do approve pedagogy or detailed standards, you will be criticized because standards are too long and complex and overly control local practice.

6. If you do not hear appeals from the public for specific content changes (e.g., inclusion of creation science) then you will be criticized for not having public participation *at the highest level* and for leaving crucial decisions to a technical panel of nonelected officials. If the state hears all these protests it will become bogged down in time-consuming and fractious disputes.

7. If you approve similar structure or dimensions for all subjects, you will be criticized for ignoring the big (structural) differences between such fields as math, science, and social studies.

8. If you hear appeals from subject matter subspecialties (too much physics, not enough biology), you will end up arbitrating balance among technical fields within a subject matter area. If you do not hear these issues, you will be accused of approving unbalanced standards within a subject area. For example, there is too much physics and not enough biology in science content standards.

9. If you wish to have standards in place by 2000, then you will contradict findings that it takes closer to five years than two years to formulate national content standards.

In short, content standards require complex trade-offs, and there is no way to avoid conflict and a sense of winners and losers. Difficult choices must be made concerning content standards and the procedures by which these standards are set. Merely following the "right" procedural steps will not be sufficient.

For instance, one constraint is school time, because not everything that all content advocates want can be taught in 180 days from 8:00 A.M. to 2:30 P.M. The history of curriculum politics has been one of jockeying for priority in an overcrowded school schedule. Some curricular priorities are politically organized into the curriculum while others are neglected. Historically, organized interests like driver education and vocational education have been more effective politically than have advocates for, say, music education.[5] Curricular priorities compete for scarce school time, and national content standards will be no exception. If states approve multiple content proposals in a field like social studies, will this provide sufficient local guidance concerning internationally competitive standards set by other countries? Changing concepts about content and new knowledge will make many of these standards quickly outdated. There needs to be a regular revision cycle such as the eight-year cycle for adopting statewide textbooks in California.

Recent indications are that content standards based on *outcomes* of what students know and can do are confronting strong counterpressures from conservative organizations. Outcome-based education (OBE) often is partially embedded in content standards like those in California and Connecticut. Opposition to OBE has forced Pennsylvania, Iowa, Ohio, Virginia, and Oklahoma to amend or drop their statewide content standards. One very outspoken outcome-based education critic is Peg Luksik, who ran a close race in a Pennsylvania Republican gubernatorial primary. Luksik calls OBE a "sham" and says the basic philosophy that all students can learn "is just rhetoric that will guarantee a standard of lowest academic achievement."[6] One critic charges that OBE "test[s] values instead of academics and emphasize[s] self-esteem and problem solving at the expense of knowledge in specific subjects."[7] The objection to problem solving is a significant problem for the early versions of content standards formulated under contracts made in 1992 by the U.S. Department of Education. All of these contractors stress problem solving.

Organizations noted in an earlier chapter that favor a limited federal or state government role in school curriculum, such as the Eagle Forum (Phyllis Schafly) and conservative Christian churches (Pat Robertson), are being opposed by statewide big business groups such as the Washington Business Roundtable. Business groups are concerned that local standards will not provide a well-prepared workforce. But the right-of-center movement is growing in strength and forming an impressive national political network, as we noted. Democrats who believe in enhanced government roles, however, may lose explicit federal opportunity-to-learn standards but will renew their battle at the state level.

THE FUTURE OF CONTENT STANDARDS

The currency of this debate ignores the fact that content standards and exams constitute a long-running saga of U.S. curriculum politics. Decisions on what knowledge is most worth knowing are at the center of school politics, even though school finance usually attracts more media attention. National curricular standards were a crucial component of the overall Clinton vision of systemic reform.[8] Content standards are now a beginning for subsequent state and local policy alignment of textbooks, assessment, staff development, categorical programs, and accreditation. All of these policy areas must be linked to teaching the content standards in America's classroom for systemic reform to succeed. Consequently, the centralization of curricular content is high-stakes politics.

Organizations formed to address state and local curriculum policy will be revamped to fight new national and state battles over national standards. Since national content standards are unlikely, the resolution of conflict will be determined by states and localities. Many Republicans will resist state standards, charging that they will lead to equal-opportunity lawsuits and will water down the rigor of national standards. The centrist coalition supporting content standards and exams will be confronted with numerous objections in each subject field from groups who want their particular content priority specified in state frameworks and assessments.

In sum, the future of standards-based reform is at a crossroads. On the one hand are many forces that have helped this reform grow and persist. Policymakers on both sides of the political aisle and across all levels of government (federal, state, and local) have broadly agreed on the merits and worth of this approach to school change, which has persisted despite substantial turnover in leadership. Further, the commitment of nongovernmental and national change agents to this agenda has been remarkable and sustaining. They have set in motion a dense array of professional networks that are connecting and providing important support to teachers and school administrators. Many of the standards themselves have moved to the middle of the change spectrum, seeking a balance between forces calling for more far-reaching innovation and those calling for conserving traditional practices. This more moderate stance may help the standards move forward politically as well as operationally by allowing teachers to incorporate new practices gradually when they make sense both for them and their students.

On the other hand, while standards reforms have been maintained on the educational agenda and while this strategy is increasingly accepted and endorsed by local policymakers, the waters have become more politically turbulent and complex. The reasons are many. One is that standards have been targeted by a politically savvy and strong religious conservative minority who see them as a strategy by liberals and the government to impose their philosophy in the schools. They are joined by a broader spectrum of parents when organizational, testing, or curricular changes create a type of schooling that departs from their own experiences and expectations, or that challenges the status quo.

Second is the hazard that any reform faces in a time of fiscal constraint. The 1990 to 1995 period is the first time in thirty plus years that schooling has received a real cut in spending after adjustment for inflation. Local officials even in the best of times often feel imposed upon by state laws and regulations, and in the mid-1990s they have been asked to shoulder more and more fiscal responsibilities. Add to this the growing fiscal burdens that states will face as the federal government devolves duties to them with limited resources. This brew is likely to at least slow the development of standards policies and the technical assistance that states can provide to districts, and give impetus to alternatives like market-based reforms and privatization.

Third are the challenges that any initiative faces when it moves into the schools: untrained teachers, confused parents, and organizational structures that resist change. Given that standards reforms ask teachers to dramatically change their practice by moving beyond the status quo of teacher-talk and drill-and-practice memorization, to know their subjects more deeply, and to help all students master more challenging material, this exponentially increases in difficulty. Compounding this is the decentralization occurring in districts via site-based management in decision making and the efforts of lawmakers in several states to reduce the numbers of central district administrators. All of these raise anew questions about what role these administrators should play in standards reform (one not well addressed by state policy), what role a reduced staff can play, and how to achieve economies of scale. Is it efficient for each school to create the wheel of curriculum, instruction, and new standards instruction and try to measure up to the new standards on their own? What can districts do to facilitate exchanges, provide support, and fight the insularity that often plagues schools and teachers?

These challenges must be faced squarely. In this era of fiscal and staffing constraints, policymakers have to learn to coordinate with and use the growing nongovernmental networks to sustain a coherent agenda and provide much-needed support to teachers and local administrators. They must look at cost savings, but they must also look frankly at how savings affect poor and special needs children. They must also look at how standards-based policies are playing out for these populations. To do this, states must collect and be able to disaggregate performance data on diverse groups of students, and to figure out how to help all students do better without blind adherence to one pedagogical position or another. Pragmatics and common sense must reign here, not ideological agendas. Finally, state and district policymakers must learn how to listen to their publics but also teach them about their reform efforts. This requires well-articulated messages and long-term efforts.

Public support and understanding of standards-based reforms remain a major obstacle to the stability of state standards. All states have developed some mechanisms for professional and public feedback during the development of their standards. But in practice these efforts were brief and looked like public-information campaigns rather than establishing on-going dialogues for mutual understanding. While some LEAs attempted to mobilize local support for standards reform, these were often isolated efforts. However, most policymakers are at a loss as to know just how to go about creating real and sustained dialogue with the public; they tend to rely on polls for their information about broader public sentiment.[9] These polls have some important limitations, for opinions expressed about education in general can generate different reactions when it comes to one's own children or one's own community. In short, the nationwide concern about inadequate public engagement in standards reform is well founded. To sustain reform, policymakers will have to learn how to do it better.

Such learning is seen in the recent challenge in California to implement a revised statewide student assessment, which illustrates the politically turbulent and complex arena of standards reform. This case highlights several political issues and barriers confronting any state attempt to revise assessment standards.

STUDENT ASSESSMENT REFORM IN CALIFORNIA*

In 1991 California became a pioneer in the effort to develop new forms of pupil assessment with the California Learning Assessment System (CLAS). For different reasons, conservative religious groups, parents, the California School Board Association, the California Teachers Association, and the governor all raised objections to the assessment during its 1993 implementation. Due to this broad opposition, CLAS is now discontinued. What happened to CLAS? Why did it generate so much opposition? Why was CLAS not able to sustain the political coalition that created it? We explore these questions about one state's failed attempt to reform assessment in order to shed light on the politics of testing in general.

The CLAS case illustrates some of the difficulties involved in wide-scale transformation of state assessment systems. For advocates of performance-based testing, the California case is an exemplar of the difficulties in moving policy toward more "authentic" forms of assessment and away from measuring basic skills through multiple-choice tests. While factors unique to California (e.g., election-year politics) partially explain the demise of CLAS, other aspects of the case offer more general lessons for reformers about the politics of testing policy in the United States.

CLAS was developed in 1991 to replace the California Assessment Program (CAP) to satisfy a number of different needs that CAP did not meet. Three goals of CLAS stand out: (1) to align California's testing system to the content of what was taught in schools—as represented in state curricular frameworks; (2) to better measure attainment of curricular content through

*The authors acknowledge the assistance of Christopher Mazzeo in this section on California.

performance-based standards setting and assessment; and (3) to provide assessment of individual student performance as well as performance data for schools and districts. The goal of the test was to create comparable scores for all parts of the state's educational system. The performance of these discrete parts of the educational system would be measured through both on-demand assessments given once a year and portfolios that track student work over a longer period of time.

The Rise and Fall of CLAS

Controversy over CLAS intensified after the first round of tests was given in Spring 1993. Rumors quickly spread among conservative groups and parents about the test's "objectionable content." These rumors were exacerbated by the secrecy that shrouded the assessment—secrecy that the California Department of Education (CDE) said was essential for retaining the integrity of the items, as developing new items was expensive. Without actual exams available for public review, rumors increased—and with them complaints by religious groups that the test's content undermined parents' moral values and invaded the privacy of students and their families. While some parents complained about privacy, others took issue with the open-ended nature of the performance assessments and the lack of "objective" scores made available by the exam. The designers of CLAS had not consulted potential critics, including religious and conservative groups, for possible objections to the wording of the questions. Figure 14.1 is a sample of a CLAS reading assessment that raised contentious issues because of the open-ended questions and requirements to include emotional reactions.

The first official response to the controversy came in January 1994 when State Senator Gary Hart put together the CLAS reauthorization bill (SB 1273). The new bill took four steps to deflect the criticism aimed at the tests:

1. A review panel would be appointed to ensure compliance with the intent of the legislation.
2. Past copies of the test would be provided each year for review by the public.

Figure 14.1
Sample Reading Test from CLAS

Read the poem that appears below and answer (on another sheet) the questions that follow. Feel free to make notes in the margins as you read.

Introductory Note: This poem, inspired by the Statue of Liberty, was written in 1883 by Emma Lazarus. Lazarus was born in Eastern Europe and immigrated to America as a young woman. Like most immigrants of that time she came to the United States by boat, entering the country through the port of New York, where the Statue of Liberty stands in New York harbor (between New York City and Jersey City, New Jersey) at the entrance to N.Y. and the USA. The poem became famous when it was later inscribed on the base of the Statue of Liberty. The original "Colossus," one of the seven wonders of the ancient world, was a huge statue that straddled the harbor of Rhodes in ancient Greece.

The New Colossus (1883)   *Notes*

Not like the brazen giant of Greek fame,
With conquering limbs astride from land to land;
Here at our sea-washed, sunset gates shall stand
a mighty woman with a torch, whose flame
Is the imprisoned lightning, and her name
Mother of Exiles. From her beacon-hand
Glows world-wide welcome; her mild eyes command
The air-bridged harbor that twin cities frame.
"Keep, ancient lands, your storied pomp!" cries she
With silent lips. "Give me your tired, your poor,
Your huddled masses yearning to breathe free,
The wretched refuse of your teeming shore.
Send these, the homeless, tempest-tossed to me,
I lift my lamp beside the golden door!"

1. What is your initial reaction or response (your thoughts, feelings, observations, questions, ideas, etc.) to this poem?

2. Pick a line in this poem that seems to you especially important or interesting. Write out the line and then explain your reasons for selecting it.

3. How do you interpret the name "Mother of Exiles" in line 6? What is the significance of this name in the poem?

4. The last part of the poem says, "Give me your tired, your poor."

a.) Who is "me" and who is you or "your?" Who is speaking in the last 5 lines of this poem and to whom are these lines addressed?

b.) Using the "Open Mind" outline provided, show with drawings, symbols, or words what the speaker of these lines is thinking or feeling or what a person hearing these lines might be expected to think and feel.

c.) Explain your graphic.

5. Use the opportunity provided by this question to say anything else you might want to say about this poem. You might want to talk about its form or language, its meaning to you personally or as a member of a group, its cultural or historical or ideological or aesthetic significance, or anything else you haven't already said about the poem.

How would average student readers answer these questions? How would weaker student readers answer them?

Source: Sheridan Blau, Santa Barbara, California, Vice President of National Council of Teachers of English. Reprinted with permission.

3. School boards could review each year's test before it was given—provided the board could guarantee test confidentiality (to answer concerns about open-ended assessments).
4. More fact-based multiple-choice and short-answer questions would be added to complement the performance tasks.

Though the Hart bill was an honest attempt to deal with the controversy, it in fact led to CLAS's demise later in the year, which was precipitated by events in the months following introduction of the bill.

The State Board of Education's removal of an Alice Walker reading selection from the 1994 test brought a firestorm of negative reaction by newspaper editorials and groups like People for the American Way. Then the scores of the 1993 tests were released in March 1994. Several schools that had done well on previous assessments fared poorly on the new tests, and some were in the wealthiest areas of the state. The results increased anger on all sides. In April the *Los Angeles Times* published an investigation critical of the test's sampling procedures. The article claimed that there were over 11,000 sampling violations in the 1993 test. Southern California school boards in two districts opted out of the 1994 tests. A conservative legal group—the Rutherford Foundation—filed suits on behalf of parents in Sacramento and San Bernadino claiming the tests violated privacy laws. The final blow of a heated month came in a scathing letter from Del Weber, the president of the California Teachers Association (CTA), to William Dawson, the Acting Superintendent of Public Instruction for the California Department of Education. Weber's letter rebuked the CDE for both its administration and its design of the assessments. While ultimately supportive of the CLAS concept, CTA's response added to the public relations nightmare for CDE and CLAS.

At the end of April Dawson addressed the criticisms, stating strongly that all districts would be required to administer the tests but could create opt-out procedures for parents who did not want their children to take the test. Defending both the confidentiality of the assessment and the scoring procedures used in the first year, Dawson claimed the *Los Angeles Times* article was inaccurate. Only 150 schools had samples that should not have been released to the public. Nonetheless, recognizing the controversy, Dawson vowed to have the public more involved in future test review. Most important, he commissioned a scholarly review board of testing experts, led by Stanford University Professor Lee Cronbach, to examine sampling and other statistical issues from the 1993 tests.

In early May the governor finally spoke out. Emphasizing the controversy over content and the sampling problem, Wilson called for the State Auditor General to review CLAS fiscal issues. Secretary DiMarco called the assessment "seriously flawed" and "disastrous." The responses to the governor and Secretary DiMarco's comments were swift. In a May 12 article from the *Los Angeles Times*, former State Superintendent Bill Honig blasted Wilson and his aide for jumping off the CLAS bandwagon. Implying that the governor did so for political gain, Honig claimed Wilson's actions played into the hands of extremists with an agenda. In the ensuing months the verbal volleys between the governor, DiMarco, and Dawson continued. In mid-July CDE put the 1993 test items on public view. Initial reports were positive—many parents who had first expressed fears indicated the tests were not as bad as they originally believed.

But whatever boost CDE might have received from the public viewing was soon nullified by the release of the report of Professor Cronbach's group, the Committee on Sampling and Statistical Procedures. Suggesting that operational problems were significant in 1993, the committee recommended some measures to ensure technical competence and quality control in future tests. The committee found the samples basically sound but poorly implemented by CDE, and also found that the assessment's school site scores were not reliable. Their concerns about large standard errors led the committee to recommend that future school-level assessments be administered on an experimental basis.

In announcing the report, Dawson emphasized the positive and implied that CDE's plan for both technical procedures and individual scores was validated by the committee. But Governor Wilson and Secretary DiMarco did not see it that way. Citing some of the conclusions of the experts' report, the Governor vetoed SB 1273 on September 27, 1994, and called for a new statewide testing program in its place. While Governor Wilson first criticized CLAS for its problems of sampling and content, his veto of SB 1273 showed his change of focus—CLAS failed to provide individual scores for students, which could enhance parental responsibility and school advising. Secretary DiMarco claimed the new bill veered away from the intent of the original CLAS bill (SB 662), which prioritized individual pupil scores as the overriding goal of CLAS. What happened instead was that in its implementation of CLAS, CDE prioritized the performance-based aspects of the test, and this decision was codified into the new bill. In a sense the governor and Secretary DiMarco were correct— many references in SB 662 to individual scores had been removed or changed in SB 1273. And the language of one section, deleted from the later bill, was ambiguous: "Comparable individual pupil results shall be completed prior to any expansion and development, or both, of new performance-based assessments *except to the extent that performance-based assessments are an integral part of the system for providing individual pupil results*" (p. 3003, emphasis added).

It can be argued that in CDE's judgment, performance-based assessment was an "integral" part of providing individual pupil results and would therefore take priority. Certainly that is what Bill Honig believed at the time of CLAS's creation in 1991. Wilson and others, however, saw the priorities differently. Given the political controversy, it is not surprising that their view won, even though CLAS was supported by most major education groups in the state including the California Teachers Association.

Why CLAS Was Discontinued

Governor Wilson's veto was merely the final blow to a new testing system that had difficulties from the beginning. Certainly, political factors unique to CLAS helped undermine it: the strength of traditional religious groups and perhaps the need for Wilson to shore up his support with these groups in an election year. Yet in addition to these specific factors, the CLAS case highlights a number of more general issues regarding the politics of assessment policy in the United States. Conflict over new performance-based assessments is not unique to California; Virginia, Arizona, and Connecticut have had similar controversies in the last year. The demise of CLAS offers a constructive lesson for policymakers committed to assessment reform rooted in performance-based testing. Three key dimensions of the CLAS case stand out as lessons for testing policy in general: (1) the tension between political and technical factors; (2) the divergent priorities and goals of key stakeholders; and (3) the extent of antigovernment feelings among the public.

The Tension Between Technical and Political Factors. While there is much agreement among policymakers and testing experts on the benefits of performance-based testing, the different world of policymakers leads technical realities to be ultimately subsumed to political ones. In the CLAS case the political reality dictated an overly optimistic 1994 time-line for implementation— against the recommendation of those familiar with performance-based examinations. The traditional requirements for a wide-scale assessment—emphasizing validity and reliability—are more problematic given the state of the art of such measures. Developing an assessment that measures the complex skills detailed in curricular frameworks is a difficult and costly process. Making such an assessment high stakes for students and schools—as CLAS did— raises the ante on technical and cost issues considerably. As the statistical review committee noted in their report, the trade-off between cost and precision in a performance-based exam is significant. Making scores reliable and valid for accountability purposes is a difficult proposition.

Further, the committee noted that a design superior for assessing schools creates difficulties for measuring individual aptitude. The chances of students getting comparable forms of the test decreases with a larger sample, making student-level accountability decisions hazardous and possibly quite unfair. Yet CDE was expected to solve these technical problems and deliver a test with both student and school scores by 1993. CDE's choice to push performance-based testing at the expense of individual scores says much about the agency's priorities. Still, it is likely whatever choice the agency had made would have alienated someone. Policymakers' need for quick and decisive action may be disastrous for performance-based reforms like CLAS that need time and a serious discussion of the trade-offs between cost, precision, and accountability.

Divergent Priorities and Goals of Key Stakeholders.   Assessment policies, like all policies, are the creation of political coalitions. Since the actors involved often have divergent goals for testing, it is often necessary to write legislation in vague terms or incorporate seemingly conflicting goals into the same policy. In the California case, the three key stakeholders who helped to create CLAS—Governor Wilson, State Senator Hart, and former State Superintendent of Education Bill Honig—all had very different priorities for the testing program.[10] Wilson's top priority was to replace the older CAP system with a new one that provided individual student scores. Student data would allow for more parent awareness and stringent accountability of teachers, an important goal of the governor. Senator Hart was much more interested in holding the schools accountable for performance. Hewing to many of the ideas of the National Governor's Association and other policy organizations, Hart wanted to trade the schools' deregulation for stricter performance accountability. Finally, Bill Honig and the state education establishment were committed to performance-based testing and to tying assessment to the curricular frameworks.

All of these goals appear in the initial legislation. However, once implementation of CLAS occurred, it was clear that not all of the priorities could be accommodated. When CDE implemented a policy closest to Honig and Hart's vision, the governor and others who supported his position balked. The controversy over testing content helped strengthen the opponents' contention that the test was "seriously flawed." What has not been resolved in either California or other states speaks to the goals of assessment policy. Should tests emphasize student or school-level accountability? Given cost and precision factors, this issue may involve a clear trade-off for many states. Are assessments predominantly informative and persuasive tools to help students and teachers to perform better, or are they regulatory instruments tied to rewards for good scores and sanctions for nonperformance? These questions and others were not resolved in the California case and led to an inevitable conflict once CLAS was implemented.

Antigovernment Feelings.   Many policymakers have been surprised by the extent of the negative reaction to reforms like performance-based assessment and OBE. Since many of the loudest cries have come from religious groups, they are often dismissed as mere "extremism." But to dismiss all criticism is to ignore the origins of much of the unrest—the extent of antigovernment feeling these complaints reflect. Nearly all criticism of CLAS has been directed at CDE and other key figures in the state capitol. And much of this criticism has focused on the privacy issue. As one of the lawyers for a parents group that sued the state put it:

> The state has an interest in assessing the quality of teaching in the schools. They also have an interest in knowing whether kids can think rather than regurgitate facts. But there's a difference between testing a student's ability to think and asking them what they think about personal things. And frankly, the latter is no business of the state.[11]

The criticism did not stop at privacy concerns. An *Orange County Daily News* editorial railed against the "Sacramento bureaucrats" to whom CLAS ceded control over "core issues of schooling."[12] The president of one of the school boards that opted out of CLAS claimed the concern was "not the moral issue as much as the absence of testing basic skills." These criticisms reflect more than just disagreement over education goals and means. Rather, they illustrate the extent of antigovernment feelings in California at the very time reforms are trying to expand the reach of the state and persuade many of the need to rethink traditional ways of testing. The convergence of these two trends does not bode well for ambitious testing reform being considered in other states. In effect, the public is being asked to reject the traditional way of thinking about testing when they themselves do not trust the questioners.

The Rise of California Assessment

CLAS ended with several unresolved issues and a well-organized opposition that also objected to California's participation in the 1994 federal law—Goals 2000. Consequently, it is surprising that a new state assessment passed in just one year after CLAS was discontinued, especially since Republicans had gained enough seats to obtain a one-vote majority in the California Assembly.

Each of the major roadblocks, however, were overcome by a winning coalition of Assembly and Senate Democrats, the governor, education groups, and big business.

The three major issues from the CLAS debacle remained, but new approaches were fashioned. A two-track assessment system was designed to develop student, school-level, and state assessment. The student track consists of districts using currently available tests (such as CTBS), with the state giving a district $5 for each of its students who takes the test. Presumably, these commercially available tests will be aligned with state curricular frameworks and textbooks that are being revised in 1996. School- and district-level assessment is to be phased in by 1998–1999 through a new instrument that will include a balance of "basic and applied skills." The bill's authors expect that "applied skills" will include performance assessments, and basic-skills assessment will emphasize multiple-choice questions.

In order to satisfy political demands for more emphasis on the basics, grade-level curriculum standards are to be formulated as a guide for teaching and for performance levels. The state will explicitly agree on how good is good enough for grade-level subject attainment. It is not clear how the new state assessment will be aligned with individual student tests from commercial publishers. The expectation is that both assessment tracks (state and pupil) can be linked to the state's curricular frameworks as well as the National Assessment of Educational Progress (NAEP).

These substantive assessment changes, however, might pass the legislature if public confidence in state government could be rebuilt after CLAS. The governor and conservative parent groups wanted more control over the design and implementation of state assessments. The CDE lost legitimacy during the CLAS dispute and needed to be less prominent. Indeed, newly elected State Schools Superintendent Delaine Eastin pledged to the legislature in public hearings that CDE staff who designed CLAS would not be involved in any new state assessment.

Two new assessment governance mechanisms were designed to provide more gubernatorial and citizen influence and to lessen CDE's visible role. A twenty-one person Commission for the Establishment of Academic Content and Performance Standards will be responsible for developing "academically rigorous" standards in all major subject areas, at every grade level. The majority of the Commission—eleven of its members—will be appointed by the governor.

The public will also participate in the approval of the tests themselves. A six-person Statewide Pupil Assessment Review Panel will review all tests to assure that they contain no questions

- About a student's or parent's personal beliefs about sex, family life, morality, or religion.
- Designed to evaluate personal characteristics such as honesty, integrity, sociability, or self-esteem.

A majority of this panel must be parents with children in public schools. Legislators and local school board members can review the contents of any approved or adopted test as long as they agree to maintain the confidentiality of test items. Easily understood materials describing the nature and purpose of the tests must be made available to members of the public, including parents and students.

The new California assessment was approved by a crucial Assembly committee by one vote. The governor seems satisfied and has provided adequate funding for 1996 test administration. While some of the assessment provisions could be inconsistent, there is a rising concern about the attainment of pupils after California finished tied with Louisiana for last (out of thirty-seven states) in the 1995 NAEP fourth-grade reading assessment. The new state assessment must be comparable to the NAEP administered by the U.S. Department of Education. It must present an appropriate balance of types of assessment instruments, including multiple-choice and short-answer questions and applied writing skills. The assessment will report on grades 4, 5, 8, and 10, but performance standards must be established for every grade level.

The opponents will focus on preventing funds for developing the new state assessment but let the individual testing proceed in 1996. The final state assessment political battle stemming from CLAS is far from over in California. Soon after the bill was signed by the governor, Orange Country conservatives attacked it: "I say kill it," said Joan Wonsley, a Dana Point mother of three who co-founded an anti-CLAS parent group. "They want to know what kids think. They're getting psychological, talking about political correctness. They're reshaping social attitudes."[13]

CONCLUSION

Both state assessments and state curriculum standards contain high-stakes political issues—what knowledge is most worth knowing.[14] Institutionalizing new forms of assessment and adopting centralized standards will require public trust and public understanding—more than just top-down state-level political marketing and campaigning.[15] California's experience suggests that an elite professional alliance cannot both set the agenda for reform and persuade the public that their agenda is best.[16] But merely responding to what the public desires does not capitalize on research and professional educators' growing knowledge base. Somehow, education leaders must find a middle ground that considers both grass-roots opinion and improved assessment and curriculum concepts. This will entail more than engagement or interactions between the public and professional educators.[17] Successful implementation of new assessments and curriculum standards requires guidance from leaders who grasp how the public interprets the various messages that they hear about testing. President Clinton's 1997 proposal for a voluntary national test will stimulate some of the same controversy that surrounded California's CLAS assessment.

NOTES

1. Frederick Wirt and Michael Kirst, *Schools in Conflict* (Berkeley, Calif.: McCutchan, 1992).

2. Charles Lindblom and David Braybrooke, *A Strategy of Decision* (New York: Free Press, 1963).

3. D. L. Ball, *Implementing the NCTM Standards* (East Lansing, Mich.: National Center for Research on Teacher Learning, 1992), pp. 2–3.

4. Diane Massell and Michael Kirst, "Formulating National Content Standards," *Education and Urban Society* 26, no. 2 (February 1994).

5. Wirt and Kirst, *Schools in Conflict.*

6. Cited in Diane Brockett, "Outcome Based Education Faces Strong Opposition," *School Board News* 13, no. 10 (1993): 1–6.

7. Cited in ibid., p. 8.

8. Smith and O'Day, "Systemic School Reform."

9. Diane Massell, Michael Kirst, and Peg Hoppe, "Persistence and Change in State Education Reform," paper presented to the 1996 annual meeting of American Education Research Association, New York, April 9, 1996.

10. Lorraine McDonnell, "Assessment Policy as Persuasion and Regulation," *American Journal of Education* 102, no. 4 (August 1994): 394–420.

11. *Ed Cal*, weekly newsletter of the Association of California Administrators, May 30, 1994, p. 8.

12. Ibid.

13. Cited in John Gittelsohn, "All Aren't Hailing CLAS Replacement," *Orange County Reporter*, October 15, 1995, p. 3.

14. See Michael W. Kirst, "Politics of Nationalizing Curricular Content," *American Journal of Education* 102, no. 4 (August 1994): 383–393.

15. Robert Rothman, *Measuring Up: Standards, Assessment, and School Reform* (San Francisco: Jossey-Bass, 1995).

16. Peter Schrag, "The New School Wars: How Outcomes Education Blew Up," *The American Prospect* (Winter 1995): 53–62.

17. Richard Elmore and Susan Fuhrman, eds., *The Governance of the Curriculum* (Alexandria, Va.: Association for Supervision and Curriculum Development, 1994).

Part V

FUTURE RESEARCH NEEDS IN EDUCATION POLITICS

15

Unexplored Dimensions of "Political" in the Politics of Education

Recent analyses of the linkages between *policy analysis,* on the one hand, and *politics,* on the other, suggest that contemporary focus on the first has been poorly linked to the theoretical needs of the second.[1] In this chapter we specify ideas for research in educational politics that should ensue if the politics of education field is to become less oriented to specific policies or to a singular paradigm. We suggest a much richer variety of research within a theoretical framework that schools might well undertake if this field is to stress politics research more than it has in the past. The larger conceptual framework of the chapter rests in the understanding of "political" as encompassing a broad range of factors within the political system that shape or influence its activities. That framework suggests a set of categories of political analysis that is drawn from the relevant subfields of political science. We review these by summarizing basic findings from the subfields and then suggesting research areas for the politics of education. Specific suggestions for future research are based on the gaps discovered as we synthesized the research for this volume.

POLITICAL LEARNING

Students of democracy have always been interested in the way in which individuals learn their roles as citizens in a democratic society. This political learning, or socialization, can be explained by theory in cognitive psychology (such as Piaget's) that asserts the young learn little about a topic until they reach an age of being open to that topic. Adults retain and expand on what they learned as children.

Relevance Outside Education

Beginning with the early studies of how Greek philosophers sought to inculcate proper values and behavior in the young, political scientists have focused on political role learning. This research has gone through periods of a new awareness of that focus with an intensive research phase in the 1960s, but a sudden loss of interest thereafter. In the 1920s researchers studied political learning among the young in a number of major nations, including the United States.[2] Interest was renewed after World War II, as University of Michigan scholars developed constructs of how such learning took place and how it continued into adult life.[3] In the 1960s detailed studies polled children in the United States and other nations to gather data on changes in their perceptions.[4] But after that surge of studies, new ideas in political socialization were limited, as if most researchers believed they had learned all there was to learn; little has been done in recent decades. What do scholars believe that they have indeed learned?

The finding that there was only limited political awareness among the young fits nicely into Piagetian theories that there are specific periods in children's development when certain ideas are "ready" to be accepted. The ability to understand politics comes in the early teen years, when children's awareness extends from the local and immediate to the larger society, where information is available about the political world and candidates.[5] While young children are apparently indifferent to politics, vague perceptions of political life shape their later voting behavior and party identifications.[6] The influences of the family, peers, and neighborhood all coalesce to form a common belief and perception, creating the cues that shape children's thinking. Of key importance here is the finding that schools do little to influence children's future political cognitions. That may be because the curriculum provides little early, structured, political learning other than creating symbolic support for the political system through flags, the pledge of allegiance, and so on.

In developmental terms, the foundation is laid early to be built on later in life. Thus, adult's political behavior, such as party identification or voting frequency, is linked to that of their parents. Incidentally, party identification has a longer life than do religious values learned in childhood. Consequently, political campaigns become efforts to recruit the party faithful, leaving only a small proportion of independents (maybe one quarter or less) who also can be solicited by candidates of the major parties.

Research Possibilities on Political Learning

Since the mid-1970s politics of education scholars have rarely studied political learning, leaving it to others who link such learning with the curriculum.[7] Consequently, there is a large opening for scholars who might explore the cognitive aspects of how political learning among the young and adults is influenced by schools. Collaboration with cognitive psychologists would illuminate certain research questions that are analyzed below.

Do Children Lack Political Understanding?   Earlier studies of children's political understanding relied on data drawn from paper-and-pencil tests,[8] which produced only narrow findings. Little used options are qualitative or small-group studies of what the youngest understand about politics. Moreover, new efforts describe not simply voting and party attitudes but the young's grasp of what the "political" is and how it applies—even to matters close to them. For example, Wirt interviewed first-graders to determine their understanding of three models of political decision making—majority rule, minority rights, and authoritarian—as applied to situations they knew in their brief lives. From their own experiences, first-graders understood the political models quite well and could apply them to test cases.

Growing Awareness in the Early Teens?   In a world saturated by media exposure and instant access by computer to a larger world, what are the political messages that teenagers detect and their reactions to them? This question goes beyond just understanding children's grasp of political personages to what they know about political events—gangs, wars, assassinations, political scandals, and so on. Is teenagers' image of a dysfunctional society reflected also in their views about political parties, voting, interest groups, and other advanced political concepts? Moreover, how does the schools' civic curriculum reinforce or alter those perceptions, often gained from the media?[9] Here again, by relying less on structured questions, polls plus small-group studies could make possible understanding these cognitive images.

The Adult Reaction to Change?   What happens in adults' lives that may alter their earlier cognitions about politics? This question does not address how adults change their party affiliation or why they choose not to vote, but rather it attempts to understand how the political learning that adults received as children affects their perceptions and voting about school matters. Also, more research is needed to link adults' evaluation of their own schooling with their views about schools or school policy. If an adult is satisfied with his or her own schooling, but is unhappy about schools in general today, what created that attitudinal change? Or does an earlier unhappiness translate into later dissatisfaction with schools?

Once again, a research area abandoned by one discipline can be reopened by another, bringing to bear new insights and methods of study.

THE MEDIA AND SCHOOL POLITICS

Until recently, the political impact of media communication was little studied in political science. Primarily, media have been seen as something that politicians manipulated for their own ends. But in recent decades, political scientists believe that the media themselves alter the democratic process, particularly in elections and policymaking, by affecting the information from which citizens make political decisions. What is striking is the absence of research within politics of education concerning media impact on school politics, even though school administrators know the political problems that the media occasion.

Studies Outside Education

Political studies of the media have centered around the classic research questions of political scientist Harold Lassell that focus on, "*Who says what to whom with what effect?*" That is, focus is on the institution of the media, on media content, on audiences, and on their consequences for citizens. Journalists—electronic or print—summarize, refine, and alter what they learn in order to make it suitable for their audiences to hear or read—and do so for a profit. But the content of these functions has consequences for shaping values and interests of audiences who listen to the messages. What they hear or see shapes their grasp of the world outside, including schools.

Some studies have demonstrated that there is a concentrated ownership and control of the media, print or electronic.[10] Others have focused on the political orientation of media employees (often criticized as "liberal"), or on how they translate news in a general way (often viewing politics as a "horse race" or essentially conflict-based).[11] Government operations, while the source of great attention, are often seen as grounds for a battle rather than for cooperation. That relationship of media and government is becoming increasingly close and increasingly less neutral.[12] In effect, media sources take on a political orientation in which their previous norm of neutrality or "objectivity" is now rarely followed. And this focus on conflict and cynicism increasingly dominates media reports on education.

The influence of the media on the political system has been given much attention in political science—but very little of this looks at local issues.[13] Research on the media's effects on politics is most often found in studies of voting. Television coverage is a main source of information on choices for the presidency, but much media trivialize policy discussions and view government as arenas of conflicting interests. Increasingly "negative" campaigning via television dominates electoral campaigns at all levels, so contact between voter and candidate is filtered through media.

Also, the media have an impact on school government—an audience itself. Research suggests that the media influence is most often employed in generating clues about the policy environment, which makes the media one of those helping to set the policy agenda of government. Governments also affect the media by "managing" the news in order to shape media coverage and hence public views of school policy, but the linkage is complex and often confused.[14] The First Amendment protects the media against government censorship, of course, but Federal Communications Commission regulation also affects the use of wave lengths and sometimes media content.

Surrounding all this has been the increasing concern for the media's responsibility in a democracy. Maybe of more importance is the problem that triviality and conflict that overwhelm media coverage can fuzzy citizens' perceptions of events.

Research Possibilities for Politics of Education

So very little politics of education research has looked at the media that the field is wide open to research possibilities. Suggestions include the following:

Elites' Use of the Media.   As school elites (e.g., school professionals, interest groups) seek to construct a "policy stream" supportive of their ideas, they will use the media to shape citizen opinion. The study of interest groups in school policymaking has dealt very little with the media, whether local, state, or national. Many case studies of local school conflict seem blind to what the media do. The central question is, What is the relationship between elites and media in shaping the decision-making process in school matters? Thus, how are agendas presented, and what is the political stance of media owners on local school issues?

The Media Role in School Politics.   In the swamp of data about school performance or reform, how do the media decide which data are useful to transmit to the public? In particular, what is the role of the Education Writers Association, and what is the quality of reporting about education among newspaper journalists? How do journalists' career changes affect their reporting on schools? We don't even know how much the media reporters know about schools. More broadly, what is the relationship between the reporters —print or electronic—and the owners of the media? Are there different agendas about school matters, and if so, what are they?

A basic fact lies behind such questions, namely, most voters get their information about schools from T.V. and radio. These electronic media often feature stories on school discipline, gangs, dress codes, violence, and drugs. Other stories focus heavily on conflict, like teacher strikes or superintendent turnover in core cities. Peripheral issues like home schooling and computer access also are important. This electronic coverage might explain why school discipline is at the top of the public's concerns reflected in the annual Gallup poll on American education. Yet politics of education research on the content and political impact of electronic media on school policy is nonexistent.

The Media Audience.   What are parents' sources of information about schools, what criteria do they employ to judge that information, and what conditions sensitize them to school news? This audience is not homogenous, so answers will be differentiated by parents' education, economic status, and possibly even gender and race. But politics of education specialists have not given thought to formalizing theories about the differing interactions between media and audience.

The Normative Structure of the Media and Schools.   These empirical questions carry normative concerns that merit research. As journalists translate information to the public, what are the expectations about school reporting required by both their own profession and their responsibility to the public? Does the debate over "neutrality" occur, and what dangers arise if a more partisan approach is taken by media journalists and owners?

Research collaboration between politics of education scholars and their colleagues in journalism schools would be quite fruitful. Survey data on the current challenge to education would be especially illuminating about answers to such questions as, Is the rapid spread of policies across states and localities (i.e., a "policy epidemic") in large or small part caused or aided by media coverage?

ELECTORAL POLITICS

Electoral studies, one part of political behavior, focus strongly on the attitudes and behaviors of voters and nonvoters as they select or reject government decision makers.[15] Such research is distinct from that studying political institutions like political parties or pressure groups that link citizens to the elected.

Studies Outside Education

Political science has focused on the attitudes and activities of citizens within the political system. Frequent elections provide a large data source for scholars of electoral politics. Research money has been substantial, creating research institutions like the University of Michigan's electoral archive. National Science Foundation research grants train new scholars to use increasingly sophisticated models and quantitative analyses of political behavior. Research findings on electoral behavior are so numerous that we will consider only a few here.

From the earliest research of polls and participation in national elections, one finding prevails. Over the past five decades fewer citizens are voting. From presidential elections down the ticket to school government, voter turnout today ranges from 51 percent to 12–15 percent. In the 1996 presidential election about 55 percent voted of those registered. A second major finding has been that while all citizens are equal, in the words of George Orwell, "Some are more equal than others." That is, the higher the status, the more citizens participate in our democracy, whether by voting or other means. The obverse is also found—the farther down the scale, the less the participation.[16] In effect, this is the "More-More" role noted in an earlier chapter. Those with more resources in society participate more in the political system, and they get more rewards, which then causes them to participate even more, and so on. For those with less resources the opposite process takes place.

Participation means not simply the act of voting, but can also involve other activities; working in an organization with a local policy emphasis; persuading others to vote; campaigning; contacting local, state, or national government officials; attending political rallies; giving money in campaigns; and so on. But the key point is that few participate in most of these activities. Roughly half do none of them, another quarter do only one (mostly voting in a presidential election), and only one percent do as many as six.[17] In the 1994 California federal election, for example, 26 percent of the adults voted because many were not registered.

Research Possibilities for Politics of Education

Research concerning the connection between electoral politics and the politics of education terminated abruptly about twenty-five years ago. In the 1960s the necessity to garner voters to support school bonds and tax levies gave rise to a brief politics of education literature. It focused primarily on keeping the voter turnout low, because most voters in local school finance elections supported more school spending.[18] After 1968 a large number of negative voters appeared, leading to the failure of most school finance referenda, noted in an earlier chapter. Rarely is this electoral connection, reflecting a new theory of voter dissatisfaction, studied in order to explain behavior. Indeed, no scholar has updated school referenda studies since Piele and Hall in 1973 and Hamilton and Cohen in 1974.[19]

Linkage of Voting and Nonvoting for Schools. In the current era of growing school expenditures, relatively few researchers have studied why voters do or do not participate in school elections. In particular, what is the relevance of the act of voting itself to citizens' sense of involvement in democracy? What attitudes shape their perception of schools and their motivations in life? As to school board elections, how do citizens perceive the relevance of voting, the presence of elections, and their dissatisfaction or satisfaction? How do local policymakers perceive citizens as they plan for elections, and what strategies do they derive—successful or not—from their perceptions?

The Social Bases of Participation. As mentioned, voting participation is positively linked to status, particularly to educational attainment. More important, how do those at different status levels perceive the electoral connection—what do they hope for from it and what evidence is there of this hope? What factors in social life, like high income or church attendance, help political participation? As racial minorities enter the middle class, does their voting behavior differ from that of other middle-class voters? Research can create complex theories of democratic participation involving school influence, but there is no active cadre of scholars doing this work.

The Multiple Acts of Participation. The variety of kinds of democratic participation in schools has been little studied. But there is a useful cross-linkage of such studies from political science to schools.[20] Specifically, other than voting, how do citizens participate in linking themselves to school policies? Or to board actions? On the one hand, there is the elite connection to study, those small numbers who regularly attend board meetings or vote in referenda. On the other, there is the large number who do neither. But what other kinds of participation take place, particularly those that boards and professionals perceive as designed to influence them, such as school-site governance?

These research possibilities necessitate new kinds of data collection, which could include community samples (used in earlier research) both before and after a referendum or board election. Or the annual Gallup poll data published in *Phi Delta Kappan* could be explored and reanalyzed. Explorations of small-group interviews at different stages of an election provide another—and most unusual—source of data. This approach would draw from qualitative studies in phenomenology to determine and analyze personal motivations concerning political behavior. Finally, instructors' easy access to collecting such data by students would facilitate such research.

POLITICS AND POLICY COMMUNITIES

Most recent research in intergovernmental relations, noted in an earlier chapter, has looked at the interactions among the levels of government and their impact on the classroom.[21] This type of analysis needs to be supplemented by a different intergovernmental perspective that uses concepts like "policy community."

One scholar provides an overview of this evolving notion of policy community:

> People working in America on policy problems . . . have enough regular contact or interaction to be regarded as members of a community or organized social system, even though they may work in hundreds of agencies spread over the country. Communities of policy experts . . . include those primarily engaged in studying the policies and procedures being employed in an area, as well as administrators of the major agencies with operating programs. The communities involve bureau chiefs and officials in operating agencies with academics and consultants employed by research and development firms, publishers and editors of professional journals and magazines, representatives from business firms that are major suppliers of goods and services employed in the area, members of legislative staffs and legislators themselves who specialize in the subject, and other elected officials with interest in the policies.[22]

It is important to note that not all community members will be directly involved in policymaking. Rather, the policy community is a constellation of intellectual ideas and social understandings that influence the policy choices of decision makers within its domain. The concept of policy community implies that individuals within it share internal norms, values, and frameworks of communication, and may engage in concerted political activities. A policy community is thus a broader concept than a policy issue network, which focuses on a particular policy at a specific level of government.[23] For example, the spread of state school finance reform in the 1970s was orchestrated by a network led by the Ford Foundation.[24] These issue networks rely on a central guidance mechanism (like Ford or the Institute for Creation Science) more than do policy communities.

Relevance of Work in Other Fields

Political science has explored policy communities by asking questions like, How does the communality of policy community members develop? How is this sustained and possibly transformed? What impact do policy communities have on paradigm shifts that undergird policy solutions? What policies are enacted, implemented, and influenced by policy communities?[25]

An important variable of success in influencing policy through a community is coherence among members' policy views.[26] Policy communities learn and change their views about appropriate policy solutions and develop new policy paradigms. One policy analyst observes:

> Asking "how" a policy means is asking how a policy accrues meaning; where meanings reside; how they are transmitted to and among various policy stakeholders; how they come to be shared or not shared; how they may be destroyed.... In suggesting that a legitimate role for policy and implementation analysis is a focus on how meanings are communicated successfully or not, I am also suggesting that the net of stakeholders needs to be more widely cast than is traditionally suggested. Not only are we interested in the actions of traditional implementors ... but also in nonparticipant observers of the policy issue: members of the greater public who have an interest in the issue and who are involved in the creation and sharing of policy meaning. While not standing to gain materially from the success of the policy, they are a part of a policy process that is also about the expression and validation of values....[27]

Political scientists have examined the path of policy from ideas embraced by a policy community to policy outcomes.[28] But these analyses are partial and preliminary, and do not focus on education policy. The concept of policy community can be linked to concepts like "powerful ideas."[29] A recent powerful idea shared by an education reform policy community concerns the linkage between better education and successful U.S. international economic competition.

Application to Education

Mazzoni provides some insights on the involvement of policy communities in recent state education reform that emphasized state subject matter standards and other policy changes.[30] He mentions such nationwide groups as:

1. *State political leaders*—Education Commission of States, National Conference of State Legislatures, Chief State School Officers, and National Governors Association.
2. *Big business*—Business Roundtable, National Alliance of Business, National Association of Manufacturers, and U.S. Chamber of Commerce.

3. *Subject matter associations*—National Council of Teachers of Mathematics, National Science Teachers Association, and many others.
4. *Teacher organizations*—AFT, NEA.
5. *Policy analysts*—Carnegie Forum on Education and the Economy, Center for Policy Research in Education.

These organizations "publicized reports, convened meetings, sponsored research, cultivated personal relationships, and lobbied state lawmakers."[31]

There are many other organizations and groups active in state education reform at the national and state levels. One group of opponents is opposed to outcome-based education, as noted in an earlier chapter. Many parts of the supportive coalition, such as business, are extremely fragmented, and can be neutralized by opponents that include Citizens for Excellence in Education, the Christian Coalition, and the Eagle Forum. These organizations are part of another policy community that uses the Heritage Foundation for policy analysis and advocacy.

Another potential construct of a policy community is found in a case study of public choice in Minnesota:

> But instead of individual entrepreneurs, suppose that *policy intellectuals* initiate an idea. They are joined in a dialogue with *policy advocates* who decide to push the idea forward. The policy advocates make the idea more explicit and tangible by drafting a proposal, and work the proposal into a bill without direct assistance from the originators of the idea. The advocates ultimately win the endorsement and support of *policy champions*, who help write the bill and support its enactment into law. Also, in anticipation of the problems and challenges of implementation, the advocates or champions build additional support by joining forces with *policy administrators* sympathetic to the new idea. Policy administrators then carry the idea through the testing and experimentation and oversee its eventual implementation into practice.[32]

In sum, the concept of policy communities within education policy needs more definition and more research on their operation and impact. Traditional research on interest groups cannot encompass the boundaries of a policy community. A major research question is how the influence of policy communities fits with pluralism or other political science theories about decision making in democracies.

COURTS AND LAW

Courts as policymakers, law as reflection of politically dominant values, and judges as agents transmitting views of what that
law looks like—all constitute crucial unresearched areas in the
politics of education. In recent decades, courts have greatly affected
school policymaking. Political science has a long tradition of
constitutional analysis supplemented in recent decades by analysis of judicial behavior and institutions. Again, though, politics
of education has done almost nothing about courts, even though
schoolpeople are everywhere facing a storm of legal change.

Studies Outside Education

Analyses of courts and law have had long roots in legal and
political science scholarship because the Constitution provides
broad parameters for the use of power in the thousands of
American governments.[33] Over time, that emphasis on legal analysis
has altered in response to new theories about the behavior of
judges, the goals of law, and the means of achieving these goals.
Starting in the 1950s, however, political science examined judicial voting patterns and the causes of judges' decisions. This
approach, noted fully in Chapter 12, sees court behavior as part
of the total political system.[34] More recently, research has focused on court interactions with other agencies[35] or with public
opinion. Consequently, the study of courts, justice, and the law
has moved well beyond constitutional interpretation into examining the institutions, roles, and post-decision consequences of
the judiciary.

A wide variety of research transcends the old tradition that
only lawyers did legal analysis.[36] New concepts involve institution, role, organization, and values that focus on topics like:

- Alternatives to formal adjudication
- Politics and judicial selection
- Contextual influences on judicial decision making
- The personal role of judges in decision making
- The nature and influence of organized litigants
- Post-decision implementation

More recent methods of analysis have turned from content analysis of court decisions to quantitative analysis of judicial behavior. These studies incorporate new methods of data analysis, running from descriptive statistics to regression analysis.

Certain theoretical orientations guide this newer judicial behavioral analysis that applies to all levels of government and all policies—like education. For example, theory asserts and evidence supports the following:

1. While courts have different rituals and pressures on them compared to other branches of government, they are, nevertheless, a major agency in policymaking and implementation. As such, they are "political" agencies of the policy system.[37] Actual decisions by judges operate within allegedly neutral or "objective" rules (imposed by the Constitution and tradition) that, however, ultimately favor one side in allocating resources and values. As such, courts are part of the political system in this allocation function.

2. The major effort of courts is to arrive at some internal agreement about their actions, whether a consensus in judgment or an agreement to be consonant with decisions over a period of time (*stare decisis*). That effort contributes to the stability of law facing an environment that often calls for change. That stability in turn adds certainty to the lives of citizens and to the operations of social institutions.

3. There is more discretion among judges in state or federal appellate courts, and so personal values can play more of a role in arriving at decisions. Custom inhibits much freedom, of course, but where it does exist, judges with common values will vote together in different blocks in decisions affecting major policy issues.

4. Finally, formal adjudication does not exhaust all methods of conflict resolution. That resolution may be achieved through informal mediation or arbitration by family heads or church leaders, or by informal courts within a social organization. Such practices involve use of third parties to deal with contestants, thereby providing decisions that lead to peaceful resolution.

In short, research portrays courts as basically political in its conflict resolution task; claimants seeking state legitimacy over such conflicts; and judges varying in decisions about constitution and statute that are linked to social context, values, and partisanship. While judges are constrained by the institution, their decisions are infused by personal values of society, party, and philosophy. The interaction of institution and person provides a rich analysis of these authorities in black robes.

Research Possibilities for Politics of Education

Few scholars of the politics of education actually study adjudication, the uses of law, or judicial behavior. They seem to avoid this legal context of politics, maybe because they think they need law degrees to do judicial analysis. However, lack of legal training has not stopped political scientists or authors from exploring the role of courts as policy innovators.[38] We next note some useful research directions for politics of education scholars.

Education Law in the American States.   Much of the research on law in the politics of education focuses on the origins, implementation, and evaluation of school *statutes*. Other legal writing—mostly before the 1980s—focuses primarily on compilations and analyses of major federal court cases affecting school policy.[39] The latter has high utility for school professionals and boards who need legal advice to wend their way through increasingly complex legal challenges to the school system.

However, meaningful analysis has been done by politics of education scholars that explains political aspects of *education law across the American states*. For example, studies of site-based management find only limited review of the state's legal issues. Within each state there does not exist a compilation of state law, but content analysis of such law or codes is sparingly employed to determine the values, purposes, and consequences of education law.[40]

Judicial Consequences of New Law.   Another priority research area is parallel studies of *judicial behavior,* namely, the role of judges and litigants when they are allocating resources and values for education.

Regarding *judicial behavior,* how are judges at any level influenced in their schooling decisions by differences in their own social background, partisan selection, and philosophy? What are the role concepts they use in their decision making? Finally, among the states, what theory helps explain conflicting decisions in judicial areas like school finance equalization. For example, New Hampshire courts declare their finance system constitutional, but New Jersey judges reach the opposite conclusion.

As to *court decisions,* what is the linkage of public opinion to legal decisions on school policy? How do differences in the adjudication systems among the states—rooted in cultures—affect the nature of court decisions? How has a set of legal decisions on a given policy—like desegregation or student discipline—altered by new ideas or evidence? How do judicial decision and administrative implementation interact, especially over time? What alternatives to formal adjudication exist to resolve school conflicts (e.g., mediation)?

Questions regarding *litigants* include, Who uses courts in conflict over school policy? How do interest groups use the courts as a lobbying process (particular attention to religious matters might be paid here)? Is there a consistent pattern of litigants as winners and losers arising from judges' decisions? Is there interstate variation in these outcomes? And what theory underlies such behavior?

COMPARATIVE EDUCATION

Politics of education scholars have conducted international case studies and comparisons for many years.[41] But most of this research was conceived before policymakers had utilized international comparative analysis of student achievement in subjects such as reading, math, and science. There is a raging debate about the alleged low performance of the United States in math and science, including results from the Second International Math and Science Study.[42] Regardless of how the United States is doing in the international achievement horse race, there is a need to link student attainment with underlying politics. How do influences on achievement from the politics of education operate in different countries? Do these political differences have much impact on U.S. achievement compared to other nations? If countries centralized at the national or state level do obtain better student achievement, what are the implications for U.S. education governance?

For example, the Third International Mathematics and Science Study (TIMSS) looked at forty countries to analyze their intended curriculum (government policies), implemented curriculum (taught in classrooms), and attained curriculum (learned by students on a common international test). Some of the key questions were: What curriculum differences exist between countries? What is taught and when? What topics are not covered? The political theory underlying such testing is, What do different political patterns have to do with these different national curriculum policies and student assessment results?

Relevance to the Politics of Education

A major theme of TIMSS is the extremely wide variation among countries in the intended and implemented curriculum.[43] Another study of university entrance exams in math and science in seven countries also stressed variation in curricular format and length, topics covered and their difficulty, and the degree to which students were given choices in answering test items.[44] So far, scholarly study of these intercountry differences focuses on whether the United States' academic standards are comparatively difficult or easy, and how much time is spent on various topics in the U.S. curriculum compared to other nations. Politics of education research in the United States focuses overwhelmingly on the English-speaking countries and other European countries like Belgium, Norway, Denmark, Switzerland, and Austria, while those in the Pacific Basin or Latin America receive less attention.[45]

Politics of education research focusing on comparative education has looked at who controls education, but *not at the differences that various policymaking structures and processes make in what students study*. A strong predictor of whether a student has learned a curricular topic is the opportunity (or its lack) to study that topic in school. This is called "opportunity to learn." For example, some countries use a central ministry of education and a national exam system to determine what students learn. What is the connection of this centralized policymaking approach to official curriculum objectives or exam content? Some countries have a much closer policymaking and political influence linkage between university admissions and secondary school curricula than does the United States. For example, in the United States exams such as the SAT and ACT drive the secondary school content, while university syllabi do so in Hong Kong and France. U.S. research on politics has rarely used a comparative perspective to pursue the influence of higher education policies on lower education curriculum. The constant theme of national variation in comparative curriculum studies suggests the need to dissect the political influences that cause and maintain intercountry differences.

Recent comparative political analysis by the Organization for Economic Co-Operation and Development(OCED)provides some hints. Table 15.1 presents a comparison of decisions about education taken by governance as a percentage of all decisions. Note that in the United States an unusually low number of decisions are made at the national level. The lack of national standards in the United States may help account for lower student assessment results compared to some other nations. In the United States local control is in accord with public opinion, and Table 15.2 demonstrates that among the surveyed nations the United States has the highest percentage of public opinion favoring local decisions in general, including the amount of time spent teaching each subject, plus how subjects are taught. Our commitment to local control inhibits our ability to politically impose national or state academic curriculum standards, as evidenced by the recent Congressional debate concerning Goals 2000.

These tables provide a view of the political influences on differences among countries in what students study and consequently learn. There is a long tradition of studies of curriculum politics in the United States, but this focus needs to be extended to the international arena.[46] Politics of education scholars need to place more emphasis on what difference that politics makes in what students learn. International comparisons of school-based management, for example, need to focus more on the opportunity to learn in various curricular contexts. A centralized curriculum might cause more standardization in what content the teachers

Table 15.1
Decisions Made by Level of Governance as a Percentage of All Decisions
(Public Lower and Secondary Education)

	Locus of decision making			
	School level	Intermediate level 1	Intermediate level 2	National level
Austria	44%	8%	26%	23%
Belgium	26	50	24	–
Denmark	39	48	–	14
Finland	38	50	–	13
France	35	–	35	30
Germany	32	44	17	7
Ireland	74	8	–	18
New Zealand	73	–	–	27
Norway	31	45	–	24
Portugal	42	–	3	55
Spain	28	26	14	32
Sweden	47	47	–	6
Switzerland	9	44	46	–
United States	26	71	3	–

* The specific decision-making level does not exist

Source: Organization for Economic Co-operation and Development, *Education at a Glance* (Paris: OECD, 1993) p. 134.

cover, especially if this central curriculum is reinforced by high-stakes exams. The international arena is an excellent place to expand the foci of studies. Some U.S. states with high achievement (Minnesota, Iowa) and low achievement (California, Louisiana) could be compared with other nations in terms of their distinctive politics of determining curriculum.

CONCLUSION

Politics of education research began with small groups of scholars in the mid-1960s and reached a high level of productivity in the 1970s. Since then, both theoretical and empirical work have not kept pace with rapid changes in the political context of education. On the other hand, *policy* analysis became more prominent

Table 15.2

Percentage of Respondents Who Thought It Was "Very Important" for Decisions to Be Made by Schools Themselves

	What subjects are taught	How subjects are taught	Amount of time spent teaching each subject	How the school budget is spent	Teacher selection and promotion	Teachers' salaries and working conditions	Items average within each entry
Austria	31%	36%	28%	33%	31%	18%	29.6%
Belgium							
(Flemish community)	22	41	27	36	39	26	31.9
Denmark	20	32	16	34	31	12	24.0
Finland	18	35	26	40	34	22	28.9
France	34	56	51	50	59	43	48.7
Netherlands	15	35	22	31	47	24	28.9
Portugal	44	55	50	56	51	37	48.8
Spain	13	19	17	19	20	13	16.9
Sweden	23	38	24	51	44	17	32.8
Switzerland	18	32	21	22	26	14	22.0
United Kingdom	39	50	44	57	50	32	45.3
United States	53	60	57	64	67	57	59.8
Country average for each item	27.7	40.6	31.8	41.0	41.6	26.2	

Source: Organization for Economic Co-operation and Development, *Education at a Glance* (Paris: OECD, 1993) p. 134.

after the 1970s, and more scholars were lured away from *politics* research itself. Theories that were developed to improve education policy have not had enough potential or been transferred adequately to help us understand the politics of education. Essential data bases such as elections and political socialization have not been updated in several decades. New conceptual frameworks or developments in political science have not been linked to education politics, for example, rational actor or political culture theories. In preparing this text, we had to shorten major chapters due to lack of recent data, and we found gaps in our basic understanding of this vital field. The gaps in education politics research will hinder our ability to devise policy solutions to many urgent education problems. Cooperative efforts among education, political science, education psychology, journalism, and comparative scholars will be needed to make progress on the research agenda presented in this chapter. But it is an agenda that is open to the complexities of steady-state and challenge in the schools of the American political system.

NOTES

1. James Cibulka, "Policy Analysis and the Study of the Politics of Education," in *The Study of Educational Politics*, J. Scribner and D. Layton, eds. (Bristol, Penn.: Falmer, 1995).

2. Charles Merriam, *The Making of a Citizen* (Chicago: University of Chicago Press, 1931). Later studies include David Easton and Jack Dennis, *Children in the Political System* (New York: McGraw-Hill, 1966), and Richard Dawson, Kenneth Prewitt, and Karen Dawson, *Political Socialization* (Boston: Little, Brown, 1977).

3. Campbell, et al., *The American Voter* (New York: Wiley, 1960)

4. Surveyed in Dawson et al., *Political Socialization;* the comparative aspect is found in Robert Hess and Judith Torney, *The Development of Political Attitudes in Children* (Chicago: Aldine, 1967).

5. Robert Weissberg, *Public Opinion and Popular Government* (Englewood Cliffs, N.J.: Prentice-Hall, 1976).

6. Campbell et al., *The American Voter.*

7. The historical framework is found in Herbert Kliebard, *The Struggle for the American Curriculum* (New York: Routledge & Kegan Paul, 1986); the contemporary view is found in Michael Apple, *Teachers and Texts* (New York: Routledge & Kegan Paul, 1986), and Richard Merelman, "Democratic Politics and the Culture of American Education," *American Political Science Review* 74 (1980): 319–32.

8. The significant research is found in Fred Greenstein, *Children and Politics* (New Haven: Yale University Press, 1965).

9. Merelman, "Democratic Politics."

10. B. Compaine, *Who Owns the Media?* 2nd edition (White Plains, N.Y.: Knowledge Industry Publications, 1982).

11. D. Altheide, *Creating Reality* (Beverly Hills, Calif.: Sage, 1976).

12. C. Steinberg, *The Information Establishment* (New York: Hastings House, 1980).

13. The leading analyst is Doris Graber, *Mass Media and American Politics*

and *Power in Politics* (Washington, D.C.: CQ Press, 1984). For a useful summary of research, see Robert Meadow, *Politics in Communication* (Norwood, N.J.: Ablex, 1980), and Sidney Kraus and Dennis David, *The Effects of Mass Communication on Political Behavior* (University Park: Penn State University Press, 1976). For an annual review of the topic, see *Mass Communication Review Yearbook* (Beverly Hills, Calif.: Sage).

14. See evidence in Kraus and David, *The Effects of Mass Communication.*

15. William Crotty (ed.), *Political Behavior* (Evanston, Ill.: Northwestern University Press, 1991).

16. Campbell et al., *The American Voter;* Sidney Verba and Norman Nie, *Participation in America* (Chicago: University of Chicago Press: 1972).

17. Listing and analysis in Verba and Nie, *Participation in America,* Chapter 2; see also Crotty, *Political Behavior.*

18. Richard Carter and James Sutthoff, *Communities and Their Schools* (Stanford, Calif.: Institute for Community Research, Stanford University, 1960); Philip Piele and John Hall, *Budgets, Bonds, and Ballots* (Lexington, Mass.: Lexington Books, 1973); Howard Hamilton and Sylvan Cohen, *Policy Making by Plebiscites* (Lexington, Mass.: Lexington Books, 1974).

19. Piele and Hall, *Budgets;* Hamilton and Cohen, *Policy Making.*

20. See different categories in Verba and Nie, *Participation in America;* Crotty, *Political Behavior.*

21. Michael Kirst, "Recent Research on Intergovernmental Relations in Education Policy, *Educational Researcher* 24. no. 9 (1995): 18–22.

22. James Walker, "The Diffusion of Knowledge, Policy Communities and Agenda Setting: The Relationship of Knowledge and Power," in *New Strategic Perspectives on Social Policy,* J.E. Tropman et al., eds. (New York: Pergamon Press, 1981).

23. Michael Kirst, Gail Meister, and Steven Rowley, "Policy Issue Networks," *Policy Studies Journal* 13, no. 1 (1984): 247–64.

24. Kirst et al., "Policy Issue Networks."

25. Hugh Heclo, "Issue Networks in the Executive Establishment," in *The New American Political System,* A. King, ed. (Washington, D.C.: AEI, 1978).

26. Susan Fuhrman, *Designing Coherent Education Policy: Improving the System* (San Francisco: Jossey-Bass, 1993).

27. D. Yanow, "The Communication of Policy Meanings: Implementation as Interpretation and Text," *Policy Science* 26 (1993): 41–61.

28. Judith Goldstein and Robert Keohane, eds., *Ideas and Foreign Policy: Beliefs, Institutions and Political Change* (Ithaca, N.Y.: Cornell University Press, 1993). See also James Kingdon, *Agendas, Alternatives, and Public Policies,* 2nd edition (New York: Harper Collins, 1995).

29. Robert Reich, *The Power of Public Ideas* (Cambridge, Mass.: Harvard University Press, 1988).

30. Tim Mazzoni, "State Policymaking and School Reform," in *The Study of Educational Politics,* J.D. Scribner and D.H. Layton, eds. (Bristol, Penn.: Falmer, 1995).

31. Mazzoni, "State Policymaking," p. 67. See also Kingdon, *Agendas.*

344   FUTURE RESEARCH NEEDS IN EDUCATION POLITICS

32. Nancy Roberts and Paula King, *Transforming Public Policy: Dynamics of Policy Entrepreneurship and Innovation* (San Francisco: Jossey-Bass, 1996).

33. The classic study is Benjamin Cardozo, *The Nature of the Judicial Press* (New Haven, Conn.: Yale University Press, 1921).

34. Reviewed in David Rohde and Harold Spaeth, *Supreme Court Decision Making* (San Francisco: Freeman, 1976).

35. Martin Shapiro, *The Supreme Court and Administrative Agencies* (New York: Free Press, 1968).

36. See examples in S. Goldman and A. Sarat, eds., *American Court Systems*, 2nd edition.

37. The classic study is Robert Dahl, "Decision Making in a Democracy: The Role of the Supreme Court as a National Policy-Maker," in *Readings in American Political Behavior*, Raymond Wolfinger, ed. (Englewood Cliffs, N.J.: Prentice-Hall, 1966).

38. See studies in Goldman and Sarat, *American Court Systems.*.

39. David Kirp and Mark Yudof, *Educational Policy and the Law* (Berkeley, Calif.: McCutchan, 1982); Tyll van Geel, *Authority to Control the School Program* (Lexington, Mass.: Lexington Books, 1976).

40. One exception is found in a six-state study of such law: Catherine Marshall, Douglas Mitchell, and Frederick Wirt, *Culture and Education Policy in the American States* (New York: Falmer, 1989)

41. Francis Fowler, "The International Arena," in Scribner and Layton, *The Study of Education Politics*, pp. 84–102.

42. David Berliner and Bruce Biddle, *The Manufactured Crisis* (Reading, Mass.: Addison-Wesley, 1995), pp. 13–65.

43. Based on presentation by Professor William Schmidt to the National Research Council, October 1995.

44. Debra Viadero, "Study Finds Variations in Math, Science Tests in Seven Nations," *Education Week*, January 10, 1996, p. 13. See also OECD, *Performance Standards in Education* (Paris: OECD, 1995); R.F. Arnove, P.G. Altbach, and G.P. Kelly, *Emergent Issues in Education* (New York: State University of New York, 1992). Hedley Beare and H. Telford, "School Reform and Restructuring," in *International Encyclopedia of Education*, Torsten Husen and Neville Postlethwaite, eds. (Oxford: Pergamon, 1994).

45. Fowler, "The International Arena."

46. Susan Fuhrman and Betty Malen, eds., *The Politics of Curriculum and Testing* (New York: Falmer, 1991). For a start on international comparisons see David Stevenson and David Baker, "Does State Control of Curriculum Matter? *Educational Evaluation and Policy Analysis* 18, no. 4 (1996): 339-342.

Subject Index

Academic reform era of 1983, 197, 201, 236. *See also A Nation At Risk*

AIDS education, 37

American Association of School Administrators (AASA), 85

American Association of University Women (AAUW), 79, 86, 230

American Business Conference, 87

American Federation of Labor-Congress of Industrial Organizations (AFL-CIO), 187

American Federation of Teachers, 44, 83-84, 96, 181, 184, 187, 190, 224, 228, 231, 333

American Library Association, 8-9

Annenberg Foundation, 19

Apolitical education, myth of, 27-32, 54-55

Bennett, William, 250

Brown v. Topeka Board of Education, 36, 47, 267, 269-270, 277, 280

Bush Administration, 247, 259

Bush, George, 113

Author Index